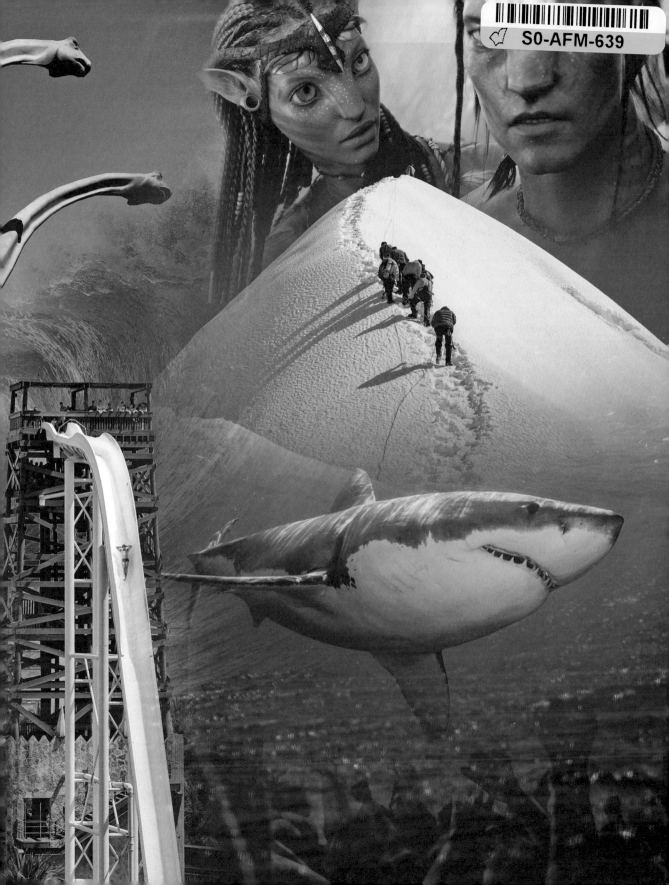

# TOP 10 OF EVERYTHING 2016

# TOP 10
## OF EVERYTHING
### 2016

hamlyn

**PAUL TERRY**

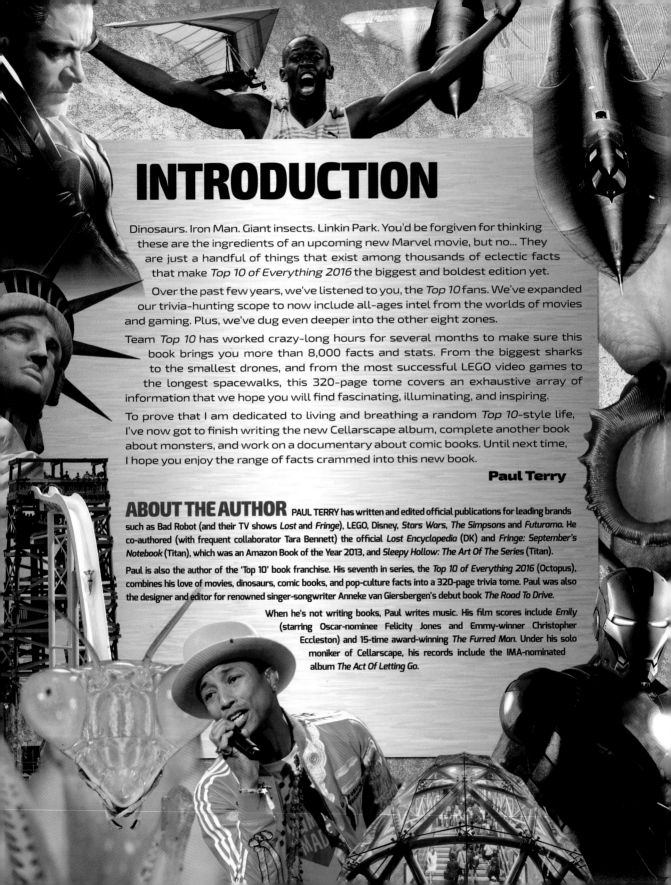

# INTRODUCTION

Dinosaurs. Iron Man. Giant insects. Linkin Park. You'd be forgiven for thinking these are the ingredients of an upcoming new Marvel movie, but no... They are just a handful of things that exist among thousands of eclectic facts that make *Top 10 of Everything 2016* the biggest and boldest edition yet.

Over the past few years, we've listened to you, the *Top 10* fans. We've expanded our trivia-hunting scope to now include all-ages intel from the worlds of movies and gaming. Plus, we've dug even deeper into the other eight zones.

Team *Top 10* has worked crazy-long hours for several months to make sure this book brings you more than 8,000 facts and stats. From the biggest sharks to the smallest drones, and from the most successful LEGO video games to the longest spacewalks, this 320-page tome covers an exhaustive array of information that we hope you will find fascinating, illuminating, and inspiring.

To prove that I am dedicated to living and breathing a random *Top 10*-style life, I've now got to finish writing the new Cellarscape album, complete another book about monsters, and work on a documentary about comic books. Until next time, I hope you enjoy the range of facts crammed into this new book.

**Paul Terry**

## ABOUT THE AUTHOR

PAUL TERRY has written and edited official publications for leading brands such as Bad Robot (and their TV shows *Lost* and *Fringe*), LEGO, Disney, *Stars Wars*, *The Simpsons* and *Futurama*. He co-authored (with frequent collaborator Tara Bennett) the official *Lost Encyclopedia* (DK) and *Fringe: September's Notebook* (Titan), which was an Amazon Book of the Year 2013, and *Sleepy Hollow: The Art Of The Series* (Titan).

Paul is also the author of the 'Top 10' book franchise. His seventh in series, the *Top 10 of Everything 2016* (Octopus), combines his love of movies, dinosaurs, comic books, and pop-culture facts into a 320-page trivia tome. Paul was also the designer and editor for renowned singer-songwriter Anneke van Giersbergen's debut book *The Road To Drive*.

When he's not writing books, Paul writes music. His film scores include *Emily* (starring Oscar-nominee Felicity Jones and Emmy-winner Christopher Eccleston) and 15-time award-winning *The Furred Man*. Under his solo moniker of Cellarscape, his records include the IMA-nominated album *The Act Of Letting Go*.

# CONTENTS

# ANIMAL
# KINGDOM

## MOSQUITO

These insects transmit several diseases including malaria, dengue fever, and yellow fever.

## INDIAN COBRA

This snake's venom, which newborns have the day they hatch from their eggs, features a toxin that paralyzes muscle tissue. Its striking hood is flared as a warning whenever it feels threatened.

### TOP 10...
# MOST DEADLY

Although humans don't have any natural predators, look at how deadly these 10 creatures are to us...

| | CREATURE | HUMAN FATALITIES PER YEAR |
|---|---|---|
| 1 | MOSQUITO | 2 million + transmits disease to 7 million |
| 2 | TSETSE FLY | 250,000–300,000 |
| 3 | INDIAN COBRA | Approx. 50,000 |
| 4 | BUTHIDAE FAMILY OF SCORPIONS | 3,250 |
| 5 | AUSTRALIAN SALTWATER CROCODILE | 1,000 |
| 6 | HIPPOPOTAMUS | 500 |
| 7 | ELEPHANT | Approx. 500 |
| 8 | CAPE BUFFALO | 200 |
| 9 | AFRICAN LION | Approx. 150 |
| 10 | AUSTRALIAN BOX JELLYFISH | Approx. 90 |

ADULT HIPPOS CAN WEIGH
## 2,722 KG

# DEATH ON FOUR LEGS

Here is how the quadrupeds featured in the above Top 10 compare in terms of how deadly they can be to humans...

AUSTRALIAN SALTWATER CROCODILE
**1,000**

AFRICAN LION APPROX.
**150**

HIPPOPOTAMUS
**500**

CAPE BUFFALO
**200**

ELEPHANT APPROX.
**500**

EARLIEST FOSSILIZED
HUMAN PARASITES
DATE BACK OVER
**8,000**
**YEARS**

## 📍 **PORK**
## **TAPEWORM**

As its name suggests, make
sure pork is thoroughly cook to
avoid this parasite.

TOP 10...
# BIGGEST HUMAN
# PARASITES

These organisms' size and behaviour may sound like
science fiction, but they're all too common...

| | PARASITE | LENGTH (M) | (FT) |
|---|---|---|---|
| 1 | PORK TAPEWORM | 50 | 164.04 |
| 2 | BEEF TAPEWORM | 12 | 39.37 |
| 3 | RAW FISH TAPEWORM | 9.14 | 30 |
| = | WHALE TAPEWORM | 9.14 | 30 |
| 5 | ROUNDWORM | 1 | 3.28 |
| 6 | RAT TAPEWORM | 0.6 | 1.97 |
| 7 | BERTIELLA TAPEWORM | 0.13 | 0.43 |
| 8 | FASCIOLA GIGANTICA FLATWORM | 0.10 | 0.33 |
| = | CYCLOPHYLLIDEA TAPEWORM | 0.10* | 0.33 |
| 10 | FASCIOLOPSIS BUSKI FLUKE | 0.075 | 0.25 |

*Larval stage

## 📍 **ROUNDWORM**

This is a threadworm, the most
common kind of roundworm in
the USA and Europe.

## 📍 **BEEF**
## **TAPEWORM**

Around 50 million people
worldwide are infected
with this parasite.

## TOP 10...
# MOST **VENOMOUS** INSECT

These creatures may be small in size, but the toxic weaponry they can deploy is immense. However intrigued you are by their appearance, look but don't touch...

| INSECT | LD50 VALUE* (LETHAL DOSE VALUE) MG PER KG OF BODY WEIGHT | | INSECT | LD50 VALUE* (LETHAL DOSE VALUE) MG PER KG OF BODY WEIGHT |
|---|---|---|---|---|
| 1 | YELLOW HARVESTER ANT | 0.12 | 6 WESTERN HONEY BEE | 2.8 |
| 2 | ASSASSIN CATERPILLAR | 0.19 | 7 YELLOW JACKET | 3.5 |
| 3 | RED HARVESTER ANT | 0.66 | 8 AFRICANIZED HONEY BEE | 7.1 |
| 4 | ASIAN HORNET | 1.6 | 9 FIRE ANT | 8 |
| 5 | PAPER WASP | 2.4 | 10 BAG-SHELTER PROCESSIONARY CATERPILLAR | 11.2 |

ASIAN HORNET
**0.12**
VENOM RATING
(LD50)

## WHAT IS LD50

Toxicology (the study of the negative effects of chemicals on organisms) uses the LD50 measure to calculate how deadly a substance is. The lower the LD50 value, the more toxic a creature's venom.

# FURTHER INVESTIGATION

**RED HARVESTER ANT**
Growing up to 10 mm (⁴/₁₀ in) long, these ants mainly eat seeds.

**PAPER WASP / UMBRELLA WASP**
These wasps will sting only if they feel threatened.

**ASSASSIN CATERPILLAR**
Multiple stings can cause death from internal bleeding.

Spiders are arachnids, not insects. Here are some venomous spiders' LD50 values...

BRAZILIAN WANDERING SPIDER
**0.00061**
LD50

BLACK WIDOW
**0.002**
LD50

SYDNEY FUNNEL-WEB SPIDER
**0.16**
LD50

BROWN SPIDER
**0.48**
LD50

MALMIGNATTE
**0.68**
LD50

TOP 10...
# BIGGEST
# BLOODSUCKERS

The most famous drinker of blood, Dracula, may be a work of fiction, but the natural world is full of real-life vampiric organisms...

| | BLOODSUCKER | (CM) | LENGTH (IN) |
|---|---|---|---|
| 1 | SEA LAMPREY | 90 | 35.5 |
| 2 | GIANT AMAZON LEECH | 45.7 | 18 |
| 3 | CANDIRÚ | 40 | 16 |
| 4 | VAMPIRE BAT | 18 | 7 |
| 5 | VAMPIRE FINCH | 12 | 4.7 |
| 6 | MADRILENIAL BUTTERFLY | 7 | 2.76 |
| 7 | ASSASSIN BUG | 4 | 1.6 |
| 8 | FEMALE MOSQUITO | 1.6 | 0.6 |
| 9 | BEDBUG | 0.5 | 0.2 |
| 10 | FLEA | 0.25 | 0.09 |

## VAMPIRE BAT

### FEEDING HABITS

Just like their mythological namesake, Vampire Bats only hunt in the dead of night. From the ground, they stealthily crawl toward their target. Cows and horses are normally on the menu, but they have been known to bite and drink blood from humans.

### SPECIES

The three kinds of bat that exclusively consume blood are the White-Winged Vampire Bat, the Hairy-Legged Vampire Bat and the Common Vampire Bat. They live in Central and South America.

### LARGE FAMILIES

These bats reside in places that have no natural light, and they favour caves. Their huge colonies can include thousands of bats that form strong familial bonds. If a mother dies, another female will tend to the orphaned young.

## ⦿ WHALE SHARK

This is the largest fish in the world. Although it grows to over 13.7 m (45 ft) long, it only eats tiny animals like plankton and larvae.

KILLER WHALE
DOCUMENTARY
BLACKFISH HAS MADE
**$2.1
MILLION**
AT THE BOX OFFICE
WORLDWIDE

## ⦿ WALRUS

Growing to over 0.9 m (3 ft) in length, the tusks of a walrus are used to assist it getting out of the sea, to make holes in ice, and to assert dominance.

### TOP 10...
# BIGGEST **CARNIVORES**

The diet of these giants ranges from tiny aquatic organisms called zooplankton to wild antelope...

| | TYPE | NAME | HEAVIEST RECORDED (KG) | (LB) |
|---|---|---|---|---|
| 1 | WHALE | Blue Whale | 189,999.4 | 418,877 |
| 2 | SHARK | Whale Shark | 21,318 | 47,000 |
| 3 | DOLPHIN | Killer Whale | 9,979 | 22,000 |
| 4 | SEAL | Southern Elephant Seal | 4,989.5 | 11,000 |
| 5 | CROCODILE | Saltwater Crocodile | 2,000 | 4,409 |
| = | WALRUS | Pacific Walrus | 2,000 | 4,409 |
| 7 | BEAR | Polar Bear | 1,002 | 2,209 |
| 8 | STINGRAY | Giant Freshwater Stingray | 600 | 1,320 |
| 9 | BIG CAT | Siberian Tiger | 500 | 1,102.3 |
| 10 | SQUID | Colossal Squid | 495 | 1,091 |

TYRANNOSAURUS REX'S
TEETH WERE UP TO

# 30.5
MM
LONG

## TOP 10...
# LARGEST PREHISTORIC
# BIPEDAL CARNIVORES

Of all the meat-eaters that roamed the lands millions of years ago, these are the biggest we have unearthed so far...

| | DINOSAUR | LENGTH (M) | (FT) |
|---|---|---|---|
| 1 | SPINOSAURUS | 18 | 59 |
| 2 | CARCHARODONTOSAURUS | 13.2 | 43.3 |
| = | GIGANTOSAURUS | 13.2 | 43.3 |
| 4 | CHILANTAISAURUS | 13 | 42.7 |
| 5 | TYRANNOSAURUS REX | 12.3 | 40.4 |
| 6 | TYRANNOTITAN | 12.2 | 40 |
| 7 | TORVOSAURUS | 12 | 39.4 |
| 8 | = ALLOSAURUS | 12 | 39.4 |
| 9 | ACROCANTHOSAURUS | 11.5 | 37.7 |
| 10 | DELTADROMEUS | 11 | 36.1 |

## ⊙ GIGANTOSAURUS

Experts calculate this predator would have weighed over 13,607.7 kg (30,000 lbs).

## ⊙ SPINOSAURUS

Its name means "spine lizard", and those back bones grew to 1.65 m (5.4 ft).

## MAKO SHARK

Two different species, the Shortfin Mako and Longfin Mako, can both be found all over the world. This, the fastest shark in the world, has a strange habit of leaping up to 6.1 m (20 ft) out of the water. Sadly, like many species of sharks, Makos are in decline due to competitive big-game fishing.

## PRONGHORN ANTELOPE

These mammals have 320° field of vision. They need to be fast to evade predators like bobcats and coyotes.

AN ADULT CHEETAH WEIGHS UP TO

# 71.7 KG

## TOP 10...
# FASTEST OF ALL

Here is how the fastest animals' speeds from all known species compare to one another...

| ANIMAL | SPEED (KPH) | (MPH) |
|---|---|---|
| 1 PEREGRINE FALCON | 389 | 242 |
| 2 SPINE-TAILED SWIFT | 171 | 106.2 |
| 3 MAGNIFICENT FRIGATEBIRD | 153 | 95.1 |
| 4 SPUR-WINGED GOOSE | 142 | 88.2 |
| 5 CHEETAH | 113 | 70.2 |
| 6 SAILFISH | 110 | 68.3 |
| 7 PRONGHORN ANTELOPE | 98 | 61 |
| 8 SPRINGBOK | 97 | 60.3 |
| 9 MAKO SHARK | 95 | 59 |
| 10 AMERICAN QUARTER HORSE | 86 | 53.4 |

## PEREGRINE FALCON

During a dive, this bird can travel as fast as a McLaren F1 car.

## ⦿ LEATHERBACK TURTLE

Estimated to live for more than 100 years, this turtle can grow to 3 m (9 ft) in length.

## ⦿ ARCTIC TERN

This, the ultimate migrator, splits its time between the Arctic and Antarctic regions.

**TOP 10...**

# LONGEST **JOURNEYS**

During migration, many animals travel thousands of miles. These are the ten that cover the most distance...

| | ANIMAL | MIGRATION DISTANCE (KM) | (MI) |
|---|---|---|---|
| 1 | ARCTIC TERN | 71,000 | 44,000 |
| 2 | SOOTY SHEARWATER | 64,000 | 40,000 |
| 3 | ELEPHANT SEAL | 32,200 | 20,000 |
| 4 | PECTORAL SANDPIPER | 28,000 | 18,000 |
| 5 | HUMPBACK WHALE | 25,700 | 16,000 |
| 6 | GREY WHALE | 22,500 | 14,000 |
| 7 | LEATHERBACK TURTLE | 19,300 | 12,000 |
| 8 | PIED WHEATEAR | 18,000 | 11,200 |
| 9 | SHORT-TAILED SHEARWATER | 17,000 | 10,600 |
| 10 | BAR-TAILED GODWIT | 11,500 | 7,200 |

EXPERTS ESTIMATE THERE ARE OVER

**8 MILLION**

PIED WHEATEARS WORLDWIDE

## ⦿ ELEPHANT SEAL

These seals spend almost all their lives in the ocean, and can hold their breath for 100 minutes. Females can live for over 20 years.

## BLACK RAT SNAKE

This is the largest snake in Canada, reaching 2.59 m (8.5 ft) in length. It is a constrictor, and like the well-known boa constrictor snake, it crushes its prey until they stop breathing before consuming them.

NEW CALEDONIAN GIANT GECKO IS

**35.5 CM**

IN LENGTH

TOP 10...

# BIGGEST **REPTILE FAMILIES**

Examining the different families of the reptile kingdom, these are the largest creatures from each of them...

| | REPTILE FAMILY | REPTILE NAME | MAXIMUM RECORDED MASS (KG) | (LB) |
|---|---|---|---|---|
| 1 | CROCODYLIDAE | Saltwater Crocodile | 2,000 | 4,400 |
| 2 | ALLIGATORIDAE | Black Caiman | 1,310 | 2,900 |
| 3 | GAVIALIDAE | Gharial | 977 | 2,150 |
| 4 | DERMOCHELYIDAE | Leatherback Sea Turtle | 932 | 2,050 |
| 5 | TESTUDINIDAE | Galápagos Tortoise | 400 | 880 |
| 6 | BOIDAE | Green Anaconda | 250 | 550 |
| 7 | VARANIDAE | Komodo Dragon | 166 | 370 |
| 8 | PYTHONIDAE | Reticulated Python | 158 | 350 |
| 9 | VIPERIDAE | Gaboon Viper | 20 | 44 |
| 10 | ELAPIDAE | King Cobra | 12.7 | 28 |

## KOMODO DRAGON

Reaching 3.1 m (10 ft) in length, these huge lizards eat mammals but are confident enough to attack humans too.

SINCE THE FIRST IN 1954,
**28**
GODZILLA FILMS HAVE BEEN MADE

📍 **GODZILLA**

Here is how the most recent *Godzilla* films' box office takings compare...

M.U.T.OS & GODZILLA
**$528,676,069**

GODZILLA & OFFSPRING
**$379,014,294**

**TOP 10...**

# BIGGEST "**MONSTER ATTACKS CITY**" MOVIES

Giant mutations, aliens, dinosaurs, and even supernatural titans have destroyed cities on the big screen...

| | CREATURE | MOVIE | YEAR OF RELEASE | BOX OFFICE ($ WORLDWIDE) |
|---|---|---|---|---|
| **1** | **THE LEVIATHAN** | The Avengers | **2012** | **1,518,594,910** |
| **2** | **T-REX** | The Lost World: Jurassic Park | **1997** | **618,638,999** |
| **3** | **TRIPOD ALIENS** | War Of The Worlds | **2005** | **591,745,540** |
| **4** | **KONG** | King Kong | **2005** | **550,517,357** |
| **5** | **M.U.T.OS & GODZILLA** | Godzilla | **2014** | **528,676,069** |
| **6** | **THE KAIJUS** | Pacific Rim | **2013** | **411,002,906** |
| **7** | **GODZILLA & OFFSPRING** | Godzilla | **1998** | **379,014,294** |
| **8** | **MIMICS** | Edge Of Tomorrow | **2014** | **369,206,256** |
| **9** | **MR. STAY PUFT** | Ghostbusters | **1984** | **295,212,467** |
| **10** | **ABOMINATION** | The Incredible Hulk | **2008** | **263,427,551** |

ALTHOUGH VERY FAST, OSTRICHES CAN WEIGH

## 156.5 KG

## ⚲ ELK

With predators like wolves and bears, these migratory mammals employ a vicious front kick, along with their antlers, for defence.

TOP 10...

# FASTEST ON LAND

Regardless of the number of legs, these are the animals that can run the fastest across the ground...

|  | ANIMAL | SPEED (KPH) | (MPH) |
|---|---|---|---|
| 1 | CHEETAH | 113 | 70.2 |
| 2 | PRONGHORN ANTELOPE | 98 | 60.9 |
| 3 | SPRINGBOK | 97 | 60.3 |
| 4 | AMERICAN QUARTER HORSE | 86 | 53.4 |
| 5 | LION | 80 | 49.7 |
| 6 | OSTRICH | 72 | 44.7 |
| = | AFRICAN WILD DOG | 72 | 44.7 |
| = | ELK | 72 | 44.7 |
| 9 | EASTERN GREY KANGAROO | 70 | 43.5 |
| 10 | COYOTE | 69 | 42.9 |

## ⚲ SPRINGBOK

This animal's name literally means "jumping antelope." Their leaps are used to display dominance and evade predators.

DUE TO POACHING
AND HABITAT
DESTRUCTION, ONLY
**3,200**
SIBERIAN TIGERS
ARE LEFT IN THE WILD

## ⚲ SNOW LEOPARD

Endemic to Central Asia, only 6,000 Snow Leopards are left in the wild. They use their tails, which can be almost as long as their 1.3 m (4.3 ft) bodies, like a scarf to keep them warm when they are sleeping.

**TOP 10…**

# LARGEST **BIG CATS**

Let's compare the weights of the big predatory relations to the domesticated cats in our neighbourhoods…

| | CAT | WEIGHT (KG) | (LB) |
|---|---|---|---|
| 1 | SIBERIAN TIGER | 500 | 1,102.3 |
| 2 | LION | 270 | 595.2 |
| 3 | JAGUAR | 140 | 308.6 |
| 4 | COUGAR | 120 | 264.5 |
| 5 | SNOW LEOPARD | 73 | 160.9 |
| 6 | LEOPARD | 64 | 141.1 |
| 7 | CHEETAH | 55 | 121.2 |
| 8 | LYNX | 35 | 77.2 |
| 9 | CLOUDED LEOPARD | 25 | 55.1 |
| 10 | CARACAL | 20 | 44.1 |

## ⚲ JAGUAR

90 percent of jaguars live in and around the Amazon rainforest. They are extremely good swimmers and have a varied diet of 85 different species.

# CAT COMPARISON

This visual chart conveys how the big cats measure up to one another…

**SNOW LEOPARD**
73
KG

**COUGAR**
120
KG

**JAGUAR**
140
KG

**LION**
270
KG

**SIBERIAN TIGER**
500
KG

THE GOLIATH BIRDEATER CAN LAY UP TO
# 200 EGGS

## ⦿ WOLF SPIDER

Female Wolf Spiders live for several years. They carry their young on their back for the first week.

## TOP 10...
# LARGEST SPIDERS

Far bigger than the species common in Western households, these are an arachnophobe's nightmare...

| | SPIDER | LEG SPAN (CM) | (IN) |
|---|---|---|---|
| 1 | HUNTSMAN | 30 | 11.8 |
| 2 | BRAZILIAN SALMON PINK | 27 | 10.6 |
| 3 | GOLIATH BIRDEATER | 25.4 | 10 |
| = | WOLF SPIDER | 25.4 | 10 |
| 5 | PURPLE BLOOM BIRD-EATING SPIDER | 23 | 9 |
| 6 | HERCULES BABOON | 20.3 | 8 |
| 7 | HYSTEROCRATES SPELLENBERGI | 17.8 | 7 |
| 8 | BRAZILIAN WANDERING SPIDER | 15 | 5.9 |
| = | CERBALUS ARAVENSIS | 15 | 5.9 |
| 10 | TEGENARIA PARIETINA | 14 | 5.5 |

## ⦿ BRAZILIAN SALMON PINK

These kinds of tarantula are popular pets. They were first discovered in 1917 in Paraíba, Brazil.

# SIZE CHART

COMMON HOUSESPIDER
1 CM

GOLIATH BIRDEATER
25.4 CM

BRAZILIAN SALMON PINK
27 CM

HUNTSMAN
30 CM

TOP 10...

# LONGEST **SNAKES**

The number one on this Top 10 is nearly nine times the average size (1.71 m / 5.6 ft) of a person...

| | SNAKE | LONGEST FOUND (M) | (FT) |
|---|---|---|---|
| 1 | RETICULATED PYTHON | 14.94 | 49 |
| 2 | GREEN ANACONDA | 11.28 | 37 |
| 3 | SCRUB PYTHON | 7.92 | 26 |
| 4 | AFRICAN ROCK PYTHON | 6.1 | 20 |
| 5 | KING COBRA | 5.64 | 18.5 |
| 6 | BOA CONSTRICTOR | 3.96 | 13 |
| 7 | BUSHMASTER | 3.05 | 10 |
| 8 | INDIAN PYTHON | 2.99 | 9.8 |
| 9 | DIAMONDBACK RATTLESNAKE | 2.74 | 8.9 |
| 10 | WESTERN RAT SNAKE | 2.44 | 8 |

## GREEN ANACONDA

This colossal snake has no venom. It overpowers, constricts, and then swallows its prey whole. This bold hunter will even attack caiman and deer.

## AFRICAN ROCK PYTHON

Africa's largest snake will not hesitate in preying on big cats or crocodiles.

NOT JUST VERY LONG, THE BOA CONSTRICTOR CAN WEIGH UP TO

## 45.3 KG

## GREAT DANE

Animation designer Iwao Takamoto (Apr 29, 1925 – Jan 8, 2007) created the character of Scooby Doo, and based him on a Great Dane.

### TOP 10...

# TALLEST DOGS

Measuring from the top of their heads to their feet, these dog breeds tower over all others...

| | DOG | HEIGHT (CM) | (IN) |
|---|---|---|---|
| 1 | GREAT DANE | 112 | 44 |
| 2 | IRISH WOLFHOUND | 86.4 | 34 |
| 3 | GREAT PYRENEES | 81.3 | 32 |
| 4 | LEONBERGER | 80 | 31.5 |
| 5 | NEAPOLITAN MASTIFF | 78.7 | 31 |
| 6 | NEWFOUNDLAND | 71.1 | 28 |
| 7 | SAINT BERNARD | 69.9 | 27.5 |
| = | BERNESE MOUNTAIN DOG | 69.9 | 27.5 |
| 9 | BULLMASTIFF | 68.6 | 27 |
| = | DOGUE DE BORDEUX | 68.6 | 27 |

ORIGINALLY FROM LEONBERG, GERMANY, LEONBERGERS CAN WEIGH

# 77 KG

# BEETHOVEN

Here is how the first two *Beethoven* movies did at the box office (Beethoven is a Saint Bernard)...

BEETHOVEN (1992)
**$147,214,049**

BEETHOVEN'S 2ND (1993)
**$118,243,066**

## IRISH WOLFHOUND

Historians believe that this breed could date back over 9,000 years. In modern times, they have appeared in popular culture such as the 2011 video game *The Elder Scrolls V: Skyrim*.

## WEIMARANER

This breed is extremely loyal. Its pack mentality is so strong that it can suffer anxiety when apart from its owner.

BEING A LEAN BREED, GREYHOUNDS WEIGH

**32** KG ON AVERAGE

TOP 10...

# FASTEST **DOGS**

Recall what it feels like to travel 50 kph in a car, and then look at the speeds of dogs in this Top 10...

| | BREED | TOP SPEED (KPH) | (MPH) |
|---|---|---|---|
| 1 | GREYHOUND | 69.2 | 43 |
| 2 | SALUKI | 64.3 | 40 |
| = | VIZSLA | 64.3 | 40 |
| 4 | DALMATIAN | 60 | 37 |
| 5 | BORZOI | 57.9 | 36 |
| 6 | WEIMARANER | 56.3 | 35 |
| = | WHIPPET | 56.3 | 35 |
| 8 | DOBERMAN PINSCHER | 48.3 | 30 |
| = | BORDER COLLIE | 48.3 | 30 |
| 10 | RUSSELL TERRIER | 40.2 | 25 |

## GREYHOUND

Unsurprisingly, the fastest dog in the world has been adopted by several sports teams as their mascot. These include Ontario, Canada's Sault Ste. Marie Greyhounds.

## 101 DALMATIANS

The 1961 animated Disney movie *101 Dalmatians* took $215,880,014 at box offices around the world. In 1996, a live-action version, starring six-time Oscar-nominee Glenn Close as Cruella De Vil, took $320,689,204.

A GIRAFFE'S NECK IS
## 2 M LONG

### 📍 AFRICAN BUSH ELEPHANT

This is the largest of the two species of African Elephant. The smaller, the Africa Forest Elephant, weighs 5,896.7 kg (13,000 lb), less than half as much as the Bush species.

## TOP 10...
# HEAVIEST ON LAND

Considering a family car weighs around 1,360.8 kg (3,000 lb), these animals really tip the scales...

| | ANIMAL | WEIGHT (KG) | (LB) |
|---|---|---|---|
| 1 | AFRICAN BUSH ELEPHANT | 12,000 | 26,455 |
| 2 | ASIAN ELEPHANT | 5,200 | 11,464 |
| 3 | SOUTHERN ELEPHANT SEAL | 4,000 | 8,818 |
| = | SOUTHERN WHITE RHINOCEROS | 4,000 | 8,818 |
| 5 | HIPPOPOTAMUS | 3,200 | 7,054 |
| 6 | PACIFIC WALRUS | 2,000 | 4,409 |
| = | SALTWATER CROCODILE | 2,000 | 4,409 |
| 8 | BLACK RHINOCEROS | 1,400 | 3,086 |
| 9 | GIRAFFE | 1,360 | 2,998 |
| 10 | WILD WATER BUFFALO | 1,200 | 2,645 |

## BLACK RHINO SUBSPECIES

The Western Black Rhino was announced officially extinct in 2011, due to poaching. Other sub-species of rhino – the Chobe Black, Uganda Black, Eastern Black, South-central Black, and South-western Black – are all in danger of becoming extinct. Conservation organizations like WWF (www.wwf.org.uk) are part of a global movement to help prevent the extinction of countless endangered species.

## DIPLODOCUS

This popular dinosaur was named by American paleontologist Othniel Charles Marsh in 1878.

EXPERTS BELIEVE PUERTASAURUS WEIGHED

**100,000 KG**

## ARGENTINOSAURUS

First discovered in Argentina (hence its name) by Guillermo Heredia, this dinosaur lived 97 million years ago.

TOP 10...

# BIGGEST PREHISTORIC HERBIVORES

Although they only consumed vegetation, the size of these creatures dwarfs anything walking the Earth today...

| | DINOSAUR | LENGTH (M) | (FT) |
|---|---|---|---|
| 1 | AMPHICOELIAS | 60 | 196.8 |
| 2 | ARGENTINOSAURUS | 36 | 118.1 |
| 3 | MAMENCHISAURUS | 35 | 114.8 |
| 4 | FUTALOGNKOSAURUS | 34 | 111.5 |
| = | SAUROPOSEIDON | 34 | 111.5 |
| 6 | DIPLODOCUS | 33 | 108.3 |
| 7 | XINJIANGTITAN | 32 | 105 |
| 8 | PUERTASAURUS | 30 | 98.4 |
| = | = TURIASAURUS | 30 | 98.4 |
| 10 | DREADNOUGHTUS | 26 | 85.3 |

## PUERTASAURUS

One of the largest fossilized Puertasaurus vertabrae found is 1.68 m (5.51 ft) wide.

THE DIRE WOLF WEIGHED **25% MORE** THAN A MODERN DAY WOLF

TOP 10...

# BIGGEST **PREHISTORIC** CARNIVOROUS MAMMALS

Millions of years ago, it wasn't just the reptilian dinosaurs that grew to enormous sizes...

| | CREATURE | WEIGHT (KG) | (LB) |
|---|---|---|---|
| 1 | ARCTOTHERIUM | 1,749 | 3,855.9 |
| 2 | ANDREWSARCHUS | 1,000 | 2,204.6 |
| 3 | SHORT-FACED BEAR | 957 | 2,109.8 |
| 4 | PSEUDOCYON | 773 | 1,704.2 |
| 5 | AMPHICYON | 600 | 1,322.8 |
| 6 | SMILODON | 470 | 1,036.2 |
| 7 | THYLACOSMILUS | 120 | 264.6 |
| 8 | PACHYCROCUTA | 110 | 242.5 |
| 9 | DIRE WOLF | 79 | 174.2 |
| 10 | EPICYON | 68 | 150 |

## SMILODON

This, the most famous sabre-toothed cat, died out around 10,000 years ago. Its front canines were 27.9 cm (11 in) long.

## SHORT-FACED BEAR

This enormous bear stood over 3.66 m (12 ft) tall.

## ⚲ COMPSOGNATHUS LONGIPES

These small dinosaurs have been seen hunting in packs in the *Jurassic Park* films.

**TOP 10...**

# SMALLEST **PREHISTORIC** ANIMALS

Compare the data to the Top 10 list on the left to truly appreciate how tiny these creatures were...

| | CREATURE | WEIGHT (KG) | (LB) |
|---|---|---|---|
| 1 | PARVICURSOR REMOTUS | 0.14 | 0.31 |
| 2 | EPIDEXIPTERYX HUI | 0.16 | 0.35 |
| 3 | COMPSOGNATHUS LONGIPES | 0.26 | 0.57 |
| 4 | CERATONYKUS OCULATUS | 0.3 | 0.66 |
| 5 | JURAVENATOR STARKI | 0.34 | 0.75 |
| 6 | LIGABUEINO ANDESI | 0.35 | 0.77 |
| 7 | MICRORAPTOR ZHAOIANUS | 0.4 | 0.88 |
| 8 | SINOSAUROPTERYX PRIMA | 0.55 | 1.2 |
| 9 | RAHONAVIS OSTROMI | 0.58 | 1.3 |
| 10 | MAHAKALA OMNOGOVAE | 0.76 | 1.7 |

PARVICURSOR REMOTUS WAS AROUND

**38 CM** LONG

## ⚲ SINOSAUROPTERYX PRIMA

A fossil of Sinosauropteryx prima, the first dinosaur to be discovered with evidence of feathers, is on display at the Geological Museum of China.

## ⚲ EPIDEXIPTERYX HUI

Minus its tail feathers, this tiny dinosaur measured 25.4 cm (10 in) in length.

## TOP 10...
# FASTEST IN THE AIR

Speeds we can experience on an average drive don't come anywhere near close to these birds' abilities...

| | BIRD | MAXIMUM KNOWN SPEED (KPH) | (MPH) |
|---|---|---|---|
| 1 | PEREGRINE FALCON | 389 | 241.7 |
| 2 | GOLDEN EAGLE | 320 | 198.8 |
| 3 | GYRFALCON | 209 | 129.9 |
| 4 | SWIFT | 171 | 106.3 |
| 5 | EURASIAN HOBBY | 161 | 100 |
| 6 | FRIGATEBIRD | 153 | 95.1 |
| 7 | SPUR-WINGED GOOSE | 142 | 88.2 |
| 8 | RED-BREASTED MERGANSER | 130 | 80.8 |
| 9 | CANVASBACK | 116 | 72.1 |
| 10 | EIDER | 113 | 70.2 |

## SWIFT

The smallest species of Swift measures 9.4 cm (3.7 in) long.

## CANVASBACK

The largest kind of these diving ducks are found in North America, with a wingspan of 88.9 cm (35 in).

THE LARGEST GOLDEN EAGLE ON RECORD WEIGHED
**7.25 KG**

## RED-BREASTED MERGANSER

This migratory bird feeds underwater, eating aquatic insects, crustaceans, and small fish.

TOP 10...

# BIGGEST **FLYING** INSECTS

From full flight to gliding abilities, these are the largest winged insects...

| | FLYING INSECT | SIZE (LENGTH) | |
|---|---|---|---|
| | | (MM) | (IN) |
| 1 | CHAN'S MEGASTICK | 567 | 22.3 |
| 2 | BORNEO STICK INSECT | 546 | 21.5 |
| 3 | WHITE WITCH MOTH | 310* | 12.2 |
| 4 | QUEEN ALEXANDRA'S BIRDWING | 310* | 12.2 |
| 5 | GIANT AFRICAN STICK INSECT | 295 | 11.6 |
| 6 | ATLAS MOTH | 262* | 10.3 |
| 7 | MEGALOPREPUS CAERULATUS DAMSELFLY | 190* | 7.5 |
| 8 | HERCULES BEETLE | 175 | 6.9 |
| 9 | TITAN BEETLE | 167 | 6.6 |
| 10 | GIANT WATER BUG | 120.7 | 4.75 |

*Wingspan, the rest are lengths

## ⦿ ATLAS MOTH

This, the biggest moth in the world, is found in Southeast Asia.

## GIANT AFRICAN MANTIS

Unlike its name suggests, this insect only grows to around 10 cm (4 in). A strange trait of this creature is that females consume the male while mating.

## ⦿ HERCULES BEETLE

This beetle gets its name from its extraordinary strength. Growing to nearly 17.8 cm (7 in), it can lift 850 times its own body weight.

## ⊙ ANDEAN CONDOR

This is one of the longest-living birds, achieving an age of over 70 years. An endangered and protected species, it is also a national symbol of several countries, including Argentina, Colombia, and Ecuador.

## ⊙ MARIBOU STORK

Like the vulture, which this bird's head resembles, the Maribou Stork is a scavenger and eater of carrion.

**TOP 10...**

# WIDEST **WINGSPANS**

These birds' dimensions mean they are expert flyers, often spending hours at a time up in the sky...

| | BIRD | WINGSPAN (M) | (FT) |
|---|---|---|---|
| 1 | WANDERING ALBATROSS | 3.6 | 11.8 |
| = | GREAT WHITE PELICAN | 3.6 | 11.8 |
| 3 | DALMATIAN PELICAN | 3.45 | 11.3 |
| 4 | MARABOU STORK | 3.4 | 11.2 |
| = | ANDEAN CONDOR | 3.4 | 11.2 |
| 6 | MUTE SWAN | 3.1 | 10.2 |
| 7 | BEARDED VULTURE | 3 | 9.8 |
| 8 | GRIFFIN VULTURE | 2.8 | 9.2 |
| = | CALIFORNIA CONDOR | 2.8 | 9.2 |
| 10 | GREY CROWNED CRANE | 2.5 | 8.2 |

ON AVERAGE, THE MUTE SWAN WEIGHS
# 14.5 KG

# EAGLE WINGSPANS

| STELLAR'S SEA EAGLE | WHITE-TAILED SEA EAGLE | MARTIAL EAGLE | HIMALAYAN GOLDEN EAGLE | WEDGE-TAILED EAGLE |
|---|---|---|---|---|
| 2.49 M | 2.52 M | 2.59 M | 2.81 M | 2.84 M |

## EMU

This is Australia's largest bird. The Emu is key in Aboriginal creation mythology (an egg thrown into the sky formed the Sun). The bird also appears on Australia's Coat of Arms, along with a Red Kangaroo.

A DALMATIAN PELICAN'S BILL IS

# 45.7 CM IN LENGTH

## TOP 10...

# HEAVIEST BIRDS

Some of these birds are unable to fly, but all of them are heavyweights with variations of wings...

| | EAGLE | WEIGHT (KG) | (LB) |
|---|---|---|---|
| 1 | OSTRICH | 156.8 | 346 |
| 2 | DOUBLE-WATTLED CASSOWARY | 85 | 190 |
| 3 | EMU | 60 | 130 |
| 4 | GOLDEN-NECK CASSOWARY | 58 | 128 |
| 5 | EMPEROR PENGUIN | 45.4 | 100 |
| 6 | GREATER RHEA | 40 | 88 |
| 7 | DARWIN'S RHEA | 28.6 | 63 |
| 8 | LITTLE CASSOWARY | 26 | 57 |
| 9 | KING PENGUIN | 16 | 35 |
| 10 | DALMATIAN PELICAN | 15 | 33 |

## EMPEROR PENGUIN

This, the largest of all penguins, is only found in the Antarctic. Its flippers mean it can swim at 9 kph (6 mph).

## GOLDEN-NECK CASSOWARY

As well as heavy, this is also a tall bird, growing to 1 m (3 ft) in height.

## GREAT GREY OWL

This striking bird has many different names, including the Spectral Owl, and the Phantom of the North.

BARN OWLS ARE KNOWN TO TRAVEL UP TO

**1,760 KM**

## SNOWY OWL

Male Snowy Owls are almost completely white, while females have the distinctive mottled black flecks.

## TOP 10...
# LARGEST OWLS

Of the 200 different species of owl, these are the 10 largest...

| | BIRD | LENGTH (CM) | (IN) |
|---|---|---|---|
| 1 | GREAT GREY OWL | 84 | 33.1 |
| 2 | BLAKISTON'S FISH OWL | 72 | 28.3 |
| 3 | SNOWY OWL | 71 | 28 |
| 4 | EURASIAN EAGLE-OWL | 70 | 27.6 |
| 5 | MILKY EAGLE OWL | 66 | 26 |
| 6 | SPOT-BELLIED EAGLE-OWL | 65 | 25.6 |
| 7 | GREAT HORNED OWL | 64 | 25.2 |
| 8 | PEL'S FISHING OWL | 63 | 24.8 |
| 9 | CAPE EAGLE-OWL | 61 | 24 |
| = | TAWNY FISH OWL | 61 | 24 |

## BEE HUMMINGBIRD

The smallest bird in the world feeds on plant nectar from 15 different species and small insects.

## TOP 10...
# SMALLEST BIRDS

Of the 10,000+ species of birds, these are the tiniest we know of...

|   | BIRD | LENGTH (CM) | (IN) |
|---|---|---|---|
| 1 | BEE HUMMINGBIRD | 5 | 1.97 |
| 2 | BANANAQUIT | 7.5 | 2.96 |
| 3 | WEEBILL | 8 | 3.15 |
| = | STRIATED PARDALOTE | 8 | 3.15 |
| 5 | GOLDCREST | 8.5 | 3.35 |
| 6 | BROWN GERYGONE | 9 | 3.54 |
| = | LESSER GOLDFINCH | 9 | 3.54 |
| 8 | CRIMSON CHAT | 10 | 3.94 |
| = | GOLDEN-HEADED CISTICOLA | 10 | 3.94 |
| 10 | TROPICAL PARULA | 11 | 4.33 |

## TROPICAL PARULA

A common bird in Central America, it has a very distinctive call that sounds like a high-pitched buzz.

THE AVERAGE WEIGHT OF A BANANAQUIT IS
# 9.9
GRAMS

# COMPARING SIZES

This chart helps to show how the five smallest birds compare...

| GOLDCREST 8.51 CM | STRIATED PARDALOTE 8 CM | WEEBILL 8 CM | BANANAQUIT 7.51 CM | BEE HUMMINGBIRD 5 CM |
|---|---|---|---|---|

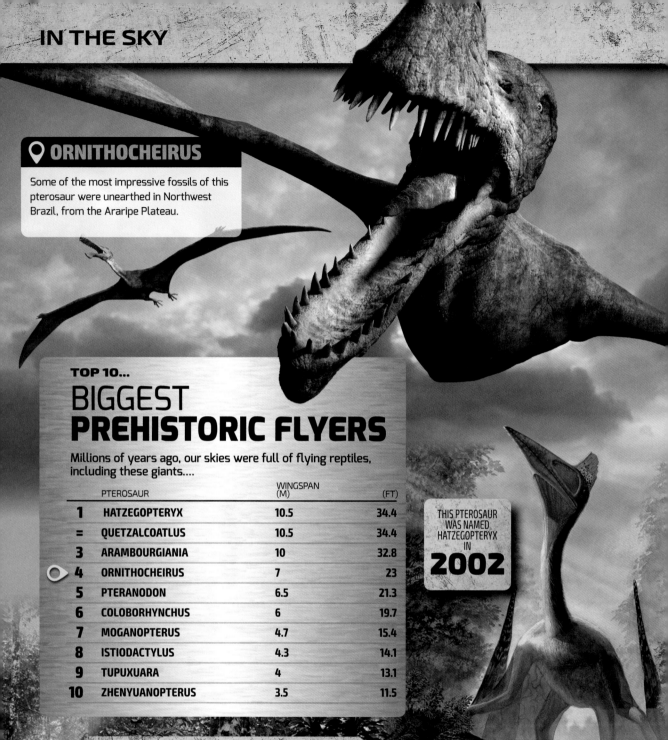

## ORNITHOCHEIRUS

Some of the most impressive fossils of this pterosaur were unearthed in Northwest Brazil, from the Araripe Plateau.

TOP 10...

# BIGGEST
# PREHISTORIC FLYERS

Millions of years ago, our skies were full of flying reptiles, including these giants....

| | PTEROSAUR | WINGSPAN (M) | (FT) |
|---|---|---|---|
| 1 | HATZEGOPTERYX | 10.5 | 34.4 |
| = | QUETZALCOATLUS | 10.5 | 34.4 |
| 3 | ARAMBOURGIANIA | 10 | 32.8 |
| 4 | ORNITHOCHEIRUS | 7 | 23 |
| 5 | PTERANODON | 6.5 | 21.3 |
| 6 | COLOBORHYNCHUS | 6 | 19.7 |
| 7 | MOGANOPTERUS | 4.7 | 15.4 |
| 8 | ISTIODACTYLUS | 4.3 | 14.1 |
| 9 | TUPUXUARA | 4 | 13.1 |
| 10 | ZHENYUANOPTERUS | 3.5 | 11.5 |

THIS PTEROSAUR WAS NAMED HATZEGOPTERYX IN
## 2002

## Q: THE WINGED SERPENT

American filmmaker Larry Cohen's 1982 monster thriller *Q: The Winged Serpent* was inspired by the mythological Aztec serpent god, Quetzalcoatl. This is also where the pterosaur Quetzalcoatlus gets its name.

## BUMBLEBEE MUSIC

One of the most famous pieces of music is 'The Flight of the Bumblebee', written by Russian composer Nikolai Rimsky-Korsakov between 1899–1900, for his opera *The Tale of Tsar Saltan*.

THE FEMALE HOUSEFLY CAN LAY
**500 EGGS**
IN HER LIFETIME

## WASP

Unlike most bees that can only sting once, wasps keep their stinger after an attack.

### TOP 10...
# FASTEST INSECT WINGS

In the world of things that buzz through the air, these beat their wings the fastest...

| | INSECT | BEATS PER SECOND (MAXIMUM) |
|---|---|---|
| 1 | MIDGE | 1,046 |
| 2 | GNAT | 950 |
| 3 | MOSQUITO | 600 |
| = | BUMBLEBEE | 600 |
| 5 | FRUIT FLY | 300 |
| 6 | WASP | 247 |
| 7 | HOUSEFLY | 190 |
| 8 | BLOWFLY | 150 |
| 9 | HOVERFLY | 120 |
| 10 | HORNET | 100 |

# BEATS PER SECOND

Here is a visual comparison of the top five fastest insects' wings...

| MIDGE | GNAT | MOSQUITO | BUMBLEBEE | FRUITFLY |
|---|---|---|---|---|
| 1,046 | 950 | 600 | 600 | 300 |

## ⦿ BLACK MARLIN

One of the most impressive fish on the planet, this lightning-fast animal can reach lengths of 4.66 m (15.3 ft) and weigh over 725.7 kg (1,600 lb).

SWORDFISH WEIGH UP TO
**648.6 KG**

## TOP 10...
# FASTEST IN THE SEA

Considering Brazil's César Cielo, the fastest swimmer on Earth, can go 5.35 mph, compare that to these speeds...

| | ANIMAL | SPEED (KPH) | (MPH) |
|---|---|---|---|
| 1 | BLACK MARLIN | 128.75 | 80 |
| 2 | SAILFISH | 110 | 68.3 |
| 3 | MAKO SHARK | 95 | 59 |
| 4 | WAHOO | 78 | 48.5 |
| 5 | BLUEFIN TUNA | 70 | 43.5 |
| 6 | GREAT BLUE SHARK | 69 | 42.9 |
| 7 | BONEFISH | 64 | 39.8 |
| = | SWORDFISH | 64 | 39.8 |
| 9 | GREAT WHITE SHARK | 56.3 | 35 |
| 10 | KILLER WHALE | 56 | 34.8 |

## WINGED FLYING FISH

There are 40 known species of flying fish. They leap out of the water and glide to avoid predators.

## BOTTLENOSE DOLPHIN

Although protected by the Marine Mammal Protection Act, many places like SeaWorld are sadly still using dolphins as a form of entertainment.

## ⚲ RIGHT WHALE

All three kinds of Right Whale are critically endangered, with as few as 50 left.

## BELUGA WHALE

This pure-white whale evolved to match its Arctic home surroundings.

THE GRAY WHALE CAN REACH
**15 M**
**IN LENGTH**

TOP 10...

# HEAVIEST IN THE OCEAN

Not only the heaviest in the ocean, these 10 are also the heaviest animals on Earth...

| | WHALE | WEIGHT (TONNE) | (LB) |
|---|---|---|---|
| **1** | BLUE WHALE | 120 | 264,554 |
| **2** | RIGHT WHALE* | 80 | 176,369 |
| **3** | FINBACK WHALE | 75 | 165,346 |
| **4** | BOWHEAD WHALE | 60 | 132,277 |
| **5** | SPERM WHALE | 50 | 110,231 |
| **6** | GRAY WHALE | 40 | 88,184 |
| **7** | HUMPBACK WHALE | 30 | 66,138 |
| **=** | BRYDE'S WHALE | 30 | 66,138 |
| **9** | SEI WHALE | 25 | 55,115 |
| **10** | GIANT BEAKED WHALE | 12 | 26,455 |

*There are three species of Right Whale: North Atlantic Right Whale, North Pacific Right Whale, and Southern Right Whale, each weighing up to 80 tonnes.

# WHALES' WEIGHTS

Here is a visual guide of how these whale's masses compare...

| COMMON MINKE WHALE | SOUTHERN MINKE WHALE | ARNOUX'S BEAKED WHALE | NORTHERN BOTTLENOSE WHALE | SOUTHERN BOTTLENOSE WHALE |
|---|---|---|---|---|
| 11 T | 10 T | 8 T | 7 T | 6 T |

GREAT WHITE SHARKS HAVE MORE THAN
**300 TEETH**
WHEN ONE BREAKS AWAY A NEW ONE GROWS.

## TOP 10...
# BIGGEST SHARKS

More than 400 species of shark have been discovered so far, and these are the largest...

| | SHARK | LENGTH (M) | (FT) |
|---|---|---|---|
| 1 | WHALE SHARK | 12.7 | 41.7 |
| 2 | BASKING SHARK | 12.3 | 40.4 |
| 3 | GREAT WHITE SHARK | 8.0 | 26.2 |
| 4 | TIGER SHARK | 7.4 | 24.3 |
| = | PACIFIC SLEEPER SHARK | 7.4 | 24.3 |
| 6 | GREENLAND SHARK | 6.4 | 21 |
| 7 | GREAT HAMMERHEAD SHARK | 6.1 | 20 |
| 8 | THRESHER SHARK | 6.0 | 19.7 |
| 9 | BLUNTNOSE SIXGILL SHARK | 4.8 | 15.7 |
| 10 | BIGEYE THRESHER SHARK | 4.6 | 15.1 |

## ⦿ GREAT WHITE SHARK

This is the largest predatory fish on Earth. One of their preferred meals is a seal for its energy-rich blubber. Great Whites strike from below at terrific speeds, taking their target by complete surprise.

## ⦿ GREENLAND SHARK

In the season five finale of *River Monsters*, host/biologist Jeremy Wade posited that the Greenland Shark's colossal size, lack of dorsal fin, and slate-grey skin, could be what many people see when they report a sighting of Scotland's Loch Ness Monster.

## ⦿ BASKING SHARK

Despite its huge mouth and size, this shark only feeds on tiny invertebrates and zooplankton, by filtering them through its jaws like a net.

## SWIMMING WITH SHARKS

The visual comparison shows how the top three largest sharks dwarf a scuba diver...

**BASKING SHARK**
12.3 M

**GREAT WHITE SHARK**
8 M

**WHALE SHARK**
12.7 M

# BITE PREVENTION

There are many things you can do to minimize your chances of being bitten by a shark, including:

• Avoid swimming at night, as sharks are mainly nocturnal hunters.

• Do not wear shiny swimsuits or jewellery as it could be mistaken for shimmering fish scales.

• Never urinate in the ocean, as this attracts sharks just like blood does.

• Do not swim when it rains, or in murky water, as both attract sharks inshore because churned water creates cover while they hunt.

TO DATE, THERE HAVE BEEN **ZERO** REPORTED SHARK ATTACKS IN CANADIAN WATERS.

## TOP 10...

# MOST **SHARK ATTACKS**

Contrary to the myth that sharks like eating people, their attacks on humans are a case of mistaken identity, as we resemble seals on the surface...

|  | LOCATION | FATAL ATTACKS | TOTAL ATTACKS |
|---|---|---|---|
| 1 | USA (EXCLUDING HAWAII) | 35 | 1,100 |
| 2 | AUSTRALIA | 153 | 572 |
| 3 | AFRICA | 94 | 345 |
| 4 | ASIA | 48 | 129 |
| 5 | HAWAII | 9 | 136 |
| 6 | OCEANIA/PACIFIC ISLANDS (EXCLUDING HAWAII) | 49 | 126 |
| 7 | SOUTH AMERICA | 24 | 117 |
| 8 | ANTILLES & BAHAMAS | 16 | 70 |
| 9 | CENTRAL AMERICA & MEXICO | 27 | 56 |
| 10 | NEW ZEALAND | 8 | 49 |

## GREECE

Not making this Top 10 by a long way is Greece. Of the 14 shark attacks reported, 12 of those were fatal. The last death from a shark attack occurred in 1969.

## ⦿ HAWAII

Hawaii is home to 40 different species of shark, including the Tiger Shark.

## BIGFIN SQUID

Rarely caught on camera, this massive creature has been seen at depths of 2,386.1 m (7,828.5 ft).

## THE KRAKEN

Tales (and illustrations) of a kraken/huge squid attacking ships date back to 1250.

**TOP 10...**

# LARGEST **SQUID/OCTOPI**

Once considered merely creatures of legend, we now know these tentacled organisms reach gigantic sizes...

| | ANIMAL | TYPE | LENGTH (M) | (FT) |
|---|---|---|---|---|
| 1 | COLOSSAL SQUID | Squid | 14 | 45.9 |
| 2 | GIANT SQUID | Squid | 13 | 42.7 |
| 3 | BIGFIN SQUID | Squid | 8 | 26.2 |
| 4 | GIANT PACIFIC OCTOPUS | Octopus | 6.1 | 20 |
| 5 | ASPEROTEUTHIS ACANTHODERMA | Squid | 5.5 | 18 |
| 6 | ROBUST CLUBHOOK SQUID | Squid | 4+ | 13.1+ |
| = | COCKATOO SQUID | Glass Squid | 4+ | 13.1+ |
| 8 | SEVEN-ARM OCTOPUS | Octopus | 4 | 13.1 |
| 9 | MEGALOCRANCHIA FISHERI | Glass Squid | 2.7 | 8.9 |
| 10 | DANA OCTOPUS SQUID | Squid | 2.3 | 7.5 |

## GIANT PACIFIC OCTOPUS

This is the largest octopus on Earth. It can weigh more than 272.2 kg (600 lb).

## BIGGEST & SMALLEST

This is how these two different species measure up...

**OCTOPUS WOLFI**
**2.54 CM**

**COLOSSAL SQUID**
**13.9 M**

THE GIANT PACIFIC OCTOPUS CAN LAY
**400,000**
**EGGS**
IN ITS LIFETIME

A BABY BLUE WHALE IS

# 7 M

**WHEN BORN**

## TOP 10...

# LONGEST **WHALES**

The heaviest whales are examined earlier in this Animal Kingdom zone, and these are the longest...

| | NAME | LENGTH (M) | (FT) |
|---|---|---|---|
| 1 | BLUE WHALE | 28 | 92 |
| 2 | FINBACK WHALE | 27.3 | 89.5 |
| 3 | SPERM WHALE | 20.4 | 67 |
| 4 | NORTH PACIFIC RIGHT WHALE | 19.8 | 65 |
| 5 | HUMPBACK WHALE | 18.9 | 62 |
| 6 | SOUTHERN RIGHT WHALE | 18 | 59 |
| = | BOWHEAD WHALE | 18 | 59 |
| 8 | SEI WHALE | 17 | 56 |
| 9 | GRAY WHALE | 14.9 | 49 |
| = | BRYDE'S WHALE | 14.9 | 49 |

## HUMPBACK WHALE

Humpbacks are found all over the world, due to their migratory behaviour. This species is famous for its long "whale song" sounds.

## BRYDE'S WHALE

These whales can stay underwater for 20 minutes on one breath. They can dive down to depths of 304.8 m (1,000 ft).

**41**

## ⊙ ELASMOSAURUS

This plesiosaur has an extremely long neck with 71 vertebrae. Experts calculate it could have weighed 2,000 kg (4,409.2 lb).

### TOP 10...
# BIGGEST PREHISTORIC OCEAN BEASTS

Reptiles, fish, and mammals all feature in this Top 10 of the largest aquatic creatures from millions of years ago...

|  | ANIMAL | TYPE | LENGTH (M) | (FT) |
|---|---|---|---|---|
| 1 | SHONISAURUS | Reptile | 21 | 66 |
| 2 | BASILOSAURUS | Mammal | 20 | 65.6 |
| 3 | LIVYATAN | Mammal | 17.5 | 57.4 |
| 4 | MEGALODON | Fish | 16 | 52.5 |
| 5 | HAINOSAURUS | Reptile | 15.2 | 49.9 |
| = | MOSASAURUS | Reptile | 15.2 | 49.9 |
| 7 | ELASMOSAURUS | Reptile | 14 | 46 |
| 8 | PLIOSAURUS | Reptile | 12.8 | 42 |
| 9 | DUNKLEOSTEUS | Fish | 10 | 32.8 |
| = | LEEDSICHTHYS | Fish | 10 | 32.8 |

## ⊙ MEGALODON

Due to the similarity in its jaws and fossilized findings, experts often refer to Megalodon as a giant-sized Great White Shark, although they are not related.

## MEGALODON

These comparisons show just how huge this prehistoric giant was.

GREAT WHITE SHARK
7.9 M

MEGALODON
16 M

MOSASAURUS LIVED AROUND
**70 MILLION** YEARS AGO

## 📍 LEEDSICHTHYS

The first remains of this huge fish were found in the 19th century, especially by Alfred Nicholson Leeds, whom the fish's name partly comes from.

CRETOXYRHINA WAS A PREHISTORIC SHARK THAT HAD

# 7
## CM-LONG TEETH

## TOP 10...
# BIGGEST
# PREHISTORIC FISH

Even the smallest fish on this list is equal to the size of a large, modern-day shark...

| | ANIMAL | LENGTH (M) | (FT) |
|---|---|---|---|
| 1 | MEGALODON | 16 | 52.5 |
| 2 | DUNKLEOSTEUS | 10 | 32.8 |
| = | LEEDSICHTHYS | 10 | 32.8 |
| 4 | ONCHOPRISTIS | 8 | 26.2 |
| 5 | RHIZODUS | 7 | 23 |
| 6 | CRETOXYRHINA | 6.1 | 20 |
| 7 | ISURUS | 6 | 19.7 |
| = | XIPHACTINUS | 6 | 19.7 |
| 9 | MAWSONIA | 4 | 13.1 |
| = | ONYCHODUS | 4 | 13.1 |

## 📍 XIPHACTINUS

This is a fossilized head of this prehistoric fish. American paleontologist George Fryer Sternberg famously found one of these with another fossilized fish inside its belly.

## 📍 RHIZODUS

This huge, bony fish had two elongated fangs (among its many teeth) that grew to 22 cm (8.6 in).

# MECHANICAL
# CREATIONS

## SEAWISE GIANT

Although scrapped in 2010, when this Japanese oil tanker (made by Sumitomo Heavy Industries, Ltd.) was fully loaded, it weighed 657,018,568.9 kg (1,448,478,000 lb).

## HINDENBURG LZ-129

During its two operational years, this airship notched up 30 flights. Its debut was on September 14, 1938.

BHP IRON ORE TRAIN HAS

**682** TRAIN CARS

## BHP IRON ORE

This train, its carriage and cargo weighed 99,790,321 kg (220 million lb).

**TOP 10...**

# BIGGEST VEHICLES OF ALL

Examining all of the different modes of transportation, including by land, sea, air, and also space explorations, these are the 10 largest machines...

| | TYPE | NAME | COUNTRY | SIZE (M) | (FT) |
|---|---|---|---|---|---|
| 1 | TRAIN | BHP Iron ore | Australia | 7,353 | 24,124 |
| 2 | LAND TRANSPORTER | F60 Overburden Conveyor | Germany | 502.01 | 1,647 |
| 3 | SHIP | Seawise Giant Oil Tanker | Japan | 458.46 | 1,504.1 |
| 4 | AIRCRAFT CARRIER | US Enterprise | USA | 342 | 1,122 |
| 5 | AIRSHIP | Hindenburg LZ-129 | Germany | 245 | 803.8 |
| 6 | SUBMARINE | Typhoon-class | Russia | 175 | 574.15 |
| 7 | SPACE STATION | International Space Station | USA, Canada, Russia, Japan, Europe | 108.5* | 356* |
| 8 | PLANE | Hughes H4 Hercules | USA | 97.51** | 319.92** |
| 9 | HELICOPTER | Mil V-12 | Russia (Soviet Union era) | 37 | 121.39 |
| 10 | TANK | Char 2C / FCM 2C | France | 10.27 | 33.69 |

All measurements are vehicles lengths except: *width and **wingspan

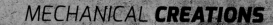

## ⦿ COLUMBIA SPACE SHUTTLE

This NASA shuttle tragically broke up when it re-entered Earth's atmosphere. All seven crewmembers were killed.

A TOTAL OF
**21**
**B-2 SPIRIT**
BOMBERS HAVE BEEN MADE

TOP 10...

# MOST EXPENSIVE VEHICLES OF ALL TIME

When technological advances add greater capabilities and size to vehicles, the price tags can soar into the billions...

| | TYPE | NAME | COUNTRY | COST ($) |
|---|---|---|---|---|
| 1 | TRAIN/RAILWAY SYSTEM | LO Series Shinkansen/Chūō Shinkansen | Japan | 75.5 billion |
| 2 | AIRCRAFT CARRIER | USS Gerald R. Ford | USA | 14 billion |
| 3 | ROCKET | Columbia Space Shuttle* | USA | 13 billion |
| 4 | TANK | K2 Black Panther | South Korea | 8.8 billion |
| 5 | PRIVATE BOAT | History Supreme | UK | 4.8 billion |
| 6 | SUBMARINE | SSN 774 Virginia-class | USA | 2.64 billion |
| 7 | PLANE | B-2 Spirit | USA | 2.4 billion |
| 8 | HELICOPTER | Bell Boeing V-22 Osprey | USA | 72.1 million |
| 9 | AIRSHIP | Zeppelin NT model LZ N07-101 | Germany | 15.9 million |
| 10 | CAR | Lamborghini Veneno | Italy | 4.5 million |

*Tragically broke up on re-entering Earth's atmosphere Feb 1, 2003

## ⦿ LO SERIES

This train will reach speeds of 505.3 kph (314 mph) once it is complete. Started in 2014, the first stage of the rail development is expected to be completed by 2027.

## 📍 EUROCOPTER X3

Only one Eurocopter X3 has been built. It has a rotor diameter of 12.6 m (41.3 ft). It is currently in France's Musée de l'Air et de l'Espace (aerospace museum).

## 📍 LOCKHEED SR-71

During its 35-year run, from 1964, 32 copies of this strategic aircraft were constructed.

TOP 10...

# FASTEST MANNED VEHICLES

To make this a comprehensive top 10 of top speeds, we've combined all the modes of transport that can be human-operated...

|  | TYPE OF VEHICLE | VEHICLE NAME | COUNTRY | YEAR | TOP SPEED (KPH) | (MPH) |
|---|---|---|---|---|---|---|
| 1 | ROCKET | Apollo 10 | USA* | 1969 | 39,897 | 24,791 |
| 2 | PLANE | Lockheed SR-71 Blackbird | USA | 1976 | 3,529.6 | 2,193.6 |
| 3 | JET-ENGINE CAR | Thrust SSC | USA | 1997 | 1,227.98 | 763.04 |
| 4 | CAR | Bluebird CN7 | Australia | 1964 | 710 | 440 |
| 5 | MOTORCYCLE | Top 1 Ack Attack | USA | 2010 | 605.7 | 376.36 |
| 6 | TRAIN** | SCMaglev | Japan | 2003 | 581 | 361 |
| 7 | BOAT | Spirit Of Australia | Australia | 1978 | 555.21 | 345 |
| 8 | HELICOPTER | Eurocopter X3 | France | 2013 | 487.63 | 303 |
| 9 | HOVERCRAFT | Jenny II | Portugal | 1995 | 137.4 | 85.38 |
| 10 | AIRSHIP | Zeppelin Luftschifftechnik LZ N07-100 | Germany | 2004 | 112 | 69.6 |

*Returning from the Moon to USA
**Magnetic Levitation Train (no contact with rail track)

THRUST SSC JET-ENGINE CAR WAS
## 16.5 M
LONG

## ◉ POWERBOAT

The sleek, modern-looking design of powerboats seen today evolved in the 1930s and 1940s to help set new speed records.

# FASTEST MACHINES IN SPORT

There are more mechanized sports that propel humans beyond 160 kph than you'd think...

| SPORT | TOP SPEED (KPH) | (MPH) |
|---|---|---|
| 1 TOP FUEL DRAGSTER | 534.59 | 332.18 |
| 2 POWERBOAT | 337.95 | 210 |
| 3 AIRSHOW STUNT PLANE | 426 | 264.7 |
| 4 INDY CAR | 413.52 | 256.95 |
| 5 FORMULA ONE CAR | 369.9 | 229.8 |
| 6 MOTOR RALLY (NASCAR, ETC.) | 342.4 | 212.8 |
| 7 SNOWMOBILE | 338 | 210.03 |
| 8 MOTORCYCLE (RACING) | 310.99 | 193.24 |
| 9 JETSKI | 180.24 | 112 |
| 10 MONSTER TRUCK | 159.48 | 99.1 |

## ◉ TOP FUEL DRAGSTER

This vehicle can travel 304.8 m (1,000 ft) in 3.7 seconds.

TOP FUEL DRAGSTERS CAN REACH **160** KPH IN **0.8 SECS**

# OTHER FAST VEHICLES

Two other popular sports vehicles that didn't make it onto this Top 10:
· Hovercraft, which can travel at 139.20 kph (86.5 mph).
· Go-Kart, which can achieve 128.7 kph (80 mph).

## GERALD R. FORD

Only one of this new class of 25-deck "supercarrier" currently exists, although 10 are planned.

THE GERALD R. FORD-CLASS AIRCRAFT CARRIER CAN HOLD

### 60 AIRCRAFT

## TOP 10...

# LONGEST
# BATTLESHIPS

Most of the these sea-faring constructions are more than 304.8 m (1,000 ft) long...

| | NAME/CLASS | COUNTRY | LENGTH (M) | (FT) |
|---|---|---|---|---|
| 1 | USS ENTERPRISE | USA | 342 | 1,122 |
| 2 | USS GERALD R. FORD | USA | 337 | 1,105.6 |
| 3 | USS NIMITZ | USA | 333 | 1,092.5 |
| 4 | USS KITTY HAWK | USA | 327 | 1,072.8 |
| 5 | FORRESTAL-CLASS | USA | 325 | 1,066.3 |
| 6 | USS JOHN F. KENNEDY | USA | 320 | 1,049.9 |
| 7 | USS MIDWAY | USA | 306 | 1,003.9 |
| 8 | ADMIRAL KUZNETSOV | Russia | 302 | 990.8 |
| 9 | HMS QUEEN ELIZABETH | UK | 284 | 931.8 |
| 10 | KIEV | Russia | 283 | 928.5 |

## NIMITZ

10 of the USA's Nimitz-class carriers have been built. The last was signed off for construction on Jan 10, 2009.

## ⦿ WESTLAND LYNX

In service for over 40 years, this helicopter's debut flight was on March 21, 1971.

## AIR SUPPORT

Here is how the flying military vehicles from below measure up...

**FALCON HTV-2**
20,921.47 KPH

**GENERAL DYNAMICS FB-111A**
2,655 KPH

**BARRACUDA**
1,041.3 KPH

**WESTLAND LYNX**
400.87 KPH

## ⦿ FALCON HTV-2

This unmanned, experimental craft is part of the USA's DARPA (Defense Advanced Research Projects Agency) program.

A DPV (DESERT PATROL VEHICLE) CAN CARRY

**680.4 KG**

## TOP 10...
# FASTEST **MILITARY VEHICLES**

Incorporating the wide range of tactical transport and craft used for military operations, these are the quickest in each of their classes...

| | TYPE | NAME | COUNTRY | SPEED (KPH) | (MPH) |
|---|---|---|---|---|---|
| 1 | HYPERSONIC CRUISE VEHICLE | Falcon HTV-2* | USA | 20,921.47 | 13,000 |
| 2 | AIRCRAFT BOMBER | General Dynamics FB-111A | USA | 2,655 | 1,650 |
| 3 | UNMANNED AERIAL VEHICLE | Barracuda | Germany/Spain | 1,041.3 | 647 |
| 4 | HELICOPTER | Westland Lynx | UK | 400.87 | 249.09 |
| 5 | TRUCK | IFAV (Interim Fast Attack Vehicle) | USA | 156.11 | 97 |
| 6 | SHIP | HMCS Bras d'Or (FHE 400) | Canada | 117 | 72 |
| 7 | LIGHT ATTACK VEHICLE | DPV (Desert Patrol Vehicle) | USA | 96.56+ | 60+ |
| 8 | TANK | S 2000 Scorpion Peacekeeper | UK | 82.23 | 51.10 |
| 9 | SUBMARINE | Alfa-class | Russia | 74 | 46 |
| 10 | AIRCRAFT CARRIER** | USS Gerald R. Ford (CVN-78) | USA | 55.56+ | 34.52+ |

*Still being tested and developed
**The actual top speed of aircraft carriers remains classified, but some have calculated they may be able to achieve up to 157.42 kph (97.82 mph / 85 knots)

## KOENIGSEGG AGERA

World-renowned *Top Gear* magazine hailed this model as 2010 Hypercar of the Year.

SALEEN S7 TWIN-TURBO HAS A

**269** CM **WHEELBASE**

## BUGATTI VEYRON GRAND SPORT VITESSE

This car was first revealed to the world at the Geneva Motor Show in 2012. Bugatti give interested owners the option to customize the exterior and interior colours.

### TOP 10...
# FASTEST CARS

Be they in production or merely concept cars, these are the quickest cars on the planet right now...

| | MODEL | TOP SPEED (KPH) | (MPH) |
|---|---|---|---|
| 1 | HENNESSEY VENOM GT | 435.31 | 270.49 |
| 2 | BUGATTI VEYRON 16.4 SUPER SPORT | 431.07 | 269.86 |
| 3 | KOENIGSEGG AGERA | 418.42 | 260 |
| 4 | SSC ULTIMATE AERO | 414.31 | 257.44 |
| 5 | 9FF GT9-R | 413.59 | 257 |
| 6 | BUGATTI VEYRON GRAND SPORT VITESSE | 408.84 | 254.04 |
| 7 | SALEEN S7 TWIN-TURBO | 399.11 | 248 |
| 8 | KOENIGSEGG CCX | 394.28 | 245 |
| 9 | MCLAREN F1 | 391.06 | 243 |
| 10 | ZENVO ST1 | 375 | 233 |

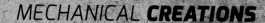

**9FF GT9-R WEIGHS**
# 1,326 KG

## ⦿ ARIEL ATOM 500

This car costs $225,000 and has a top speed of 270.36 kph (168 mph).

## TOP 10...
# FASTEST 0-60MPH CARS

In terms of acceleration, these are the 10 that triumph over all other cars...

| | MODEL | TIME TO GO FROM 0-60MPH (SECS) |
|---|---|---|
| 1 | LINGENFELTER CHEVROLET CORVETTE | 1.97 |
| 2 | SRT VIPER HENNESSEY VENOM 1000TT | 2.2 |
| 3 | ARIEL ATOM 500 (V-8) | 2.3 |
| 4 | BUGATTI VEYRON 16.4 SUPER SPORT | 2.4 |
| = | BUGATTI VEYRON EB 16.4 | 2.4 |
| 6 | CAPARO T1 | 2.5 |
| = | HENNESSEY VENOM GT | 2.5 |
| = | BUGATTI VEYRON 16.4 GRAND SPORT VITESSE | 2.5 |
| 9 | PAGANI ZONDA R | 2.6 |
| = | ULTIMA GTR 720 | 2.6 |

# CAR TYPES

Since the first steam-powered automobile appeared in 1768, the shape, technology, and abilities of cars has changed dramatically. Hundreds of years, and thousands of car designs later, the options for gearheads remains bountiful today. In 2015, in the USA alone, there were over 260 kinds of car available.

## ⦿ CAPARO T1

This car was designed by former McLaren F1 engineers Ben Scott-Geddes and Graham Halstead.

SUZUKI HAYABUSA
GSX1300R
WEIGHS

## 214.5
**KG**

# COMPARING KAWASAKIS

Here's how the speeds of the featured four compare...

| KAWASAKI ZX-14 299.3 KPH | KAWASAKI ZX-12R 299.2 KPH | KAWASAKI NINJA ZX-11 282 KPH | KAWASAKI GPZ900R NINJA 254 KPH |
|---|---|---|---|

**TOP 10...**

# FASTEST PRODUCTION BIKES

These are the fastest vehicles on two wheels that money can buy...

| | MODEL | TOP SPEED (KPH) | (MPH) |
|---|---|---|---|
| **1** | SUZUKI HAYABUSA GSX1300R | 312 | 194 |
| **2** | DUCATI DESMOSEDICI RR | 307.3 | 191 |
| **3** | BMW S1000RR | 303 | 188 |
| **=** | MV AGUSTA F4 R 312 | 303 | 188 |
| **5** | KAWASAKI ZX-14 | 299.3 | 186 |
| **6** | KAWASAKI ZX-12R | 299.2 | 185.8 |
| **7** | HONDA CBR1100XX SUPER BLACKBIRD | 290 | 180 |
| **8** | KAWASAKI NINJA ZX-11 | 282 | 175 |
| **9** | BIMOTA YB6 EXUP | 270 | 170 |
| **10** | KAWASAKI GPZ900R NINJA | 254 | 158 |

## ⊙ BMW S1000RR

This was the winner of several Bike of the Year awards in 2010, the year that it became commercially available. Previously, it was only made for the Superbike World Championships.

LAMBORGHINI VENENO
FUEL CONSUMPTION:

**20** KM
PER GALLON

## 📍 LAMBORGHINI VENENO

This has a 6.5 litre V12 engine, with a 7-speed automatic gearbox.

## DIE ANOTHER DAY

This 2002 James Bond film features an Aston Martin Vanquish as its star car. It costs $300,000 to buy.

KE02 EWW

### TOP 10...
# MOST **EXPENSIVE** PRODUCTION CARS

If money is no object, these 10 cars are the priciest designs out there...

| | NAME | PURCHASE COST ($) |
|---|---|---|
| 1 | LAMBORGHINI VENENO | 4,500,000 |
| 2 | BUGATTI VEYRON LEGEND MEO CONSTANTINI | 2,800,000 |
| 3 | BUGATTI VEYRON 16.4 SUPER SPORT | 2,400,000 |
| 4 | ASTON MARTIN ONE-77 | 1,850,000 |
| 5 | PAGANI ZONDA CINQUE ROADSTER | 1,800,000 |
| 6 | LAMBORGHINI REVENTÓN | 1,600,000 |
| = | KOENIGSEGG AGERA R | 1,600,000 |
| 8 | MAYBACH LANDAULET | 1,380,000 |
| 9 | PAGANI HUAYRA | 1,300,000 |
| = | FERRARI LAFERRARI | 1,300,000 |

## ASTON MARTIN'S 007 LEGACY

Several different models of Aston Martin cars have been featured multiple times in *James Bond* films over the past 43 years, including:
· The DB5 in *Goldfinger*.
· The DBS V12 in *Quantum of Solace*.
· The DB10 in *Spectre*.

## BAGGER 288

This colossal machine has been featured in movies such as 2012's *Ghost Rider: Spirit of Vengeance.*

NASA'S CRAWLER-TRANSPORTER IS
# 40 M
LONG

## CRAWLER-TRANSPORTER

This mammoth transporter boasts a base containing eight tracks. Each track has 57 "shoes" to allow the vehicle to grip into the ground whilst moving its heavy payload.

TOP 10...

# HEAVIEST LAND TRANSPORTERS

When the items that have to be moved weigh thousands of tons, the device performing the task needs to weigh way more...

| | NAME | FUNCTION | WEIGHT (TONS) |
|---|---|---|---|
| 1 | BAGGER 288 | Power Shovel Excavator | 45,500 |
| 2 | MARION 5960-M "BIG DIGGER" | Power Shovel Excavator | 17,825 |
| 3 | MARION 6360 "THE CAPTAIN" | Power Shovel Excavator | 15,000 |
| 4 | TAKRAF BAGGER 293 | Power Shovel Excavator | 14,200 |
| = | TENOVA TAKRAF SRS 8000 | Power Shovel Excavator | 14,200 |
| 6 | F60 OVERBURDEN CONVEYOR BRIDGE | Moving bridges | 13,600 |
| 7 | 4250-W "BIG MUSKIE" | Power Shovel Excavator | 13,500 |
| 8 | SRS(H) 1050 | Bucket Wheel Excavator | 6,000 |
| 9 | HERRENKNECHT EPB SHIELD S-300 | Tunnel maker | 4,364 |
| 10 | CRAWLER-TRANSPORTER | NASA shuttle transport | 2,400 |

# TOP THREE TITANS

Here is how the heaviest transporters compare...

**BAGGER 288**
45,500 T

**MARION 6360 "THE CAPTAIN"**
15,000 T

**MARION 5960-M "BIG DIGGER"**
17,825 T

## LNER SILVER LINK

Built in 1935, its first journey on Sep 29 became a record-breaking one from London's King's Cross station, setting a new speed record at that time.

TOP 10...

# FASTEST STEAM LOCOMOTIVES

In the age before electricity revolutionized the train industry, these steam engines held the speed records...

| | TRAIN | COUNTRY | YEAR | TOP SPEED (KPH) | (MPH) |
|---|---|---|---|---|---|
| 1 | LNER CLASS A4 NO. 4468 MALLARD | UK | 1939 | 202.6 | 126 |
| 2 | BORSIG DRG SERIES 05 002 | Germany | 1936 | 200.4 | 125 |
| 3 | PENNSYLVANIA RAILROAD E2 #7002 | USA | 1905 | 185.07 | 115 |
| 4 | BR 18 201 | Germany | 1972 | 182.4 | 113 |
| 5 | MILWAUKEE ROAD CLASS A | USA | 1935 | 181.1 | 112.5 |
| 6 | LNER CLASS A4 2509 SILVER LINK | UK | 1935 | 180.3 | 112 |
| 7 | LNER CLASS A3 NO. 2750 PAPYRUS | UK | 1935 | 168.5 | 105 |
| 8 | MILWAUKEE ROAD CLASS F6 | USA | 1934 | 166.6 | 104 |
| 9 | GWR 3700 CLASS 3440 CITY OF TRURO | UK | 1904 | 164 | 102 |
| 10 | LNER CLASS A3 4472 FLYING SCOTSMAN | UK | 1934 | 161 | 100 |

MILWAUKEE ROAD CLASS A COULD WEIGH MORE THAN **226,800 KG** WITH A FULL TENDER ATTACHED

## LNER COMPARISON

This graph looks at the LNER trains featured above...

| LNER CLASS A4 NO. 4468 MALLARD | LNER CLASS A4 2509 SILVER LINK | LNER CLASS A3 NO. 2750 PAPYRUS | LNER CLASS A3 4472 FLYING SCOTSMAN |
|---|---|---|---|
| 202.6 KPH | 180.3 KPH | 168.5 KPH | 161 KPH |

## BORSIG DRG SERIES 05 002

This German train has up to 2,367 horsepower. It had 24 smoke tubes and 106 heating tubes.

# LOCKHEED MODELS

This visual guide examines the three Lockheeds from the below chart...

**LOCKHEED SR-71 BLACKBIRD**
3,529.6 KPH

**LOCKHEED YF-12A**
3,331.5 KPH

**LOCKHEED F-104C STARFIGHTER**
2,259.5 KPH

## 77 MCDONNELL F-101A VOODOOS
WERE BUILT

## X-15

Only three models of the X-15 were ever built. One of them is on display at the USA's National Air and Space Museum in Washington D.C.

## PHANTOM II

More than 5,000 units of this twin-engine jet fighter have been made since it was developed in the 1950s.

TOP 10...

# FASTEST MANNED AIRCRAFT

Piloting the aircraft in this Top 10 requires intense training sessions to cope with the physical effects of flying at these extreme speeds...

|   | AIRCRAFT | PILOT(S) | DATE | TOP SPEED (KPH) | (MPH) |
|---|---|---|---|---|---|
| 1 | NORTH AMERICAN X-15 | William J. "Pete" Knight | Oct 3, 1967 | 7,273 | 4,519 |
| 2 | LOCKHEED SR-71 BLACKBIRD | Eldon W. Joersz & George T. Morgan | July 28, 1976 | 3,529.6 | 2,193.2 |
| 3 | LOCKHEED YF-12A | Robert L. Stephens & Daniel Andre | May 1, 1965 | 3,331.5 | 2,070.1 |
| 4 | MIKOYAN GUREVICH YE-166 | Georgii Mosolov | July 7, 1962 | 2,681 | 1,665.9 |
| 5 | MCDONNELL-DOUGLAS F-4 PHANTOM II | Robert G. Robertson | Nov 22, 1961 | 2,585.1 | 1,606.3 |
| 6 | CONVAIR F-106 DELTA DART | Joseph Rogers | Dec 15, 1959 | 2,455.7 | 1,525.9 |
| 7 | LOCKHEED F-104C STARFIGHTER | Walter W. Irwin | May 16, 1958 | 2,259.5 | 1,404 |
| 8 | MCDONNELL F-101A VOODOO | Adrian Drew | Dec 12, 1957 | 1,943.5 | 1,207.6 |
| 9 | FAIREY DELTA 2 | Peter Twiss | Mar 10, 1956 | 1,833.31 | 1,139.2 |
| 10 | F-100C SUPER SABRE | Horace A. Hanes | Aug 20, 1955 | 1,323 | 822.1 |

TOP 10...
# PLANES WITH
# LARGEST WINGSPANS

Although aviation technology is constantly being improved, the record for the widest aircraft has not been superseded in nearly 70 years...

| | NAME | COUNTRY | DEBUT FLIGHT | WINGSPAN (M) | (FT) |
|---|---|---|---|---|---|
| 1 | HUGHES H-4 SPRUCE GOOSE | USA | Nov 2, 1947 | 97.5 | 319.8 |
| 2 | ANTONOV AN-225 MRIYA | Russia (Soviet Union era) | Nov 21, 1988 | 88.4 | 290 |
| 3 | AIRBUS A380-800 | Europe (various) | Apr 21, 2005 | 79.8 | 261.8 |
| 4 | ANTONOV AN-124 | Russia (Soviet Union era) | Dec 26, 1982 | 73.3 | 240.5 |
| 5 | CONVAIR B-36J-III | USA | Aug 8, 1946 | 70.1 | 230 |
| = | CONVAIR XC-99 | USA | Nov 23, 1947 | 70.1 | 230 |
| 7 | BOEING 747-8F | USA | Feb 8, 2010 | 68.5 | 224.7 |
| 8 | LOCKHEED C-5B | USA | June 30, 1968 | 67.9 | 222.7 |
| 9 | BOEING 747-400 | USA | Feb 9, 1969 | 64.4 | 211.3 |
| = | ANTONOV AN-22 | Russia (Soviet Union era) | Feb 27, 1965 | 64.4 | 211.3 |

CONVAIR
**XC-99'S**
FINAL FLIGHT
WAS IN
**1957**

# HISTORY OF BOEING

William E. Boeing (Oct 1, 1881 – Sep 28, 1956) joined forces with George Conrad Westervelt (Dec 30, 1879 – Mar 15, 1956) and founded Pacific Aero Products. 1916's Boeing Model 1, a seaplane, was their first aircraft. After Westervelt left, the company's name was simplified to the Boeing Airplane Company in 1917.

📍 **ANTONOV AN-124**

55 of these strategic Russian planes have been produced since 1982.

**EC 665 TIGER'S** DEBUT FLIGHT WAS IN **1991**

### ⦿ BELL BOEING

More than 200 units of this helicopter have been built since 1988.

## TOP 10...

# MOST EXPENSIVE
# MILITARY
# HELICOPTERS

The development funding behind these helicopters exceeds a total of $440 million...

| | NAME | COUNTRY OF MANUFACTURE | COST ($ MILLIONS) |
|---|---|---|---|
| 1 | SIKORSKY CH-53K KING STALLION | USA | 84.9 |
| 2 | BELL BOEING V-22 OSPREY | USA | 72.1 |
| 3 | NHINDUSTRIES NH90 | Germany | 59 |
| 4 | SIKORSKY SH-60 SEAHAWK | USA | 42.9 |
| 5 | EC 665 TIGER | France | 39.2 |
| 6 | BOEING CH-47F CHINOOK | USA | 38.5 |
| 7 | BOEING AH-64E APACHE | USA | 35.5 |
| 8 | BELL AH-1Z VIPER | USA | 31 |
| 9 | KAMAN SH-2G SUPER SEASPRITE | USA | 26 |
| 10 | AGUSTAWESTLAND AW101 | UK/Italy | 21 |

# HELICOPTER COSTS

Here is how the top three of the chart compare...

SIKORSKY CH-53K KING STALLION **84.9**

NH INDUSTRIES NH90 **59**

BELL BOEING V-22 OSPREY **72.1**

### ⦿ NHINDUSTRIES NH90

In service for more than 20 years since its debut in December 1995, this helicopter can carry up to 20 troops.

ROBOBEE'S WINGS CAN BEAT
**120**
TIMES PER SECOND

## 📍 ZANO

Zano captures video in high definition and can be controlled via a smartphone.

## 📍 DELFLY MICRO

This tiny drone weighs 3.07 g (0.02 oz).

TOP 10...
# SMALLEST **DRONES**

Drones are becoming more and more commonplace for military, delivery, and hobbiest purposes, and they're getting tinier each year...

| | NAME | DEVELOPED BY | WINGSPAN (CM) | (IN) |
|---|---|---|---|---|
| 1 | ROBOBEE | Harvard's School of Engineering and Applied Sciences, USA | 3 | 1.18 |
| 2 | SKEYE NANO DRONE | TRBDlabs | 4 | 1.57 |
| = | CHANNEL MICRO QUAD COPTER TR-MQ1 | Top Race | 4 | 1.57 |
| 4 | CX10 | Cheerson | 4.4 | 1.73 |
| 5 | Q4 NANO MINI QUADCOPTER | Husban | 4.5 | 1.77 |
| 6 | ZANO | Torquing Group Ltd | 6.5 | 2.56 |
| 7 | CODE BLACK DRONE | Code Black | 8.15 | 3.25 |
| 8 | DELFLY MICRO | DelFly, Netherlands | 10 | 3.94 |
| 9 | FPV X4 MINI RTF QUADCOPTER | Hubsan | 10.2 | 4.02 |
| 10 | PD-100 BLACK HORNET PRS | Prox Dynamics | 12 | 4.72 |

## HANG GLIDER

Since 1997, the sixth-generation design of hang gliders, featuring carbon-fibre crossbars, has been used by hobbyists and professionals.

HANG GLIDING WAS INVENTED

**1,500 YEARS AGO**

## PARAGLIDER

Paragliders often seek out "thermals" to increase their lift. These are pockets of air that are warmer as a result of the sun heating the ground beneath the area.

TOP 10...

# HIGHEST **HANG GLIDING & PARAGLIDING** CHAMPIONS

These champions have a head for extreme heights, piloting their craft to altitudes that planes regularly inhabit...

| | NAME | COUNTRY | HEIGHT ACHIEVED (M) | (FT) |
|---|---|---|---|---|
| 1 | ROBBIE WHITTALL | UK | 4,526 | 14,849.08 |
| 2 | RICHARD WESTGATE | UK | 4,380 | 14,370.08 |
| 3 | LARRY TUDOR | USA | 4,343 | 14,248.69 |
| 4 | KAT THURSTON | UK | 4,325 | 14,189.63 |
| 5 | IAN E. KIBBLEWHITE | New Zealand | 4,175 | 13,697.51 |
| 6 | URS HAARI | Switzerland | 4,150 | 13,615.49 |
| 7 | MICHAEL KOBLER | Switzerland | 4,050 | 13,287.40 |
| 8 | JUDY LEDEN | UK | 3,970 | 13,024.93 |
| 9 | RAINER M. SCHOLL | Germany | 3,820 | 12,532.81 |
| 10 | SEAN M. DOUGHERTY | Canada | 3,671 | 12,043.96 |

## MICROLIGHT

In competitive microlight sports events, the craft must weigh no more than 450 kg (992 lb).

## MICRO MOTOR CHAMPS

These graphics compare the top five entries of the below chart...

| SERGE ZIN 9,720 M | ERIC SCOTT WINTON 9,144 M | JAN BÈM 8,072 M | ALEXIS ANASTASIOU 7,608 M | RAMÓN MORILLAS SALMERON 7,589 M |

FRANCE HAS MORE THAN
**26,000**
REGISTERED PARAGLIDERS

**TOP 10...**

# HIGHEST **MICROLIGHT** **& PARAMOTOR** CHAMPIONS

The addition of an engine means that these light-frame craft can reach even more dizzying heights...

| | NAME | COUNTRY | HEIGHT ACHIEVED (M) | (FT) |
|---|---|---|---|---|
| 1 | SERGE ZIN | France | 9,720 | 31,889.76 |
| 2 | ERIC SCOTT WINTON | Australia | 9,144 | 30,000 |
| 3 | JAN BÈM | Czech Republic | 8,072 | 26,482.94 |
| 4 | ALEXIS ANASTASIOU | Greece | 7,608 | 24,960.63 |
| 5 | RAMÓN MORILLAS SALMERON | Spain | 7,589 | 24,898.29 |
| 6 | MARK JACKSON | UK | 7,395 | 24,261.81 |
| 7 | WALTER MAURI | Italy | 7,143 | 23,435.04 |
| 8 | ROLAND GODDENS | Belgium | 7,000 | 22,965.88 |
| 9 | KAREN SKINNER | Spain | 6,250 | 20,505.25 |
| 10 | ROBERT MAIR | UK | 6,245 | 20,488.85 |

## PARAMOTOR

This word describes the engine aspect of a paraglider that has a motor.

## 📍 GAR WOOD

The legendary Iowa, USA-born record-setter was born Dec 4, 1880, and died June 19, 1971.

**GAR WOOD'S MISS AMERICA X WAS**

## 11.5 M LONG

**TOP 10...**

# FASTEST ON WATER RECORD HOLDERS

The number one speed record on this chart has not been broken in over 30 years...

| | SKIPPER | VESSEL | COUNTRY | YEAR | BEST SPEED ACHIEVED (KPH) | (MPH) |
|---|---|---|---|---|---|---|
| 1 | KEN WARBY | Spirit of Australia | **Australia** | 1978 | 511.12 | 317.6 |
| 2 | LEE TAYLOR | Hustler | **USA** | 1967 | 459.02 | 285.22 |
| 3 | DONALD CAMPBELL | Bluebird K7 | **UK** | 1964 | 444.71 | 276.33 |
| 4 | STANLEY SAYRES, ELMER LENINSCHMIDT | Slo-Mo-Shun IV | **USA** | 1952 | 287.26 | 178.5 |
| 5 | MALCOLM CAMPBELL | Bluebird K4 | **UK** | 1939 | 228.11 | 141.74 |
| 6 | GAR WOOD | Miss America X | **USA** | 1932 | 200.94 | 124.86 |
| 7 | KAYE DON | Miss England III | **Italy** | 1932 | 192.82 | 119.81 |
| 8 | HENRY SEGRAVE | Miss England II | **UK** | 1930 | 158.94 | 98.76 |
| 9 | GEORGE WOOD | Miss America II | **USA** | 1928 | 149.41 | 92.84 |
| 10 | JULES FISHER | Farman Hydroglider | **USA** | 1924 | 140.64 | 87.39 |

## 📍 MALCOLM CAMPBELL

During his career, as well as setting four water speed records, Campbell also broke nine land speed records.

### ADRIENNE CAHALAN

Aside from being a World Yachtswoman of the Year nominee, Cahalan also has a Master's degree in Applied Meteorology.

### BRUNO PEYRON

In 1993, Bruno Peyron became the first recipient of the Jules Verne Trophy, the award for the fastest circumnavigation of the Earth.

**TOP 10...**

# FURTHEST DISTANCE SAILING IN 24 HOURS

As this Top 10 proves, long-distance sailing is not only very popular in France, it has also produced some of the most skilled yachtsmen...

| | SKIPPER | VESSEL | COUNTRY | YEAR | BEST DISTANCE ACHIEVED IN 24 HOURS (KM) | (MI) |
|---|---|---|---|---|---|---|
| 1 | PASCAL BIDÉGORRY | Banque Populaire V | France | 2009 | 1,681.4 | 1,044.8 |
| 2 | FRANCK CAMMAS | Groupama 3 | France | 2007 | 1,470 | 914 |
| 3 | BRUNO PEYRON | Orange II | France | 2006 | 1,420.1 | 882.4 |
| 4 | ADRIENNE CAHALAN | Maiden II | Australia | 2002 | 1,286.73 | 799.54 |
| 5 | STEVE FOSSETT | PlayStation | USA | 2001 | 1,272.64 | 790.78 |
| 6 | GRANT DALTON | Club Med | France | 2001 | 1,213.4 | 754.0 |
| 7 | LOÏCK PEYRON | Innovation Explorer | France | 2001 | 1,165.8 | 724.4 |
| 8 | LAURENT BOURGNON | Primagaz | France | 1994 | 1,000 | 620 |
| 9 | OLIVIER DE KERSAUSON | Lyonnaise des eaux | France | 1994 | 971.61 | 603.73 |
| 10 | SERGE MADEC | Jet Services V | France | 1990 | 968.10 | 601.55 |

BANQUE POPULAIRE V TRIMARAN IS

## 39.6 M
LONG

**THE U.S. NAVY FEATURES OVER 326,000 PERSONNEL**

## ⚲ USA

Along with its array of aircraft carriers and planes, the U.S. Navy also has 71 submarines in its arsenal.

## CARRIER CONSTRUCTIONS

This pie-chart gives a visual representation of how the different nations' aircraft carrier achievements compare...

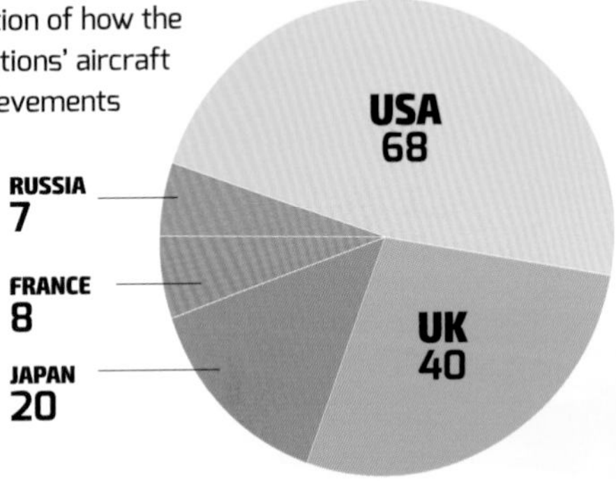

RUSSIA
**7**

FRANCE
**8**

JAPAN
**20**

USA
**68**

UK
**40**

TOP 10...

# MOST AIRCRAFT CARRIERS

These colossal seacraft are often key components in international military operations...

| | COUNTRY | NUMBER IN SERVICE | TOTAL NUMBER EVER BUILT |
|---|---|---|---|
| 1 | USA | 10 | 68 |
| 2 | UK | 0 | 40 |
| 3 | JAPAN | 0 | 20 |
| 4 | FRANCE | 1 | 8 |
| 5 | RUSSIA | 1 | 7 |
| 6 | INDIA | 2 | 3 |
| = | SPAIN | 1 | 3 |
| = | AUSTRALIA | 0 | 3 |
| = | CANADA | 0 | 3 |
| 10 | ITALY | 2 | 2 |

## ⚲ UNITED KINGDOM

The Royal Navy was formerly established as a national institution in 1660.

## VANGUARD

This British-made class of submarine can carry 16 Trident II missiles, which each weigh 58,967 kg (130,000 lb).

**TOP 10...**

# LONGEST
# SUBMARINES

Russia's navy has produced six of the 10 biggest submarines in history...

| | CLASS | COUNTRY | LENGTH (M) | (FT) |
|---|---|---|---|---|
| 1 | TYPHOON | Russia | 175 | 574.14 |
| 2 | BOREI | Russia | 170 | 557.74 |
| = | OHIO | USA | 170 | 557.74 |
| 4 | DELTA III | Russia | 166 | 544.62 |
| 5 | OSCAR II | Russia | 155 | 508.53 |
| 6 | VANGUARD | UK | 149.9 | 491.8 |
| 7 | TRIOMPHANT | France | 138 | 452.76 |
| 8 | YASEN | Russia | 120 | 393.7 |
| 9 | VIRGINIA | USA | 115 | 377.3 |
| 10 | SIERRA II | Russia | 111 | 364.17 |

# SEAWOLF

Just missing out on a place in the above Top 10 is USA's *Seawolf* submarine. It is 108 m (354.33 ft) long.

JAPAN'S
SŌRYŪ
SUBMARINE
IS
**84 M**
IN LENGTH

AUSTRALIA HAS WON
**10**
GOLD MEDALS
FOR WORLD CUP
SAILING

## TOP 10...
# WORLD CUP
# SAILING NATIONS

These are the countries that have produced the greatest wave-based racers...

| | COUNTRY | TOTAL GOLD | TOTAL SILVER | TOTAL BRONZE | TOTAL MEDALS |
|---|---|---|---|---|---|
| 1 | AUSTRALIA | 10 | 8 | 9 | 27 |
| 2 | GREAT BRITAIN | 7 | 7 | 2 | 16 |
| 3 | FRANCE | 2 | 4 | 3 | 9 |
| 4 | NORWAY | 4 | 1 | 2 | 7 |
| = | CHINA | 3 | 2 | 2 | 7 |
| = | NEW ZEALAND | 3 | 2 | 2 | 7 |
| 7 | RUSSIA | 1 | 2 | 3 | 6 |
| 8 | CROATIA | 1 | 4 | 0 | 5 |
| = | GREECE | 1 | 3 | 1 | 5 |
| 10 | AUSTRIA | 2 | 0 | 1 | 3 |

## ◉ FRANCE

Founded in 1946, the French Sailing Federation incorporates over 1,000 sailing clubs all over France. 176 French Federation members have competed at an Olympic level.

## ◉ NORWAY

The Norwegian Sailing Federation was established in 1970.

## TOTAL MEDALS

This chart compares the total number of medals from the top five sailing nations...

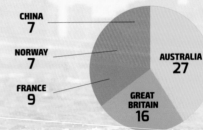

CHINA
**7**

NORWAY
**7**

FRANCE
**9**

AUSTRALIA
**27**

GREAT BRITAIN
**16**

## ⦿ ALLURE OF THE SEAS

This cruise ship is 361.8 m (1,187 ft) long and has 25 dining options.

ALLURE OF THE SEAS' CREW:

# 2,384
**PEOPLE**

**TOP 10...**

# VESSELS WITH MOST PASSENGERS

These cruise-liners can hold enough people to match the population of some cities...

| | NAME | MAIDEN VOYAGE | MAX PASSENGERS |
|---|---|---|---|
| 1 | ALLURE OF THE SEAS | Dec 1, 2010 | 6,296 |
| = | OASIS OF THE SEAS | Dec 5, 2009 | 6,296 |
| 3 | NORWEGIAN EPIC | July 10, 2009 | 5,183 |
| 4 | COSTA DIADEMA | Nov 1, 2014 | 4,928 |
| 5 | CARNIVAL SPLENDOR | Aug 18, 2008 | 4,914 |
| 6 | QUANTUM OF THE SEAS | Nov 2, 2014 | 4,905 |
| 7 | CARNIVAL MAGIC | May 1, 2011 | 4,720 |
| = | CARNIVAL BREEZE | June 3, 2012 | 4,720 |
| 9 | CARNIVAL DREAM | Sep 21, 2009 | 4,631 |
| 10 | INDEPENDENCE OF THE SEAS | May 2, 2008 | 4,375 |

## ⦿ OASIS OF THE SEAS

Although they share the same capacity, this ship is 5 cm (1.97 in) shorter than *Allure Of The Seas.*

# CRUISE LINERS

Luxury cruise ships date back to the mid-1800s when British company Peninsular and Oriental Steam Navigation Company (better known now as P&O) began offering long sea-bound trips to faraway countries. The technology has changed over the centuries that followed, but the core experience of the cruise holiday has not.

# MACHINES ON SCREENS

📍 **FAST & FURIOUS 6**

More than 400 different cars were featured on screen in this sequel.

**TOP 10...**

# BIGGEST **ICONIC CAR** MOVIES

Comparing the big-screen adventures that feature cars as the stars, these are the most successful motor-movies...

| | MOVIE | ICONIC CAR | YEAR RELEASED | BOX OFFICE ($ WORLDWIDE) |
|---|---|---|---|---|
| 1 | FURIOUS 7 | Various | 2015 | 1,499,723,320 |
| 2 | SKYFALL | 1965 Aston Martin DB5 | 2012 | 1,108,561,013 |
| 3 | THE DARK KNIGHT | The Tumbler | 2008 | 1,004,558,444 |
| 4 | FAST & FURIOUS 6 | Various | 2013 | 788,679,850 |
| 5 | FAST FIVE | Various | 2011 | 626,137,675 |
| 6 | MIB 3 | Ford Taurus SHO, 1964 Ford Galaxie | 2014 | 624,026,776 |
| 7 | CASINO ROYALE | Aston Martin DBS V12 | 2006 | 599,045,960 |
| 8 | MEN IN BLACK | Ford LTD Crown Victoria | 1997 | 589,390,539 |
| 9 | QUANTUM OF SOLACE | Aston Martin DBS V12 | 2008 | 586,090,727 |
| 10 | CARS 2 | Various | 2011 | 559,852,396 |

CARS (2006) MADE **461.9 MILLION** AT THE BOX OFFICE

📍 **QUANTUM OF SOLACE**

This, the second Daniel Craig outing as James Bond, was released in 2008. It featured an array of cars, including the Alpha Romeo 159, the Aston Martin DBS V12, the Ford Edge, and the Jaguar XJ8.

## GRAND THEFT AUTO: VICE CITY

This game featured a huge amount of licensed songs, including Tears For Fears' "Pale Shelter."

## TOP 10...
# BIGGEST DRIVING GAMES

Just three game franchises feature in this Top 10, with GTA dominating the chart...

| | NAME | PLATFORM | RELEASED | UNIT SALES (MILLIONS) |
|---|---|---|---|---|
| 1 | MARIO KART WII | Wii | 2008 | 35.11 |
| 2 | MARIO KART DS | DS | 2005 | 23.10 |
| 3 | GRAND THEFT AUTO: SAN ANDREAS | PS2 | 2004 | 20.81 |
| 4 | GRAND THEFT AUTO V | PS3 | 2013 | 19.36 |
| 5 | GRAND THEFT AUTO: VICE CITY | PS2 | 2002 | 16.15 |
| 6 | GRAND THEFT AUTO V | Xbox 360 | 2013 | 15.03 |
| 7 | GRAN TURISMO 3: A-SPEC | PS2 | 2001 | 14.98 |
| 8 | GRAND THEFT AUTO III | PS2 | 2001 | 13.10 |
| 9 | GRAN TURISMO 4 | PS2 | 2004 | 11.66 |
| 10 | GRAN TURISMO | PS | 1997 | 10.95 |

# GT COMPARED

These graphics show how the three *Gran Turismo* entries on this chart compare...

**GRAN TURISMO 3: A-SPEC**
14.98

**GRAN TURISMO 4**
11.66

**GRAN TURISMO**
10.95

## GRAN TURISMO 5

This sequel brought a choice of 1,000 different cars to choose from, and 71 race tracks across 26 locations. *GT5* also allowed players to compete with as many as 15 other players via an online race option.

GRAN TURISMO 5 (2010) HAS SOLD
**10.59 MILLION** UNITS WORLDWIDE

## ⊙ IRON MAN 3

This, the seventh Marvel Cinematic Universe production is the eighth most successful movie of all time.

## THE MATRIX RELOADED

Just missing out on a place in the below Top 10 the second *Matrix* movie featured squid-like sentinels and made $742,128,461 at the box office.

## TOP 10...
# BIGGEST ROBOT MOVIES

Sentient machines have been cropping up in movies for nearly 100 years. These are the 10 robot-filled productions that have made the most at the box office...

| | MOVIE | ROBOT(S) FEATURED | YEAR OF RELEASE | BOX OFFICE ($ WORLDWIDE) |
|---|---|---|---|---|
| 1 | AVENGERS: AGE OF ULTRON | Ultron and his army | 2015 | 1,277,969,385 |
| 2 | IRON MAN 3 | Remote-controlled Iron Man suits | 2013 | 1,215,439,994 |
| 3 | TRANSFORMERS: DARK OF THE MOON | Alien robots Autobots & Decepticons | 2011 | 1,123,794,079 |
| 4 | TRANSFORMERS: AGE OF EXTINCTION | Alien robots Autobots & Decepticons | 2014 | 1,091,405,097 |
| 5 | STAR WARS: EPISODE I – THE PHANTOM MENACE | Clone Troopers & others | 1999 | 1,027,044,677 |
| 6 | STAR WARS: EPISODE III – REVENGE OF THE SITH | General Grievous & others | 2005 | 848,754,768 |
| 7 | TRANSFORMERS: REVENGE OF THE FALLEN | Alien robots Autobots & Decepticons | 2009 | 836,303,693 |
| 8 | STAR WARS: EPISODE IV – A NEW HOPE | C-3PO, R2-D2 & many more | 1977 | 775,398,007 |
| 9 | GUARDIANS OF THE GALAXY | Cyborg Nebula | 2014 | 774,176,600 |
| 10 | X-MEN: DAYS OF FUTURE PAST | Sentinels | 2014 | 748,121,534 |

AUTOBOT BUMBLEBEE HAS STARRED IN
**5**
TRANSFORMERS FILMS SINCE THE 1986 ANIMATED MOVIE

## ⦿ TITANFALL

Featuring the ability to do battle with 49 other Xbox One owners, *Titanfall* focuses on your skill in controlling a massive mech called a Titan. A sequel is being developed now.

TITANFALL WAS RELEASED FOR
**3**
PLATFORMS: XBOX ONE, XBOX 360 AND PC

TOP 10...
# BIGGEST SELLING **MECH GAME FRANCHISES**

The fusion between humans and mech(anical) suits has exploded in popularity in gaming over the past decade...

| | FRANCHISE | BEST-SELLING GAME | RELEASED | ALL PLATFORMS' UNIT SALES (MILLIONS) |
|---|---|---|---|---|
| 1 | HALO | Halo 3 | 2007 | 12.02 |
| 2 | GEARS OF WAR | Gears of War 2 | 2008 | 6.72 |
| 3 | METAL GEAR SOLID | Metal Gear Solid 2: Sons Of Liberty | 2001 | 6.05 |
| 4 | MASS EFFECT | Mass Effect 3 | 2012 | 5.48 |
| 5 | BIOSHOCK | BioShock | 2007 | 4.55 |
| 6 | TITANFALL | Titanfall | 2014 | 4.27 |
| 7 | LOST PLANET | Lost Planet: Extreme Condition | 2006 | 1.95 |
| 8 | MECHASSAULT | MechAssault | 2002 | 1.13 |
| 9 | ARMORED CORE | Armored Core 2 | 2000 | 0.79 |
| 10 | ZONE OF THE ENDERS | Zone of the Enders | 2001 | 0.75 |

## ⦿ MASS EFFECT 3

Released across six gaming platforms, this sequel outsold *Mass Effect 2* by one million copies.

# METAL GEAR SOLID HISTORY

From the first *Metal Gear* release for the MSX2 console in 1987, through to 2015's *Metal Gear Solid V: The Phantom Pain*, Japanese game designer Hideo Kojima's initial ideas have spawned 27 releases for the franchise.

## INDEPENDENCE DAY

A sequel is confirmed for release summer 2016. Jeff Goldblum reprises his role as David Levinson.

E.T. ACTRESS DREW BARRYMORE WAS

**7**

**YEARS OLD**

WHEN THE 1982 FILM WAS RELEASED

TOP 10...

# BIGGEST SPACESHIP MOVIES

Countless films feature spacecrafts, but these 10 are the biggest box office successes...

| | MOVIE | YEAR RELEASED | BOX OFFICE ($ WORLDWIDE) |
|---|---|---|---|
| 1 | AVATAR | 2009 | 2,787,965,087 |
| 2 | THE AVENGERS | 2012 | 1,518,594,910 |
| 3 | TRANSFORMERS: DARK OF THE MOON | 2011 | 1,123,794,079 |
| 4 | TRANSFORMERS: AGE OF EXTINCTION | 2014 | 1,091,405,097 |
| 5 | STAR WARS: EPISODE I – THE PHANTOM MENACE | 2009 | 1,027,044,677 |
| 6 | STAR WARS: EPISODE III – REVENGE OF THE SITH | 2005 | 848,754,768 |
| 7 | TRANSFORMERS: REVENGE OF THE FALLEN | 2009 | 836,303,693 |
| 8 | INDEPENDENCE DAY | 1996 | 817,400,891 |
| 9 | E.T.: THE EXTRA-TERRESTRIAL | 1982 | 792,910,554 |
| 10 | STAR WARS: EPISODE IV – A NEW HOPE | 1977 | 775,398,007 |

## TRANSFORMERS: AGE OF EXTINCTION

Although used extensively in the promos, the Dinobots only appear on screen for 5 minutes of the film's 165-minute running time.

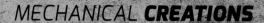

LEGO STAR WARS:
THE COMPLETE SAGA
FOR THE WII HAS SOLD
**5.51**
MILLION UNITS
WORLDWIDE

TOP 10...

# BIGGEST SELLING
# SPACECRAFT GAMES

The gaming world is full of science-fiction realms and intergalactic battles. These spaceship-starring games have outsold all the rest...

| NAME | PLATFORM | RELEASED | UNIT SALES (MILLIONS) |
|---|---|---|---|
| 1 HALO 3 | Xbox 360 | 2007 | 12.02 |
| 2 SUPER MARIO GALAXY | Wii | 2007 | 11.23 |
| 3 FINAL FANTASY VII | PlayStation | 1997 | 9.72 |
| 4 HALO: REACH | Xbox 360 | 2010 | 9.71 |
| 5 HALO 2 | Xbox | 2004 | 8.49 |
| 6 FINAL FANTASY X | PS2 | 2001 | 8.05 |
| 7 FINAL FANTASY VIII | PlayStation | 1999 | 7.86 |
| 8 SUPER MARIO GALAXY 2 | Wii | 2010 | 7.40 |
| 9 CRASH BANDICOOT 3: WARPED | PlayStation | 1998 | 7.13 |
| 10 HALO: COMBAT EVOLVED | Xbox | 2001 | 6.43 |

## ⦿ SUPER MARIO GALAXY

The first *Mario* game to truly take the protagonist into outer space, this title gives the player 42 different galaxies to explore. *Super Mario Galaxy* was awarded Game of the Year by several major publications.

## ⦿ HALO 3

This game is also featured in *Halo: The Master Chief Collection*, created for the Xbox One in 2014.

## THE HALO UNIVERSE

Examining all of the *Halo* games made so far, this chart reveals the most successful releases...

HALO: COMBAT EVOLVED
6.43

HALO 3
12.02

HALO 2
8.49

HALO: REACH
9.71

# FORCES OF NATURE

## CHINA

One of the deadliest periods of the 1931 floods was between July and August. During this time, more than 0.6 m (2 ft) of rain fell and nine cyclones struck the country.

## ICELAND

Over an eight-month period between 1783-84, Iceland's volcanic system of Lakagígar, Grímsvötn, and Þórðarhyrna erupted. More than half the country's livestock died, contributing towards the death of a quarter of Iceland's population.

## TOP 10...

# DEADLIEST **DISASTERS** OF ALL TIME

The forces of nature at work on our planet are unpredictable, ever-changeable, and can cause utter devastation...

| | TYPE | LOCATION | YEAR | FATALITIES |
|---|---|---|---|---|
| 1 | VOLCANIC ERUPTION | Iceland | 1783 | 6 million (est) |
| 2 | FLOOD | China | 1931 | 2.5-3.7 million |
| 3 | EARTHQUAKE | Shaanxi, China | 1556 | 820,000–830,000 (est) |
| 4 | CYCLONE | Bangladesh (formerly East Pakistan) | 1970 | 500,000 |
| 5 | TSUNAMI | Several affected by Indian Ocean tsunami | 2004 | 230,000-310,000 |
| 6 | HEATWAVE | Europe | 2003 | 70,000 |
| 7 | AVALANCHE | Peru | 1970 | 20,0000 |
| 8 | STORM | Venezuela | 1999 | 15,100 |
| 9 | BLIZZARD | Iran | 1972 | 4,000 |
| = | LIGHTNING | Greece | 1856 | 4,000 |

PERU'S 1970 AVALANCHE CONSISTED OF

# 80

**MILLION M³** OF WATERY MUD AND DEBRIS

## BANGLADESH

The November 3-13, 1970 cyclone was the sixth to strike the country that year. Ravi Shankar and George Harrison's benefit concert in 1971, The Concert for Bangladesh, raised money for the reparations. This picture shows a survivor among damage caused by a devastating tornado that struck the country on April 26, 1989.

LUZON'S MOUNT PINATUBO EXPELLED
**100 KM³**
OF MAGMA IN 1991

## 📍 KOLUMBO

This active volcano is located 8 km (4.9 miles) north-east of the Greek island of Santorini. Its 1650 eruption created Kolumbo, which is Greek for "swimming."

**TOP 10...**

# BIGGEST VOLCANIC ERUPTIONS

In Roman mythology, Vulcan was the god of fire and the forging of metals, apt attributes for "volcano" to take its name from...

| | NAME | LOCATION | YEAR | AMOUNT OF VOLCANIC DISCHARGE (CUBIC KM) | (CUBIC MI) |
|---|---|---|---|---|---|
| 1 | UNKNOWN | The Tropics | 1258 | 200–800 | 48-192 |
| 2 | MOUNT TAMBORA | Lesser Sunda Islands (Indonesia) | 1815 | 150 | 36 |
| 3 | UNKNOWN | New Hebrides (Vanuatu) | 1452–53 | 36–96 | 8.6-23 |
| 4 | KOLUMBO | Santorini (Greece) | 1650 | 60 | 14.4 |
| 5 | HUAYNAPUTINA | Peru | 1600 | 30 | 7.2 |
| = | LONG ISLAND (PAPUA NEW GUINEA) | New Guinea | 1660 | 30 | 7.2 |
| 7 | KRAKATOA | Indonesia | 1883 | 21 | 5 |
| = | QUILOTOA | Ecuador | 1280 | 21 | 5 |
| 9 | SANTA MARIA | Guatemala | 1902 | 20 | 4.8 |
| 10 | PINATUBO | Luzon (Philippines) | 1991 | 6-16 | 1.4-3.8 |

# GRAPH OF ERUPTIONS

Here is a visual representation of how the first five eruptions compare...

UNKNOWN THE TROPICS
**800 km³**

MOUNT TAMBORA LESSER SUNDA ISLANDS (INDONESIA)
**150 km³**

UNKNOWN NEW HEBRIDES (VANUATU)
**96 km³**

KOLUMBO SANTORINI (GREECE)
**60 km³**

HUAYNAPUTINA PERU
**30 km³**

## 📍 VANUATU

82 islands make up the archipelago called Vanuatu. Many of its volcanoes are active.

## VALDIVIA

The most powerful earthquake ever recorded lasted 10 minutes. The subsequent tsunamis it triggered featured 35-ft (10.7-m)-high waves.

## SUMATRA

Its epicentre was off the Sumatran coast. The earthquake's effects killed nearly a quarter of a million people across 14 countries, including Thailand, Sri Lanka, and India.

## TOP 10...

# BIGGEST EARTHQUAKES

A colossal release of energy through our planet's crust leads to earthquakes. Often, this can trigger further devastation in the form of volcanic activity and tsunamis...

| | LOCATION | DATE | MAGNITUDE (RICHTER SCALE) |
|---|---|---|---|
| 1 | VALDIVIA (CHILE) | May 22, 1960 | 9.5 |
| 2 | SUMATRA (INDONESIA) | Dec 26, 2004 | 9.3 |
| 3 | ALASKA (USA) | Mar 27, 1964 | 9.2 |
| 4 | TŌHOKU REGION (JAPAN) | Mar 11, 2011 | 9.0 |
| = | KAMCHATKA (RUSSIA) | Nov 4, 1952 | 9.0 |
| = | ARICA (CHILE) | Aug 13, 1868 | 9.0 |
| 7 | SUMATRA (INDONESIA) | Nov 25, 1833 | 8.9 |
| = | TŌHOKU REGION (JAPAN) | July 9, 869AD | 8.9 |
| 9 | ECUADOR (COLUMBIA) | Jan 31, 1906 | 8.8 |
| = | MAULE (CHILE) | Feb 27, 2010 | 8.8 |

1964 ALASKAN EARTHQUAKE LASTED

**278 SECONDS**

## ALASKA

The 1964 earthquake and tsunami resulted in a total of 139 deaths. The tallest wave measured 67 m (220 ft).

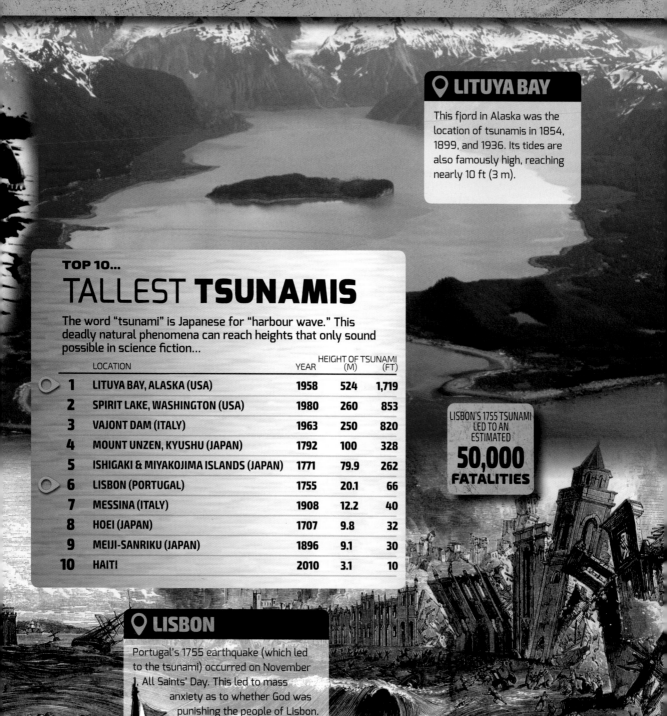

## ⦿ LITUYA BAY

This fjord in Alaska was the location of tsunamis in 1854, 1899, and 1936. Its tides are also famously high, reaching nearly 10 ft (3 m).

**TOP 10...**

# TALLEST **TSUNAMIS**

The word "tsunami" is Japanese for "harbour wave." This deadly natural phenomena can reach heights that only sound possible in science fiction...

| | LOCATION | YEAR | HEIGHT OF TSUNAMI (M) | (FT) |
|---|---|---|---|---|
| 1 | LITUYA BAY, ALASKA (USA) | 1958 | 524 | 1,719 |
| 2 | SPIRIT LAKE, WASHINGTON (USA) | 1980 | 260 | 853 |
| 3 | VAJONT DAM (ITALY) | 1963 | 250 | 820 |
| 4 | MOUNT UNZEN, KYUSHU (JAPAN) | 1792 | 100 | 328 |
| 5 | ISHIGAKI & MIYAKOJIMA ISLANDS (JAPAN) | 1771 | 79.9 | 262 |
| 6 | LISBON (PORTUGAL) | 1755 | 20.1 | 66 |
| 7 | MESSINA (ITALY) | 1908 | 12.2 | 40 |
| 8 | HOEI (JAPAN) | 1707 | 9.8 | 32 |
| 9 | MEIJI-SANRIKU (JAPAN) | 1896 | 9.1 | 30 |
| 10 | HAITI | 2010 | 3.1 | 10 |

LISBON'S 1755 TSUNAMI LED TO AN ESTIMATED

**50,000 FATALITIES**

## ⦿ LISBON

Portugal's 1755 earthquake (which led to the tsunami) occurred on November 1, All Saints' Day. This led to mass anxiety as to whether God was punishing the people of Lisbon.

## ⊙ SS ATLANTIC EXPRESS

At 7:15pm, on July 19, 1979, the collision between the two Greek tankers, the SS *Atlantic Express* and the *Aegean Captain*, led to the the fifth-worst oil spillage in history.

## TOP 10...
# LARGEST SHIPS SUNK BY NATURE

Many vessels have become shipwrecks during wars and collisions, but these are the ten biggest to be affected by natural phenomena...

| | SHIP | COUNTRY | YEAR SUNK | HOW IT SANK | WEIGHT (T) |
|---|---|---|---|---|---|
| 1 | SS ATLANTIC EXPRESS | Greece | 1979 | Tanker collision during storm | 293,000 |
| 2 | COSTA CONCORDIA | Italy | 2012 | Ran aground on rocks | 114,000 |
| 3 | MV DERBYSHIRE | UK | 1980 | Sank in tropical storm | 92,000 |
| 4 | RMS TITANIC | UK | 1912 | Iceberg collision | 46,000 |
| 5 | ANDREA DORIA LINER | Italy | 1956 | Hit another ship in fog | 30,000 |
| 6 | MV PRINCESS OF THE STARS | Philippines | 2008 | Capsized during a typhoon | 24,000 |
| 7 | SS EDMUND FITZGERALD | USA | 1975 | Storm and high waves | 16,000 |
| 8 | RMS REPUBLIC | UK | 1909 | Hit another ship in fog | 15,000 |
| 9 | RMS EMPRESS OF IRELAND | Canada | 1914 | Hit another ship in fog | 14,000 |
| 10 | MS AL-SALAM BOCCACCIO | Egypt | 2006 | Capsized in heavy storm | 5,600 |

## ⊙ TITANIC

More than 1,500 people died after the RMS *Titanic* struck an iceberg on April 14, 1912, just four days into its maiden voyage to New York, USA from Southampton, England.

COSTA CONCORDIA DISASTER:
# 64
**PEOPLE** INJURED

# HEAVIEST TO BE SUNK

These graphics give an at-a-glance guide to how the ships' weights compare...

SS ATLANTIC EXPRESS
293,000 T

COSTA CONCORDIA
114,000 T

MV DERBYSHIRE
92,000 T

RMS TITANIC
46,000 T

ANDREA DORIA LINER
30,000 T

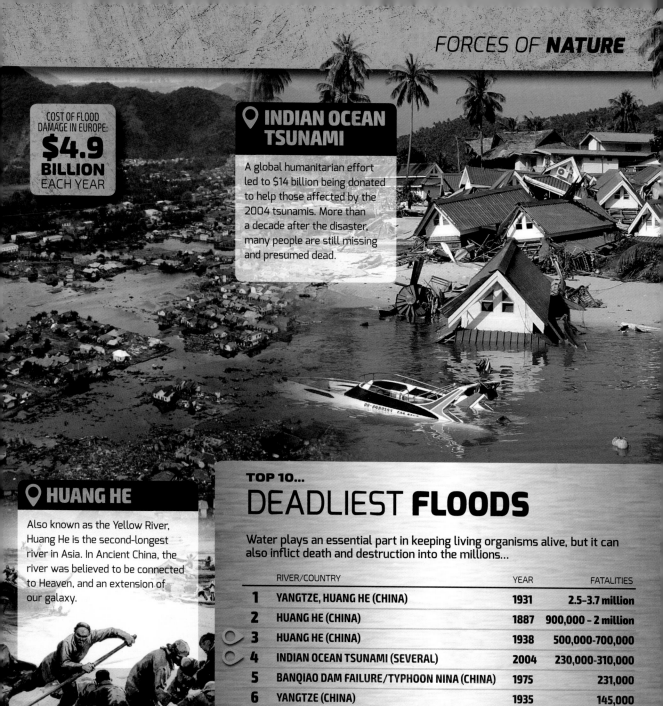

COST OF FLOOD DAMAGE IN EUROPE:

# $4.9 BILLION

EACH YEAR

## 📍 INDIAN OCEAN TSUNAMI

A global humanitarian effort led to $14 billion being donated to help those affected by the 2004 tsunamis. More than a decade after the disaster, many people are still missing and presumed dead.

## 📍 HUANG HE

Also known as the Yellow River, Huang He is the second-longest river in Asia. In Ancient China, the river was believed to be connected to Heaven, and an extension of our galaxy.

TOP 10...

# DEADLIEST **FLOODS**

Water plays an essential part in keeping living organisms alive, but it can also inflict death and destruction into the millions...

| | RIVER/COUNTRY | YEAR | FATALITIES |
|---|---|---|---|
| 1 | YANGTZE, HUANG HE (CHINA) | 1931 | 2.5–3.7 million |
| 2 | HUANG HE (CHINA) | 1887 | 900,000 – 2 million |
| 3 | HUANG HE (CHINA) | 1938 | 500,000-700,000 |
| 4 | INDIAN OCEAN TSUNAMI (SEVERAL) | 2004 | 230,000-310,000 |
| 5 | BANQIAO DAM FAILURE/TYPHOON NINA (CHINA) | 1975 | 231,000 |
| 6 | YANGTZE (CHINA) | 1935 | 145,000 |
| 7 | MESSINA EARTHQUAKE & TSUNAMI (ITALY) | 1908 | 123,000 |
| 8 | ST. FELIX'S FLOOD (NETHERLANDS) | 1530 | 100,000+ |
| 9 | HANOI & RED RIVER DELTA FLOODS (N. VIETNAM) | 1971 | 100,000 |
| = | LISBON EARTHQUAKE & TSUNAMI | 1755 | 100,000 |

## TRI-STATE TORNADO

This tornado tore through three American states and left a path of destruction 378 km (235 miles) long.

# DEADLIEST TORNADOES

These spinning cones of air can tear through the most fortified man-made structures like a hot knife through butter...

| | LOCATION | COUNTRY | DATE | FATALITIES |
|---|---|---|---|---|
| 1 | DAULTIPUR & SALTURIA | Bangladesh | Apr 26, 1989 | 1300 |
| 2 | EAST PAKISTAN | (now Bangladesh) | Apr 14, 1969 | 923 |
| 3 | MISSOURI, ILLINOIS, INDIANA | USA | Mar 18, 1925 | 695 |
| 4 | MANIKGANJ, SINGAIR & NAWABGANJ | Bangladesh | Apr 17, 1973 | 681 |
| 5 | VALLETTA'S GREAT HABOUR | Malta | Sep 23, 1551 | 600 |
| 6 | MAGURA & NARAIL | Bangladesh | Apr 11, 1964 | 500 |
| = | SICILY | Italy | Dec 1851 | 500 |
| = | MADARIPUR, SHIBCHAR | Bangladesh | Apr 9, 1984 | 500 |
| 9 | BELYANITSKY, IVANOVO, BALINO | Russia | June 9, 1984 | 400 |
| 10 | NATCHEZ, MISSISSIPPI | USA | May 6, 1840 | 317 |

RUSSIA'S 1984 EVENT FEATURED

**3** TORNADOES

## BANGLADESH

Due to its monsoon season (June to October), Bangladesh suffers tornadoes and floods annually.

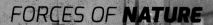

## ⦿ TYPHOON VIOLET

Incredibly, only two fatalities occurred in Japan during this typhoon.

## ⦿ CYCLONE INIGO

Between April 1-8, 2003 this cyclone affected Indonesia (where 58 people were killed and over 100 injured), East Timor, West Timor, and Australia.

TOP 10...

# FASTEST **CYCLONIC STORMS**

Beyond tornadoes, nature can serve up cyclones, hurricanes, and typhoons as well...

| | NAME | YEARS | AFFECTED AREAS | HIGHEST SPEED (KPH) | (MPH) |
|---|---|---|---|---|---|
| 1 | CYCLONE ZOE | 2002-03 | Solomon Islands, Fiji, Vanuatu, Rotuma | 350 | 217.5 |
| 2 | CYCLONE INIGO | 2003 | Indonesia, Australia | 335 | 208.2 |
| = | TYPHOON VIOLET | 1961 | Pacific Ocean | 335 | 208.2 |
| 4 | SUPER TYPHOON IDA | 1958 | Japan | 325 | 202 |
| 5 | SUPER TYPHOON OPAL | 1964 | Kosrae, Chuuk, Philippines | 315 | 195.7 |
| = | SUPER TYPHOON KIT | 1967 | Japan | 315 | 195.7 |
| = | TYPHOON JOAN | 1959 | Taiwan, China | 315 | 195.7 |
| = | SUPER TYPHOON SALLY | 1964 | Philippines, China | 315 | 195.7 |
| 9 | TYPHOON TIP | 1979 | Guam, Japan | 305 | 189.5 |
| 10 | CYCLONE GLENDA | 2006 | Australia | 300 | 186.4 |

## ⦿ CYCLONE GLENDA

Causing nearly a billion dollars in damages, but no fatalities, Cyclone Glenda swept through Australia from March 23-31, 2006.

EACH YEAR
**86**
**TROPICAL CYCLONES**
OCCUR WORLDWIDE

**SALANG PASS DEALS WITH 250 AVALANCHES ANNUALLY**

## 📍 AFGHANISTAN

A storm in the Hindu Kush mountains triggered dozens of avalanches across the Salang Pass that killed 172 people.

## TOP 10...
# MOST FATAL **AVALANCHES**

The massive flow of snow, ice, rock or mud is referred to as an avalanche. They can be triggered by an earthquake, climate change, or humans causing disruption...

| | LOCATION | EVENT | YEAR | FATALITIES |
|---|---|---|---|---|
| 1 | PERU | Huascarán avalanche (caused by Ancash earthquake) | 1970 | 20,000 |
| 2 | PERU | Huascarán avalanche | 1962 | 4,000 |
| 3 | AUSTRIA, SWITZERLAND | 649 avalanches (the 'Winter of Terror') | 1951 | 265 |
| 4 | AFGHANISTAN | Salang avalanches (minimum of 36 avalanches) | 2010 | 172 |
| 5 | PAKISTAN | Siachen Glacier avalanche | 2012 | 140 |
| 6 | RUSSIA | Kolka-Karmadon rock ice slide | 2002 | 125 |
| 7 | PAKISTAN | Kohistan avalanche | 2010 | 102 |
| 8 | USA | Wellington, Washington avalanche | 1910 | 96 |
| 9 | CANADA | Frank Slide (buried part of the mining town in Frank, Northwest Territories) | 1903 | 90 |
| 10 | AFGHANISTAN | Afghanistan avalanches (north-eastern province of Badakhshan) | 2012 | 50 |

## 📍 PERU

The Huascarán mountain is located in Peru's Yungay province. The 1970 avalanche saw landslides of 335 kph (208 mph) completely smother the village of Ranrahirca and the town of Yungay.

# AVALANCHE FATALITIES

**PERU HUASCARÁN AVALANCHE 20,000**

This graph shows just how deadly the incidents in Peru were...

**PERU HUASCARÁN AVALANCHE 4,000**

**AUSTRIA, SWITZERLAND 649 AVALANCHES 265**

**AFGHANISTAN SALANG AVALANCHES 172**

**PAKISTAN SIACHEN GLACIER AVALANCHE 140**

📍 **2012**

To tie-in with this movie's name, many cinemas decided to start the evening screenings at 20:12. The date was based on the last date on the Mayan calendar: December 20, 2012.

📍 **THE DAY AFTER TOMORROW**

This film's director Roland Emmerich enjoys making movies about destruction. He also helmed *Godzilla* (1998) and the alien invasion *Independence Day* films, the first in 1996, and its sequel in 2016.

TOP 10...

# BIGGEST **DISASTER MOVIES**

Of all the films made that feature natural phenomena wreaking havoc on our planet, these are the most successful...

| | MOVIE | TYPE OF DISASTER | YEAR OF RELEASE | BOX OFFICE ($ WORLDWIDE) |
|---|---|---|---|---|
| 1 | 2012 | A natural apocalypse | 2009 | 769,679,473 |
| 2 | ARMAGEDDON | Giant asteroid on course for Earth | 1998 | 553,709,788 |
| 3 | THE DAY AFTER TOMORROW | Global warming causes a new ice age | 2004 | 544,272,402 |
| 4 | TWISTER | Tornadoes | 1996 | 494,471,524 |
| 5 | DEEP IMPACT | Comet hits planet Earth | 1998 | 349,464,664 |
| 6 | THE PERFECT STORM | A huge wave | 2000 | 328,718,434 |
| 7 | WATERWORLD | Polar caps melt, covering Earth in water | 1995 | 264,218,220 |
| 8 | POSEIDON | 150-ft wave capsizes a cruise liner | 2006 | 181,674,817 |
| 9 | DANTE'S PEAK | Volcanic eruption in Colombia | 1997 | 178,127,760 |
| 10 | THE IMPOSSIBLE | 2004 Tsunami that devastated Thailand | 2012 | 172,419,882 |

INTO THE STORM (2014) MADE

**$160.6 MILLION** AT THE BOX OFFICE

📍 **TWISTER**

One of the sound effects used for the tornado was a camel's groan, but slowed right down.

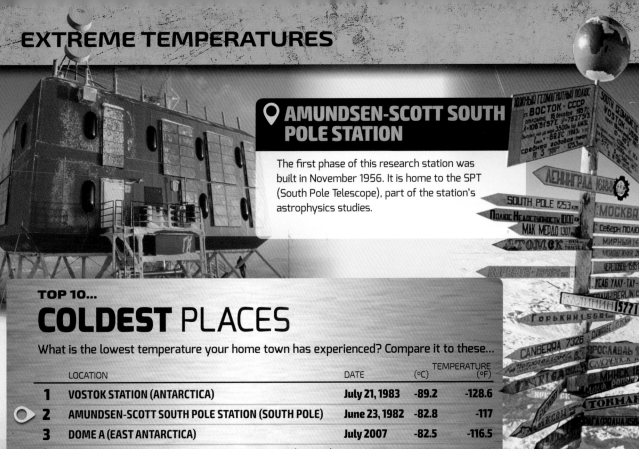

## AMUNDSEN-SCOTT SOUTH POLE STATION

The first phase of this research station was built in November 1956. It is home to the SPT (South Pole Telescope), part of the station's astrophysics studies.

## TOP 10...
# COLDEST PLACES

What is the lowest temperature your home town has experienced? Compare it to these...

| | LOCATION | DATE | TEMPERATURE (°C) | (°F) |
|---|---|---|---|---|
| **1** | VOSTOK STATION (ANTARCTICA) | July 21, 1983 | -89.2 | -128.6 |
| **2** | AMUNDSEN-SCOTT SOUTH POLE STATION (SOUTH POLE) | June 23, 1982 | -82.8 | -117 |
| **3** | DOME A (EAST ANTARCTICA) | July 2007 | -82.5 | -116.5 |
| **4** | VERKHOYANSK & OYMYAKONM SAKHA REPUBLIC (RUSSIA) | Feb 6, 1933 | -68 | -90 |
| **5** | NORTH ICE (GREENLAND) | Jan 9, 1954 | -66.1 | -87 |
| **6** | SNAG, YUKON (CANADA) | Feb 3, 1947 | -63 | -81 |
| **7** | PROSPECT CREEK, ALASKA (USA) | Jan 23, 1971 | -62 | -80 |
| **8** | UST-SHCHUGER (RUSSIA) | Dec 31, 1978 | -58.1 | -72.6 |
| **9** | MALGOVIK, VÄSTERBOTTEN (SWEDEN) | Dec 13, 1941 | -53 | -63.4 |
| **10** | MOHE COUNTY (CHINA) | Feb 13, 1969 | -52.3 | -62.1 |

THE COLDEST PLANET IS NEPTUNE:
# -214°C

## MOHE COUNTY (CHINA)

With a population of 83,500, Mohe County covers an area of 18,233 km² (7,040 miles²).

VENUS IS THE
HOTTEST PLANET:

# 462°C

## ⦿ KEBILI

This town in South Tunisia has evidence humans
have resided there for over 200,000 years.
Areas of Tunisia have been used as locations for
every *Star Wars* film to date, except *The Empire
Strikes Back* (1980).

TOP 10...

# HOTTEST PLACES

You may have experienced temperatures of over 38°C during a summer
holiday in a hot country, but these temperatures far exceed that...

| | LOCATION | DATE | TEMPERATURE (°C) | (°F) |
|---|---|---|---|---|
| 1 | DEATH VALLEY, CALIFORNIA (USA) | July 10, 1913 | 56.7 | 134 |
| 2 | KEBILI (TUNISIA) | July 7, 1931 | 55 | 131 |
| 3 | TIRAT ZVI (ISRAEL) | June 21, 1942 | 54 | 129 |
| 4 | SULAIBYA (KUWAIT) | July 31, 2012 | 53.6 | 128.5 |
| 5 | KUWAIT INTERNATIONAL AIRPORT (KUWAIT) | Aug 3, 2011 | 53.5 | 128.3 |
| = | MOHENJO-DARO, SINDH (PAKISTAN) | May 26, 2010 | 53.5 | 128.3 |
| 7 | NASIRIYAH, ALI AIR BASE (IRAQ) | Aug 3, 2011 | 53 | 127.4 |
| 8 | BASRA (IRAQ) | June 14, 2010 | 52 | 125.6 |
| = | SAN LUIS RÍO COLORADO (MEXICO) | July 6, 1966 | 52 | 125.6 |
| = | JEDDAH (SAUDI ARABIA) | June 22, 2010 | 52 | 125.6 |

## CAUTION!
## EXTREME
## HEAT
## DANGER

## ⦿ DEATH VALLEY

The hottest location on Earth is also home
to one of the biggest subterranean aquifers
in America, where the tiny, and endangered,
Devil's Hole Pupfish lives.

# OCEANIC AREAS

These graphics show how the biggest oceans compare in square km...

| PACIFIC | ATLANTIC | INDIAN | SOUTHERN | ARCTIC |
|---------|----------|--------|----------|--------|
| 166,266,876 | 86,505,602 | 73,555,662 | 52,646,688 | 13,208,939 |

THE PACIFIC OCEAN COVERS

## 46%
### OF EARTH

## TOP 10...
# LARGEST OCEANS & SEAS

With 72 per cent of our planet covered with water, this Top 10 features areas that are millions of miles in size...

| | NAME | TYPE | (SQUARE KM) | SIZE (SQUARE MI) |
|---|------|------|-------------|------------------|
| 1 | PACIFIC | Ocean | 166,266,876 | 64,196,000 |
| 2 | ATLANTIC | Ocean | 86,505,602 | 33,400,000 |
| 3 | INDIAN | Ocean | 73,555,662 | 28,400,000 |
| 4 | SOUTHERN | Ocean | 52,646,688 | 20,327,000 |
| 5 | ARCTIC | Ocean | 13,208,939 | 5,100,000 |
| 6 | PHILIPPINE | Sea | 5,179,976 | 2,000,000 |
| 7 | CORAL | Sea | 4,791,478 | 1,850,000 |
| 8 | ARABIAN | Sea | 3,861,672 | 1,491,000 |
| 9 | SOUTH CHINA | Sea | 2,973,306 | 1,148,000 |
| 10 | CARIBBEAN | Sea | 2,514,878 | 971,000 |

## 📍 INDIAN OCEAN

This ocean covers 20 per cent of our planet's surface. Fishing industries focus on the tuna and shrimp in this region.

# MARINE LIFE

The water on our planet is home to an eclectic range of organisms. There are 32,000 species of fish alone, 500 of which are different species of shark. A truly prehistoric creature, the earliest form of shark dates back over 420 million years.

**TOP 10...**

# BIGGEST **COUNTRIES** (LAND MASS)

Even though these land masses are vast, compare their areas to the size of Earth's oceans and seas...

| | COUNTRY | SIZE (SQUARE KM) | (SQUARE MI) |
|---|---|---|---|
| 1 | RUSSIA | 17,098,242 | 6,601,668 |
| 2 | CANADA | 9,984,670 | 3,855,100 |
| 3 | CHINA | 9,706,961 | 3,747,879 |
| 4 | USA | 9,629,091 | 3,705,407 |
| 5 | BRAZIL | 8,514,877 | 3,287,612 |
| 6 | AUSTRALIA | 7,692,024 | 2,969,907 |
| 7 | INDIA | 3,166,414 | 1,222,559 |
| 8 | ARGENTINA | 2,780,400 | 1,073,500 |
| 9 | KAZAKHSTAN | 2,724,900 | 1,052,100 |
| 10 | ALGERIA | 2,381,741 | 919,595 |

## ⊙ RUSSIA

The largest country on Earth is home to over 144 million people. Russia is so vast it has nine different time zones.

## ⊙ CANADA

This country's name comes from *kanata*, the Saint-Lawrence Iroquoian word for "settlement" or "village." Canada is now home to more than 35 million people.

AUSTRALIA'S POPULATION:

**23.8 MILLION**

## PANGEA

Scientists believe that the Earth's singular land mass, known as Pangea, began to separate 200 million years ago. Its name comes from the Greek words for "entire" (*pan*) and "Earth" (*Gaia*).

## CHILE

Home to more than 18 million people, Chile covers an area of 756,096.3 square km (291,930.4 square miles).

THE MID-ATLANTIC RIDGE SPREADS

**2.5 CM EACH YEAR**

## CANADA

Prince Edward Island, located off the East Coast of Canada and home to 140,000 people, became an island 6,000 years ago when the sea level rose.

TOP 10...

# LONGEST COASTLINES

This Top 10 is the best way to appreciate not only the size of these countries, but their connection to the oceans...

| | COUNTRY | (KM) | LENGTH OF COASTLINE (MI) |
|---|---|---|---|
| 1 | CANADA | 265,523 | 164,988.34 |
| 2 | UNITED STATES | 133,312 | 828,36.24 |
| 3 | RUSSIA | 110,310 | 68,543.46 |
| 4 | INDONESIA | 95,181 | 59,142.73 |
| 5 | CHILE | 78,563 | 48,816.78 |
| 6 | AUSTRALIA | 66,530 | 41,339.83 |
| 7 | NORWAY | 53,199 | 33,056.33 |
| 8 | PHILIPPINES | 33,900 | 21,064.48 |
| 9 | BRAZIL | 33,379 | 20,740.75 |
| 10 | FINLAND | 31,119 | 19,336.45 |

## ◉ MID-ATLANTIC RIDGE

Scottish oceanographer Sir Charles Wyville Thomson (Mar 5, 1830 – Mar 10, 1882) and a team of explorers on the HMS *Challenger* discovered the Mid-Atlantic Ridge in 1872.

## ◉ HIMALAYAS

The name of this mountain range appropriately comes from the Sanskrit word for "abode of the snow". The Himalayas are home to many sightings of the cryptozoological creature, the Yeti.

**TOP 10...**

# LONGEST **MOUNTAIN RANGES**

You may think the biggest mountains are icy rocks scaled by explorers, but the largest exist deep below the surface of our seas...

| | RANGE | MOUNTAIN TYPE | LOCATION | LENGTH (KM) | (MI) |
|---|---|---|---|---|---|
| 1 | MID-OCEANIC RIDGE | Oceanic | Global | 65,000 | 40,389 |
| 2 | MID-ATLANTIC RIDGE | Oceanic | Atlantic Ocean | 10,000 | 6,214 |
| 3 | ANDES | Land | South America | 7,000 | 4,350 |
| 4 | ROCKIES | Land | North America | 4,800 | 2,983 |
| 5 | TRANSANTARCTIC | Land | Antarctica | 3,542 | 2,201 |
| 6 | GREAT DIVING RANGE | Land | Australia | 3,059 | 1,901 |
| 7 | HIMALAYAS | Land | Asia | 2,576 | 1,601 |
| 8 | SOUTHEAST INDIAN RIDGE | Oceanic | Indian Ocean | 2,300 | 1,429 |
| 9 | SOUTHWEST INDIAN RIDGE | Oceanic | Rodriguez Island to Prince Edward Island | 1,931 | 1,200 |
| 10 | PACIFIC-ANTARCTIC RIDGE | Oceanic | South Pacific Ocean | 1,029 | 639 |

AUSTRALIA'S GREAT DIVING RANGE REACHES

# 305.8 KM WIDE

## ◉ ANDES

A wide range of organisms live in the Andes region. This includes 1,700 species of birds, 600 different kinds of both reptiles and mammals, and 400 species of fish.

## TOP 10...
# LARGEST CAVE SYSTEMS

The ground beneath your feet is not as solid as you might think.
These underground labyrinths are the largest currently known...

| | CAVE NAME | LOCATION | LENGTH (KM) | (MI) |
|---|---|---|---|---|
| 1 | MAMMOTH CAVE | Kentucky (USA) | 643.7 | 400 |
| 2 | SISTEMA SAC ACTUN/SISTEMA DOS OJOS | Quintana Roo (Mexico) | 311 | 193.3 |
| 3 | JEWEL CAVE | South Dakota (USA) | 267.6 | 166.3 |
| 4 | SISTEMA OX BEL HA | Quintana Roo (Mexico) | 244.3 | 151.8 |
| 5 | OPTYMISTYCHNA CAVE | Korolivka (Ukraine) | 236 | 146.6 |
| 6 | WIND CAVE | South Dakota (USA) | 226.1 | 140.5 |
| 7 | LECHUGUILLA CAVE | New Mexico (USA) | 222.6 | 138.3 |
| 8 | HÖLLOCH | Muotathal (Switzerland) | 200.4 | 124.5 |
| 9 | FISHER RIDGE CAVES | Kentucky (USA) | 191.7 | 119.1 |
| 10 | GUA AIR JERNIH | Sarawak (Malaysia) | 189.1 | 117.5 |

## ⚲ LECHUGUILLA CAVE

This cave is home to many rare rock formations including tubular stalactites. Its name comes from a plant that grows near the cave's mouth called Agave lechuguilla.

MAMMOTH CAVE NATIONAL PARK COVERS

**8,652 HECTARES**

# CAVES' LENGTHS

Here is a visual comparison of the top five longest cave systems...

**MAMMOTH CAVE**
643.7 km

**SISTEMA SAC ACTUN/SISTEMA DOS OJOS**
311 km

**JEWEL CAVE**
267.6 km

**SISTEMA OX BEL HA**
244.3 km

**OPTYMISTYCHNA CAVE**
236 km

## ANGEL FALLS

American aviator Jimmie Angel flew over this place on Nov 18, 1933. The discovery led to it being named after him. On July 2, 1960, his ashes were scattered over the waterfall.

## BROWNE FALLS

The fjord called Doubtful Sound, in Fiordland, located in the lower-left corner of New Zealand's South Island, is home to Browne Falls. The area has no permanent residents.

**TOP 10...**

# HIGHEST **WATERFALLS**

There are many famous waterfalls around the world, but these 10 provide the greatest views...

| | NAME | LOCATION | HEIGHT (M) | (FT) |
|---|---|---|---|---|
| 1 | ANGEL FALLS | Bolívar State (Venezuela) | 979 | 3,212 |
| 2 | TUGELA FALLS | KwaZulu-Natal (South Africa) | 948 | 3,110 |
| 3 | CATARATAS LAS TRES HERMANAS | Ayacucho (Peru) | 914 | 3,000 |
| 4 | OLO'UPENA FALLS | Molokai, Hawaii (USA) | 900 | 2,953 |
| 5 | CATARATA YUMBILLA | Amazonas (Peru) | 896 | 2,940 |
| 6 | VINNUFOSSEN | Møre og Romsdal (Norway) | 860 | 2,822 |
| 7 | BALÅIFOSSEN | Hordaland (Norway) | 850 | 2,788 |
| 8 | PU'UKA'OKU FALLS | Hawaii (USA) | 840 | 2,756 |
| = | JAMES BRUCE FALLS | British Columbia (Canada) | 840 | 2,756 |
| 10 | BROWNE FALLS | South Island (New Zealand) | 836 | 2,743 |

NEW ZEALAND'S BROWNE FALLS HAS

# 6
**DROPS**

## 📍 MOUNT EVEREST

Although this mountain was named after Welsh surveyor George Everest, its Tibetan name is Qomolangma. It is also known as Deodungha (which means "Holy mountain").

## EDMUND HILARY

On May 29, 1953, New Zealander Sir Edmund Hillary (July 20, 1919 – Jan 11, 2008) and Nepalese Tenzing Norgay (May 29, 1914 – May 9, 1986) were the first people to reach Mount Everest's summit.

## TOP 10...

# HIGHEST MOUNTAINS

Many famous explorers have scaled this planet's tallest peaks. These are the 10 that are on every mountain climber's to-do list...

| | PLACE | PART OF MOUNTAIN RANGE | HEIGHT (M) | (FT) |
|---|---|---|---|---|
| 1 | MOUNT EVEREST/SAGARMATHA/CHOMOLUNGMA | Mahalangur Himalaya | 8,848 | 29,029 |
| 2 | K2/QOGIR/GODWIN AUSTEN | Baltoro Karakoram | 8,611 | 28,251 |
| 3 | KANGCHENJUNGA | Kangchenjunga Himalaya | 8,586 | 28,169 |
| 4 | LHOTSE | Mahalangur Himalaya | 8,516 | 27,940 |
| 5 | MAKALU | Mahalangur Himalaya | 8,485 | 27,838 |
| 6 | CHO OYU | Mahalangur Himalaya | 8,188 | 26,864 |
| 7 | DHAULAGIRI I | Dhaulagiri Himalaya | 8,167 | 26,795 |
| 8 | MANASLU | Manaslu Himalaya | 8,163 | 26,781 |
| 9 | NANGA PARBAT | Nanga Parbat Himalaya | 8,126 | 26,660 |
| 10 | ANNAPURNA I | Annapurna Himalaya | 8,091 | 26,545 |

FATALITIES WHILE CLIMBING K2:

## 80

## 📍 KANGCHENJUNGA

To respect the mountain's sacred significance to its people, British explorers George Band and Joe Brown stopped short of its summit on May 25, 1955.

## ◉ BAIKAL

Possibly the world's oldest lake (25 million years), Lake Baikal is also the largest freshwater lake. It contains 20 per cent of the world's fresh water.

**TOP 10...**

# DEEPEST **LAKES**

With these depths it's hardly surprising that lakes around the world are home to tales of monsters...

| | NAME | LOCATION | DEPTH (M) | (FT) |
|---|---|---|---|---|
| 1 | BAIKAL | Siberia, Russia | 1,637 | 5,371 |
| 2 | TANGANYIKA | Tanzania, Democratic Republic of the Congo, Burundi, Zambia | 1,470 | 4,823 |
| 3 | CASPIAN SEA | Iran, Russia, Turkmenistan, Kazakhstan, Azerbaijan | 1,025 | 3,363 |
| 4 | VOSTOK | Antarctica | 1,000 | 3,281 |
| 5 | O'HIGGINS-SAN MARTIN | Chile, Argentina | 836 | 2,743 |
| 6 | PINATUBO | Philippines | 800 | 2,625 |
| 7 | MALAWI | Mozambique, Tanzania, Malawi | 706 | 2,316 |
| 8 | ISSYK KUL | Kyrgyzstan | 668 | 2,192 |
| 9 | GREAT SLAVE | Canada | 614 | 2,015 |
| 10 | CRATER | Oregon, USA | 594 | 1,949 |

## ◉ O'HIGGINS-SAN MARTIN

Non-natives didn't live by this Chile lake until 1910. Wool production became a growing industry for Swiss, Scandinavian, and British settlers.

LOCH NESS HAS HAD
**3,000**
SIGHTINGS OF "NESSIE"

# LOCH NESS

Just off the chart is this world-famous Scottish loch, with a depth of 132 m (433 ft). There have been reports of people claiming to see the "Nessie" monster since the 7th century.

IT WAS SUSPECTED YUCATÁN HAD A CRATER IN
**1960**

## ⦿ CHICXULUB

Part of the Mexican state of Yucatán, Chicxulub is a town with just over 5,000 residents. Its name means "devil flea."

**TOP 10...**

# LARGEST **CRATERS** ON EARTH

Craters are huge indentations caused by a celestial body such as a meteorite colliding into a planet. These are Earth's biggest known dents...

| | NAME | LOCATION | AGE (MILLIONS OF YEARS) | DIAMETER (KM) | (M) |
|---|---|---|---|---|---|
| 1 | VREDEFORT | Free State (South Africa) | 2,023 | 300 | 186.4 |
| 2 | SUDBURY | Ontario (Canada) | 1,849 | 250 | 155 |
| 3 | CHICXULUB | Yucatán (Mexico) | 65 | 170 | 105 |
| 4 | KARA | Nenetsia (Russia) | 70.3 | 120 | 75 |
| 5 | MANICOUAGAN | Quebec (Canada) | 215 | 100 | 62 |
| = | POPIGAI | Siberia (Russia) | 35.7 | 100 | 62 |
| 7 | ACRAMAN | South Australia | 580 | 85-90 | 53-55 |
| 8 | CHESAPEAKE BAY | Virginia (USA) | 35.5 | 85 | 53 |
| 9 | PUCHEZH-KATUNKI | Nizhny Novgorod Oblast (Russia) | 167 | 80 | 50 |
| 10 | MOROKWENG | Kalahari Desert (South Africa) | 145 | 70 | 43 |

## ⦿ VREDEFORT

Due to its geological significance, the impact's natural structure, known as the Vredefort Dome, was added to UNESCO (United Nations Educational, Scientific and Cultural Organization) World Heritage Sites in 2005.

## AGE OF THE CRATERS

Here are the top five from the above list, but in order of age...

| VREDEFORT | SUDBURY | ACRAMAN | MANICOUAGAN | PUCHEZH-KATUNKI |
|---|---|---|---|---|
| 2,023 | 1,849 | 580 | 215 | 167 |

## ⦿ MARS

Experts believe Mars' Hellas Planitia was created over 4 billion years ago.

## ⦿ MOON

Its indentations are called *lunar maria*, latin for "seas," which they were originally misidentified as.

## TOP 10...
# LARGEST CRATERS IN OUR SOLAR SYSTEM

Of all the surface impacts we know of in our galaxy, these are the widest...

| | NAME | LOCATION | DIAMETER (KM) | (M) |
|---|---|---|---|---|
| 1 | UTOPIA PLANITIA | Mars | 3,300 | 2050.5 |
| 2 | SOUTH POLE–AITKEN BASIN | The Moon | 2,500 | 1553.4 |
| 3 | HELLAS PLANITIA | Mars | 2,300 | 1429.2 |
| 4 | CALORIS BASIN | Mercury | 1,550 | 963.1 |
| 5 | MARE IMBRIUM | The Moon | 1,145 | 711.5 |
| 6 | REMBRANDT | Mercury | 715 | 444.3 |
| 7 | TURGIS | Iapetus | 580 | 360.4 |
| 8 | RHEASILVIA | Vesta | 505 | 313.8 |
| 9 | ENGELIER | Iapetus | 504 | 313.2 |
| 10 | MAMALDI | Rhea | 480 | 298.3 |

## ⦿ MERCURY

After Earth, Mercury is the second-densest planet in our solar system. Its metallic core makes up 80 per cent of the planet's radius.

MERCURY'S CALORIS BASIN WAS DISCOVERED IN

# 1974

BY U.S. PROBE

**COBRA LILY**

This Californian plant gets its name from resembling a hooded cobra rearing backwards.

GIANT MALAYSIAN PITCHER PLANT HAS
**2.5 LITRES**
OF DIGESTIVE LIQUID

**GIANT MALAYSIAN PITCHER PLANT**

The largest-size cup of this species is 41 cm (16 in), found in 2011 in East Malaysia.

TOP 10...
# MOST CARNIVOROUS PLANTS

Meat-eating vegetation in science fiction is inspired by the horrors in the real world...

| | NAME | LOCATION | TRAP TYPE | TRAPS & EATS |
|---|---|---|---|---|
| 1 | GIANT MALAYSIAN PITCHER PLANTS | Malaysia (Borneo) | Pitfall/cup trap | Rats, mice, lizards, frogs, insects |
| 2 | COBRA LILY | California (USA) | Cobra-like pitcher trap | Flies, ants, beetles, crawling insects |
| 3 | COMMON BLADDERWORT | 50 States (USA) | Aquatic hair-trigger bladder traps | Fish fry, tadpoles, round worms |
| 4 | WATERWHEEL PLANT | Africa, Asia, Australia, Europe | Aquatic hair-trigger bristle trap | Water fleas, tadpoles. |
| 5 | WEST AUSTRALIAN PITCHER PLANT | Albany (Australia) | Pitfall/cup trap | Ants, small insects |
| 6 | GREEN PITCHER PLANT | N.Carolina, Georgia (USA) | Pitfall/cup trap | Wasps and other small insects |
| 7 | VENUS FLYTRAP | East Coast wetlands (USA) | Hair-trigger jaws/trap | Small insects and arachnids |
| 8 | CAPE SUNDEW | Cape Of Good Hope (S.Africa) | Sticky tentacles | Small insects and arachnids |
| 9 | RAINBOW PLANT | Australia, Papua New Guinea, Indonesia | Sticky barbs | Small insects |
| 10 | YELLOW BUTTERWORT | Coast of SE. USA | Sticky leaves | Flies and small insects |

# DAY OF THE TRIFFIDS

English writer John Wyndham's 1951 sci-fi thriller *The Day Of The Triffids* features huge, predatory plants, inspired by pitchers. French actress Nicole Maurey starred alongside Howard Keel in the 1962 film adaptation. The UK's BBC adapted the novel for a successful television series in 1981.

BEWARE THE TRIFFIDS... they grow ...know...walk...talk...stalk...and KIL

THE DAY OF THE TRIFFIDS

CINEMASCOPE
EASTMANCOLOR

HOWARD KEEL
NICOLE MAUREY

## ⊙ DOUGLAS SPRUCE

This tree gets its name from Scottish botanist David Douglas (June 25, 1799 – July 12, 1834).

THE SITKA SPRUCE
CAN REACH
**4.9 M**
IN DIAMETER

TOP 10...

# TALLEST **TREES**

Investigate the tallest species of trees that live near you, and compare them to these...

| | SPECIES | LOCATION | MAXIMUM KNOWN HEIGHT (M) | (FT) |
|---|---|---|---|---|
| 1 | COAST REDWOOD | California (USA) | 115.72 | 379.65 |
| 2 | DOUGLAS SPRUCE | Oregon (USA) | 99.76 | 327.3 |
| 3 | VICTORIAN ASH | Tasmania (Australia) | 99.6 | 327 |
| 4 | SITKA SPRUCE | California (USA) | 96.7 | 317 |
| 5 | GIANT SEQUOIA | California (USA) | 95.8 | 314 |
| 6 | TASMANIAN BLUE GUM | Tasmania (Australia) | 90.7 | 298 |
| 7 | MANNA GUM | Tasmania (Australia) | 89 | 292 |
| 8 | YELLOW MERANTI | Sabah (Borneo) | 88.3 | 290 |
| 9 | ALPINE ASH | Tasmania (Australia) | 87.9 | 288 |
| 10 | KLINKI PINE* | Morobe Province (Papua New Guinea) | 70+ | 229.7 |

*Was one of the tallest trees in 1941 but has not been measured accurately. There are only nine officially recognised tallest trees.

# THE ENTS

Ents are tree-like creatures in J. R. R. Tolkien's *The Lord Of The Rings* books. In filmmaker Peter Jackson's adaptations, this Ent, Treebeard, is voiced by Welsh actor John Rhys-Davies, who also played dwarf Gimli in the films.

## ⊙ COAST REDWOOD

This ancient tree is believed to live for over 2,000 years. Tragically, 95 per cent of the original redwoods have been felled.

# GAMING

## GAMEBOY COLOR

This handheld console was available in 36 different colours/designs, including a Special Pikachu Pokémon Edition.

TOTAL PS2 GAMES SOLD:
## 1,662 MILLION UNITS

### TOP 10...
# BIGGEST SELLING GAMING CONSOLES/PLATFORMS

Of every video game console, from the home entertainment systems to portable handhelds, these are the most popular platforms of all time...

| | PLATFORM | MADE BY | RELEASED | UNIT SALES (MILLIONS) |
|---|---|---|---|---|
| 1 | PLAYSTATION 2 | Sony | 2000 | 157.68 |
| 2 | NINTENDO DS | Nintendo | 2004 | 154.88 |
| 3 | GAME BOY / GAME BOY COLOR | Nintendo | 1989/1998 | 118.69 |
| 4 | PLAYSTATION | Sony | 1994 | 104.25 |
| 5 | WII | Nintendo | 2006 | 101.17 |
| 6 | PLAYSTATION 3 | Sony | 2006 | 85.15 |
| 7 | XBOX 360 | Microsoft | 2005 | 84.54 |
| 8 | GAME BOY ADVANCE | Nintendo | 2001 | 81.51 |
| 9 | PLAYSTATION PORTABLE | Sony | 2004 | 80.82 |
| 10 | NINTENDO ENTERTAINMENT SYSTEM | Nintendo | 1983 | 61.91 |

## PLATFORM WARS

Here is how the above chart measures up by manufacturer...

**NINTENDO** 518.16

**SONY** 427.9

**MICROSOFT** 84.54

## PLAYSTATION 2

Sony's hugely successful PS2 was first launched in Japan on March 4, 2000.

## NINTENDO DS

The design of the DS (Dual Screen) was partly inspired by Nintendo's 1982 two-screen Game & Watch games machines like *Oil Panic* and *Donkey Kong*.

NINTENDO DS HAS HAD **3,994** GAMES MADE FOR IT

**TOP 10...**

# BIGGEST SELLING HANDHELD CONSOLES/PLATFORMS

Portable gaming has never been as popular as it is now, and these are the overall market leaders since the trend took hold...

| | PLATFORM | MADE BY | RELEASED | UNIT SALES (MILLIONS) |
|---|---|---|---|---|
| 1 | NINTENDO DS | Nintendo | 2004 | 154.88 |
| 2 | GAME BOY / GAME BOY COLOR | Nintendo | 1989/1998 | 118.69 |
| 3 | GAME BOY ADVANCE | Nintendo | 2001 | 81.51 |
| 4 | PLAYSTATION PORTABLE | Sony | 2004 | 80.82 |
| 5 | NINTENDO 3DS | Nintendo | 2011 | 50.63 |
| 6 | GAME GEAR | Sega | 1990 | 10.62 |
| 7 | PLAYSTATION VITA | Sony | 2011 | 9.90 |
| 8 | LEAPSTER | LeapFrog Enterprises | 2003 | 4.00 |
| 9 | NEO GEO POCKET/POCKET COLOR | SNK | 1998/1999 | 2 |
| 10 | TURBOEXPRESS | NEC | 1990 | 1.50 |

## LEAPSTER

This educational handheld game system first appeared in 2003. Increased hardware and software capabilities were added to the Leapster 2 in 2008, and the LeapsterGS Explorer is the latest incarnation. Among its educational titles are several major licenses including *SpongeBob SquarePants*, *Transformers*, and various Disney properties.

105

TOP 10...

# BIGGEST SELLING
# PS4 GAMES

Although only launched Nov 13, 2013, the PS4 has already notched up a Top 10 of multi-million-selling games...

| | NAME | GENRE | RELEASED | UNIT SALES (MILLIONS) |
|---|---|---|---|---|
| 1 | CALL OF DUTY: ADVANCED WARFARE | Shooter | 2014 | 6.18 |
| 2 | GRAND THEFT AUTO V | Action | 2014 | 6.05 |
| 3 | FIFA 15 | Sports | 2014 | 5.51 |
| 4 | DESTINY | Action | 2014 | 4.53 |
| 5 | WATCH DOGS | Action | 2014 | 3.53 |
| 6 | ASSASSIN'S CREED: UNITY | Action | 2014 | 3.02 |
| 7 | CALL OF DUTY: GHOSTS | Shooter | 2013 | 3.00 |
| 8 | FAR CRY 4 | Shooter | 2014 | 2.90 |
| 9 | THE LAST OF US | Adventure | 2014 | 2.79 |
| 10 | FIFA 14 | Sports | 2013 | 2.70 |

## ⦿ FIFA 15

This is the 22nd release under the FIFA brand. The first game was 1993's *FIFA International Soccer*.

## ⦿ DESTINY

This 2014 first-person shooter was created by Bungie, the developers behind the *Halo* franchise.

IN TOTAL, DESTINY HAS SOLD
# 10.28
**MILLION**
ACROSS FOUR GAMING PLATFORMS

## GRAN TURISMO FRANCHISE

This car racing series has seen 28 editions and more than 70 million units sold since the 1997 debut.

METAL GEAR SOLID 4: GUNS OF THE PATRIOTS (2008) SOLD

## 5.95 MILLION
UNITS ON THE PS3

TOP 10...

# BIGGEST SELLING PS3 GAMES

Launched Nov 11, 2006, Sony's predecessor to its PS4 remains a very popular gaming system...

| | NAME | GENRE | RELEASED | UNIT SALES (MILLIONS) |
|---|---|---|---|---|
| 1 | GRAND THEFT AUTO V | Action | 2013 | 19.34 |
| 2 | CALL OF DUTY: BLACK OPS II | Shooter | 2012 | 13.36 |
| 3 | CALL OF DUTY: MODERN WARFARE 3 | Shooter | 2011 | 13.19 |
| 4 | CALL OF DUTY: BLACK OPS | Shooter | 2010 | 12.43 |
| 5 | GRAN TURISMO 5 | Racing | 2010 | 10.57 |
| 6 | CALL OF DUTY: MODERN WARFARE 2 | Shooter | 2009 | 10.53 |
| 7 | GRAND THEFT AUTO IV | Action | 2008 | 10.35 |
| 8 | CALL OF DUTY: GHOSTS | Shooter | 2013 | 9.53 |
| 9 | FIFA 13 | Sports | 2012 | 8.13 |
| 10 | BATTLEFIELD 3 | Shooter | 2011 | 7.09 |

# WAR GAMES

Here is how the five *Call Of Duty* games from the above chart compare...

| CALL OF DUTY: BLACK OPS II | CALL OF DUTY: MODERN WARFARE 3 | CALL OF DUTY: BLACK OPS | CALL OF DUTY: MODERN WARFARE 2 | CALL OF DUTY: GHOSTS |
|---|---|---|---|---|
| 13.36 | 13.19 | 12.43 | 10.53 | 9.53 |

NEED FOR SPEED GAMES HAVE SOLD
## 96.51 MILLION
UNITS WORLDWIDE

## PS VITA

The original version of the PSV (PlayStation Vita) was released December 2011. Less than two years later, Sony reworked their handheld console and issued an improved edition in October 2013. Sony are now focusing more on the PSV's ability to integrate with the PS4 rather than releasing Vita-specific titles.

## ⦿ NEED FOR SPEED

The first title in this gaming series was *The Need For Speed*, published by Electronic Arts in 1994 for the 3DO console. The PlayStation and Saturn versions followed later in 1996.

TOP 10...

# BIGGEST SELLING PSVITA GAMES

Sony's successor to its PSP (PlayStation Portable) also has the ability to provide remote play from a PS4...

## ⦿ UNCHARTED: GOLDEN ABYSS

This, the fourth *Uncharted* game, was the first one in the series to be created for a handheld console.

| | | NAME | GENRE | RELEASED | UNIT SALES (MILLIONS) |
|---|---|---|---|---|---|
| ⦿ | 1 | UNCHARTED: GOLDEN ABYSS | Action | 2011 | 1.41 |
| | 2 | ASSASSIN'S CREED III: LIBERATION | Action | 2012 | 1.23 |
| | 3 | CALL OF DUTY BLACK OPS: DECLASSIFIED | Action | 2012 | 1.20 |
| | 4 | LITTLEBIGPLANET PS VITA | Platform | 2012 | 1.06 |
| | 5 | PERSONA 4: THE GOLDEN | RPG | 2012 | 0.87 |
| ⦿ | 6 | NEED FOR SPEED: MOST WANTED | Racing | 2012 | 0.86 |
| | 7 | FINAL FANTASY X / X-2 HD REMASTER | RPG | 2013 | 0.70 |
| | 8 | KILLZONE: MERCENARY | Shooter | 2013 | 0.68 |
| | 9 | TEARAWAY | Action | 2013 | 0.56 |
| | = | FIFA SOCCER | Sports | 2012 | 0.56 |

## PSP CONSOLE

This console debuted on Dec 12, 2004. It used UMDs (Universal Media Discs) as its game format.

## ⦿ RATCHET & CLANK

An animated movie based on *Ratchet & Clank*, and a tie-in game (the 13th in the series) are due to be released April 2016...

SEGA'S GAME GEAR CONSOLE WAS IN PRODUCTION FOR

## 6.5 YEARS

### TOP 10...
# BIGGEST SELLING PSP GAMES

Sony ceased manufacturing this handheld console in December 2014. These are its biggest selling games...

| | NAME | GENRE | RELEASED | UNIT SALES (MILLIONS) |
|---|---|---|---|---|
| 1 | GRAND THEFT AUTO: LIBERTY CITY STORIES | Action | 2005 | 7.65 |
| 2 | MONSTER HUNTER FREEDOM UNITE | RPG | 2008 | 5.46 |
| 3 | GRAND THEFT AUTO: VICE CITY STORIES | Action | 2006 | 5.01 |
| 4 | MONSTER HUNTER FREEDOM 3 | RPG | 2010 | 4.87 |
| 5 | DAXTER | Platform | 2006 | 4.15 |
| 6 | RATCHET & CLANK: SIZE MATTERS | Platform | 2007 | 3.72 |
| 7 | MIDNIGHT CLUB 3: DUB EDITION | Racing | 2005 | 3.63 |
| 8 | GRAN TURISMO | Racing | 2009 | 3.21 |
| 9 | GOD OF WAR: CHAINS OF OLYMPUS | Action | 2008 | 3.15 |
| 10 | CRISIS CORE: FINAL FANTASY VII | RPG | 2007 | 3.14 |

## ⦿ GTA ON PSP

Aside from the two *GTA* titles in the above chart, *Grand Theft Auto: Chinatown Wars* (2009) sold 1.05 million copies for the PSP.

TOP 10...

# BIGGEST SELLING
# XBOX ONE GAMES

Microsoft's latest gaming system, released Nov 22, 2013, has some familiar franchises among its Top 10 games...

| | NAME | GENRE | RELEASED | UNIT SALES (MILLIONS) |
|---|---|---|---|---|
| 1 | CALL OF DUTY: ADVANCED WARFARE | Shooter | 2014 | 4.17 |
| 2 | TITANFALL | Shooter | 2014 | 2.56 |
| 3 | ASSASSIN'S CREED: UNITY | Action | 2014 | 2.55 |
| 4 | DESTINY | Action | 2014 | 2.48 |
| 5 | GRAND THEFT AUTO V | Action | 2014 | 2.43 |
| 6 | CALL OF DUTY: GHOSTS | Shooter | 2013 | 2.37 |
| 7 | ASSASSIN'S CREED IV: BLACK FLAG | Action | 2013 | 2.05 |
| 8 | HALO: THE MASTER CHIEF COLLECTION | Shooter | 2014 | 1.94 |
| 9 | FORZA MOTORSPORT 5 | Racing | 2013 | 1.91 |
| 10 | FIFA 15 | Sports | 2014 | 1.71 |

## GENRE WARS

This visual chart conveys the popularity of genres for the Xbox One...

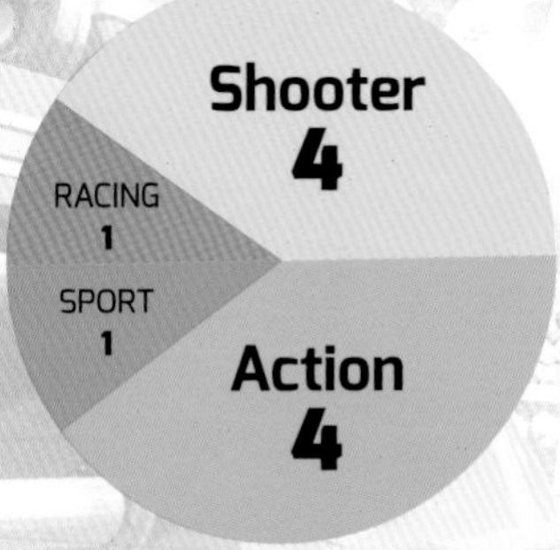

Shooter
4

RACING
1

SPORT
1

Action
4

LEGO MARVEL SUPER HEROES (2013) HAS SOLD
**0.66**
MILLION UNITS ON THE XBOX ONE

## ◉ TITANFALL

This first-person mech-enhanced shooter has won more than 60 international awards.

## KINECT ADVENTURES!

Launched with the Xbox's Kinect motion sensor device, this game features 5 mini-games that require full body motion to play.

TOP 10...

# BIGGEST SELLING XBOX 360 GAMES

These are the most successful games released for the follow-up console to the Xbox (available between 2001-08)...

| | NAME | GENRE | RELEASED | UNIT SALES (MILLIONS) |
|---|---|---|---|---|
| 1 | KINECT ADVENTURES! | Party | 2010 | 21.42 |
| 2 | GRAND THEFT AUTO V | Action | 2013 | 15.01 |
| 3 | CALL OF DUTY: MODERN WARFARE 3 | Shooter | 2011 | 14.49 |
| 4 | CALL OF DUTY: BLACK OPS | Shooter | 2010 | 14.27 |
| 5 | CALL OF DUTY: MODERN WARFARE 2 | Shooter | 2009 | 13.37 |
| 6 | CALL OF DUTY: BLACK OPS II | Shooter | 2012 | 13.28 |
| 7 | HALO 3 | Shooter | 2007 | 12.02 |
| 8 | GRAND THEFT AUTO IV | Action | 2008 | 10.88 |
| 9 | HALO: REACH | Shooter | 2010 | 9.71 |
| 10 | CALL OF DUTY: GHOSTS | Shooter | 2013 | 9.53 |

## HALO FRANCHISE

12 *Halo* titles have been released since *Halo: Combat Evolved* was launched Nov 15, 2001. The latest, *Halo 5: Guardians*, out Oct 2015, ties in with the TV series produced by filmmaker Steven Spielberg.

HALO: REACH IS THE

# 6TH

GAME OF THE SERIES

## ZELDA LEGACY

Created by Japanese game designers Shigeru Miyamoto and Takashi Tezuka, the latest *Zelda* game, *The Legend Of Zelda: Majora's Mask 3D* sold 1.56 million units in the first four months following its Feb 13, 2015 release. Miyamoto is also the creator of several other multi-million-dollar game franchises including *Mario*, *Donkey Kong*, and the Wii's party games, all of which Tezuka has been involved with as a director/producer.

## 📍 DONKEY KONG FRANCHISE

Since the 1981 arcade hit *Donkey Kong*, the franchise has expanded to more than 30 games. Over 65 million units have been sold worldwide.

THE ZELDA FRANCHISE HAS SHIFTED
**77.62**
**MILLION**
UNITS

### TOP 10...
# BIGGEST **WII U** GAMES

Although not as popular as Nintendo's previous console, the Wii, millions of Wii U games have been sold...

| | NAME | GENRE | RELEASED | UNIT SALES (MILLIONS) |
|---|---|---|---|---|
| 1 | NEW SUPER MARIO BROS. U | Action | 2012 | 4.66 |
| 2 | MARIO KART 8 | Racing | 2014 | 4.21 |
| 3 | NINTENDO LAND | Action | 2012 | 3.83 |
| 4 | SUPER SMASH BROS. FOR WIIU AND 3DS | Fighting | 2014 | 3.08 |
| 5 | SUPER MARIO 3D WORLD | Platform | 2013 | 3.00 |
| 6 | NEW SUPER LUIGI U | Platform | 2013 | 2.04 |
| 7 | WII PARTY U | Party | 2013 | 1.57 |
| 8 | THE LEGEND OF ZELDA: THE WIND WALKER | Action | 2013 | 1.29 |
| 9 | DONKEY KONG COUNTRY: TROPICAL FREEZE | Platform | 2014 | 1.01 |
| 10 | LEGO CITY UNDERCOVER | Action | 2013 | 0.81 |

## 📍 NEW SUPER MARIO BROS. U

This 2012 game allows up to five players to join in at the same time via four Wii remotes and the Wii U GamePad.

## SUPER SMASH BROS. BRAWL

After debuting on the N64 in 1999, Nintendo's face-off franchise started to incorporate non-Nintendo universe characters. *Super Smash Bros. Brawl* (2008) saw Sega's Sonic the Hedgehog and Mario do battle.

ALL WII SPORTS RELEASES (2006-14) HAVE SOLD

# 115.27 MILLION
UNITS COMBINED

TOP 10...

# BIGGEST **WII** GAMES

Nintendo stopped making Wii consoles on Oct 20, 2013, but games for the system are still being made...

| | NAME | GENRE | RELEASED | UNIT SALES (MILLIONS) |
|---|---|---|---|---|
| 1 | WII SPORTS | Sports | 2006 | 82.39 |
| 2 | MARIO KART WII | Racing | 2008 | 35.11 |
| 3 | WII SPORTS RESORT | Sports | 2009 | 32.61 |
| 4 | WII PLAY | Party | 2006 | 28.88 |
| 5 | NEW SUPER MARIO BROS. WII | Platform | 2009 | 27.92 |
| 6 | WII FIT | Sports | 2007 | 22.69 |
| 7 | WII FIT PLUS | Sports | 2009 | 21.69 |
| 8 | SUPER SMASH BROS. BRAWL | Fighting | 2008 | 12.55 |
| 9 | SUPER MARIO GALAXY | Platform | 2007 | 11.22 |
| 10 | JUST DANCE 3 | Party | 2011 | 10.07 |

## LUIGI'S MANSION

*Mario Is Missing* (1992) was the first game to feature Mario's brother Luigi as the lead character, and this 2001 game was the second. The sequel *Dark Moon* appeared 12 years later.

GAME BOY ADVANCE SHIFTED
**377.41 MILLION** UNITS OF ITS GAMES

## TOP 10...
# BIGGEST SELLING 3DS GAMES

This Nintendo console has gone through various iterations, the latest being the New Nintendo 3DS XL, released Oct 11, 2014. These are its hit games...

| | NAME | GENRE | RELEASED | UNIT SALES (MILLIONS) |
|---|---|---|---|---|
| 1 | POKÉMON X/Y | RPG | 2013 | 12.64 |
| 2 | MARIO KART 7 | Racing | 2011 | 10.57 |
| 3 | SUPER MARIO 3D LAND | Platform | 2011 | 10.05 |
| 4 | NEW SUPER MARIO BROS. 2 | Platform | 2012 | 8.57 |
| 5 | POKÉMON OMEGA RUBY/ ALPHA SAPPHIRE | RPG | 2014 | 7.71 |
| 6 | ANIMAL CROSSING: NEW LEAF | Action | 2012 | 7.63 |
| 7 | SUPER SMASH BROS. FOR WII U AND 3DS | Fighting | 2014 | 5.68 |
| 8 | LUIGI'S MANSION: DARK MOON | Adventure | 2013 | 4.10 |
| 9 | TOMADACHI LIFE | Simulation | 2013 | 3.89 |
| 10 | THE LEGEND OF ZELDA: OCARINA OF TIME | Action | 2011 | 3.59 |

## SUPER MARIO 3D LAND

This was the first *Mario* game to be made for the Nintendo 3DS handheld console.

# FRANCHISE SUMMARY

Here is how the game franchises in this Top 10 compare...

| POKÉMON | MARIO/LUIGI | ANIMAL CROSSING | TOMADACHI | ZELDA |
|---|---|---|---|---|
| 20.35 | 38.97 | 7.63 | 3.89 | 3.59 |

SUPER MARIO 3D LAND

## GAME BOY ADVANCE

Released March 2001, the Game Boy Advance was in production for just under seven years.

NINTENDO CONSOLES HAVE SEEN **15** POKÉMON GAMES RELEASED

## MARIO KART 7

Exclusively released for the 3DS in 2011, its sequel *Mario Kart 8* came out for the Wii U in 2014.

TOP 10...
# LONGEST RUNNING PLATFORMS

The length of time a gaming console is kept in production is a good reflection of its global success and popularity...

| | PLATFORM | MADE BY | YEARS IN PRODUCTION | TOTAL YEARS |
|---|---|---|---|---|
| 1 | NINTENDO ENTERTAINMENT SYSTEM | Nintendo | 1983-2003 | 20 |
| 2 | GAME BOY / GAME BOY COLOR | Nintendo | 1989-2003 | 14 |
| 3 | PLAYSTATION | Sony | 1994-2006 | 12 |
| = | PLAYSTATION 2 | Sony | 2000-12 | 12 |
| 5 | NINTENDO DS / 3DS / 3DSI XL | Nintendo | 2004-PRESENT | 11 |
| 6 | PLAYSTATION PORTABLE | Sony | 2004-14 | 10 |
| = | SUPER NINTENDO ENTERTAINMENT SYSTEM | Nintendo | 1993-2003 | 10 |
| = | XBOX 360 | Microsoft | 2005-PRESENT | 10 |
| 9 | PLAYSTATION 3 | Sony | 2006-PRESENT | 9 |
| 10 | WII | Nintendo | 2006-13 | 7 |

## GAME BOY HISTORY

Nintendo's original Game Boy graphics used four shades of grey on an LCD screen. Released April 21, 1989, it faced competition from full-colour handhelds like Atari's Lynx (1989) and Sega's Game Gear (1990), but outsold both by more than ten times their combined sales.

# FOUR VERSUS ONE

Rival manufacturers Sony and Microsoft both launched their new consoles in late 2013. Sony's PlayStation 4 has sold over 23 million units worldwide compared to Microsoft's Xbox One's 12.63 million sales. The PS4 has also had 380 games released for it, with Xbox One only hosting 256 titles.

XBOX 360 CAN ALSO PLAY

**468**

OLDER XBOX GAMES

### TOP 10...

# MOST GAMES **PER PLATFORM**

Another clear indication of the success of a games console is the amount of software made and released for it...

|  | PLATFORM | MADE BY | YEAR RELEASED | TOTAL GAMES MADE |
|---|---|---|---|---|
| 1 | NINTENDO DS | Nintendo | 2004 | 3,994 |
| 2 | XBOX 360 | Microsoft | 2005 | 3,608 |
| 3 | PLAYSTATION 2 | Sony | 2000 | 3,549 |
| 4 | PS3 | Sony | 2006 | 3,170 |
| 5 | WII | Nintendo | 2006 | 2,792 |
| 6 | PLAYSTATION | Sony | 1994 | 2,680 |
| 7 | PLAYSTATION PORTABLE (PSP) | Sony | 2004 | 1,800 |
| 8 | GAME BOY ADVANCE | Nintendo | 2001 | 1,640 |
| 9 | GAME BOY / GAME BOY COLOR | Nintendo | 1989 / 1998 | 1,607 |
| 10 | SUPER NINTENDO ENTERTAINMENT SYSTEM (SNES) | Nintendo | 1990 | 1,207 |

## 📍 PS4 DUAL-SHOCK 4

One of its new features is a touch-pad for enhanced gameplay on the front of the controller.

XBOX ONE IS CAPABLE OF
**7.1**
**SURROUND**
SOUND

## 📍 XBOX 360

The Xbox 360 controller requires batteries or a battery pack, rather than charging from the main console like the PS3's.

# FRANCHISE CONTROLLERS

Here is how the below chart looks when viewed per manufacturer/ franchise...

| SONY (PLAYSTATION) | NINTENDO (WII, N64, GAMECUBE) | MICROSOFT (XBOX) | SEGA (DREAMCAST) |
|---|---|---|---|
| 4 | 3 | 2 | 1 |

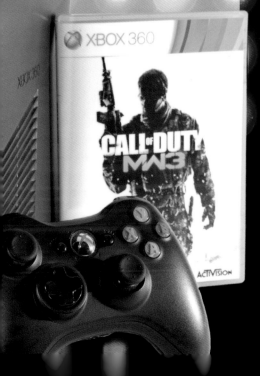

## TOP 10...

# CONTROLLERS WITH THE MOST BUTTONS

As video gaming has evolved, so have the controllers and the number of things a player can do in the on-screen world...

| | | CONTROLLER | YEAR RELEASED | TOTAL BUTTONS |
|---|---|---|---|---|
| 👁 | 1 | PLAYSTATION 4 DUALSHOCK 4 | 2013 | 17 |
| | = | PLAYSTATION 3 DUALSHOCK 3 SIXAXIS | 2007 | 17 |
| | = | PLAYSTATION 2 DUALSHOCK 2 | 2000 | 17 |
| | = | PLAYSTATION DUAL ANALOG | 1997 | 17 |
| | 5 | GAMECUBE WAVEBIRD | 2002 | 14 |
| | = | XBOX 360 | 2005 | 14 |
| | 7 | WII U | 2012 | 13 |
| | = | XBOX ONE | 2013 | 13 |
| | 9 | DREAMCAST CONTROLLER AND VMU | 1998 | 12 |
| | 10 | N64 | 1996 | 11 |

## WORLD OF WARCRAFT

The extremely popular role-playing series from publishers Activision debuted in 2004.

## TOP 10...

# MOST SUCCESSFUL GENRES

Of all the different kinds of video game made, these are the genres that sell the most...

| | GENRE | ALL PLATFORMS' UNIT SALES (MILLIONS) |
|---|---|---|
| 1 | ACTION | 1,439.18 |
| 2 | SPORTS | 1,249.02 |
| 3 | SHOOTER | 908.33 |
| 4 | RPG | 861.26 |
| 5 | PLATFORM | 832.08 |
| 6 | PARTY | 761.84 |
| 7 | RACING | 704.08 |
| 8 | FIGHTING | 421.86 |
| 9 | ADVENTURE | 397.33 |
| 10 | SIMULATION | 377.16 |

## OFF THE CHART GENRE

The one kind of game that didn't make it into this Top 10 is the Puzzle genre. 207.69 million units of puzzle games have been sold worldwide.

## NBA 2K14

This hit basketball game has contributed over 6 million in unit sales to the Sports genre total. The game features Miami Heat's LeBron James as the cover star.

THE STREET FIGHTER FRANCHISE HAS SOLD

## 32.27 MILLION
COPIES WORLDWIDE

## RACING

More than 3,000 racing games have been released.

## ⦿ GRAN TURISMO 5

This racing game is actually the 13th *Gran Turismo* franchise release.

## TWO-SERIES RACE

Here is how the below chart's contents look when summarized by its two franchises:

MARIO KART
**87.41**
million

GRAN TURISMO
**57.65**
million

INCLUDING ARCADE GAMES, THERE ARE
**11**
**MARIO KART** TITLES

## TOP 10...
# BIGGEST **RACING GAMES**

From fantasy realms, to hyper-realistic computer-generated versions of real vehicles, these racing titles outperform all others...

| | NAME | PLATFORM | RELEASED | UNIT SALES (MILLIONS) |
|---|---|---|---|---|
| 1 | MARIO KART WII | Wii | 2008 | 35.11 |
| 2 | MARIO KART DS | DS | 2005 | 23.10 |
| 3 | GRAN TURISMO 3: A-SPEC | PS2 | 2001 | 14.98 |
| 4 | GRAN TURISMO 4 | PS2 | 2004 | 11.66 |
| 5 | GRAN TURISMO | PS | 1997 | 10.95 |
| 6 | MARIO KART 7 | 3DS | 2011 | 10.57 |
| = | GRAN TURISMO 5 | PS3 | 2010 | 10.57 |
| 8 | MARIO KART 64 | N64 | 1996 | 9.87 |
| 9 | GRAN TURISMO 2 | PS | 1999 | 9.49 |
| 10 | SUPER MARIO KART | SNES | 1992 | 8.76 |

## ZUMBA FITNESS

As well as dance moves, Zumba incorporates elements of martial arts, and so qualifies as a type of Sports game.

HOT

FIVE DIFFERENT ZUMBA-THEMED VIDEO GAMES HAVE SOLD OVER
**13 MILLION** COPIES WORLDWIDE

TOP 10...

# BIGGEST SPORTS GAMES

Combining every kind of sport, including martial arts fitness games, here are the 10 best sellers...

| | NAME | PLATFORM | RELEASED | UNIT SALES (MILLIONS) |
|---|---|---|---|---|
| 1 | WII SPORTS | Wii | 2006 | 82.39 |
| 2 | WII SPORTS RESORT | Wii | 2009 | 32.61 |
| 3 | WII FIT | Wii | 2007 | 22.69 |
| 4 | WII FIT PLUS | Wii | 2009 | 21.69 |
| 5 | MARIO & SONIC AT THE OLYMPIC GAMES | Wii | 2007 | 7.97 |
| 6 | FIFA 14 | PS | 2013 | 6.74 |
| 7 | ZUMBA FITNESS | Wii | 2010 | 6.66 |
| 8 | FIFA 12 | PS3 | 2011 | 6.62 |
| 9 | KINECT SPORTS | Xbox 360 | 2010 | 6.04 |
| 10 | FIFA 15 | PS4 | 2014 | 5.51 |

## WII SPORTS

The *Will Sports* franchise has sold in excess of 115 million copies of its three titles.

2nd

0

0

# WII FIT

Since the first *Wii Fit* appeared on the Nintendo Wii in 2007, the franchise has gone on to sell more than 45 million units. The latest version, *Wii Fit U*, was released in 2013.

SMASH IT

Club

Fastball
**92** mph

IN DONKEY KONG JNR,
RELEASED IN
**1982**
MARIO PLAYED
THE VILLAIN

## 📍 SUPER MARIO BROS.

Before the 1985 NES game, Mario and
Luigi starred in the 1983 arcade classic
*Mario Bros.*

TOP 10...

# BIGGEST PLATFORM GAMES

Nintendo's Mario franchise conquers this Top 10, featuring on every
single entry...

| | NAME | PLATFORM | RELEASED | UNIT SALES (MILLIONS) |
|---|---|---|---|---|
| 1 | SUPER MARIO BROS. | NES | 1985 | 40.24 |
| 2 | NEW SUPER MARIO BROS. | DS | 2006 | 29.65 |
| 3 | NEW SUPER MARIO BROS. WII | Wii | 2009 | 27.92 |
| 4 | SUPER MARIO WORLD | SNES | 1990 | 20.61 |
| 5 | SUPER MARIO LAND | Game Boy | 1989 | 18.14 |
| 6 | SUPER MARIO BROS. 3 | NES | 1988 | 17.28 |
| 7 | SUPER MARIO 64 | N64 | 1996 | 11.89 |
| 8 | SUPER MARIO GALAXY | Wii | 2007 | 11.22 |
| 9 | SUPER MARIO LAND 2: 6 GOLDEN COINS | Game Boy | 1992 | 11.18 |
| 10 | SUPER MARIO ALL-STARS | SNES | 1993 | 10.55 |

## MARIO BY PLATFORM

Ranked by gaming
platform, the
above Top 10 is
quite an even split:

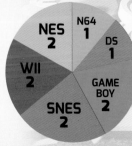

NES 2
N64 1
DS 1
WII 2
GAME BOY 2
SNES 2

## 📍 SUPER MARIO LAND

This 1989 game was the first
*Mario* adventure to be made
for the Nintendo Game Boy.

## POKÉMON

There have been 14 official soundtracks released containing *Pokémon* movie and video game music.

THE POKÉMON TRADING CARD GAME FIRST DEBUTED IN THE USA IN
# 1999

## TOP 10...
# BIGGEST RPG GAMES

All but one of this chart's entries are games spun out of the 20-year-old Pokémon franchise...

| | NAME | PLATFORM | RELEASED | UNIT SALES (MILLIONS) |
|---|---|---|---|---|
| 1 | POKÉMON RED/BLUE/GREEN VERSION | Game Boy | 1996 | 31.37 |
| 2 | POKÉMON GOLD/SILVER VERSION | Game Boy | 1999 | 23.10 |
| 3 | POKÉMON DIAMOND/PEARL VERSION | Game Boy | 2006 | 18.21 |
| 4 | POKÉMON RUBY/SAPPHIRE VERSION | Game Boy | 2002 | 15.85 |
| 5 | POKÉMON BLACK/WHITE VERSION | Game Boy | 2010 | 15.05 |
| 6 | POKÉMON YELLOW: SPECIAL PIKACHU EDITION | Game Boy | 1998 | 14.64 |
| 7 | POKÉMON X/Y | 3DS | 2013 | 12.64 |
| 8 | POKÉMON HEART GOLD/SOUL SILVER VERSION | DS | 2009 | 11.71 |
| 9 | POKÉMON FIRERED/LEAFGREEN VERSION | GBA | 2004 | 10.49 |
| 10 | FINAL FANTASY VII | PS | 1997 | 9.72 |

## LEGO HISTORY

Although the first official LEGO video game was 1997's *LEGO Island*, the company expansion into movie licenses saw *LEGO Creator: Harry Potter* released in 2001. Since then, 21 official LEGO movie games have been made.

## PROFESSOR LAYTON

Seven *Professor Layton* video games were released between 2007-14 with a total of 17.98 million units sold.

## MINECRAFT

All *Minecraft* releases across all consoles amount to 14 million copies sold.

THE ASSASSIN'S CREED FRANCHISE HAS SOLD

**74.13**
**MILLION**
COPIES

**TOP 10...**

# BIGGEST ADVENTURE GAMES

This popular genre encompasses titles that span all age groups, from LEGO titles to more adult adventuring games...

| | NAME | PLATFORM | RELEASED | UNIT SALES (MILLIONS) |
|---|---|---|---|---|
| 1 | MINECRAFT | Xbox 360 | 2013 | 6.99 |
| 2 | ASSASSIN'S CREED | Xbox 360 | 2007 | 5.49 |
| 3 | THE LAST OF US | PS3 | 2013 | 5.45 |
| 4 | TOMB RAIDER II | PS | 1997 | 5.24 |
| 5 | PROFESSOR LAYTON AND THE CURIOUS VILLAGE | DS | 2007 | 5.17 |
| 6 | ASSASSIN'S CREED | PS3 | 2007 | 4.79 |
| 7 | ZELDA II: THE ADVENTURE OF LINK | NES | 1987 | 4.38 |
| 8 | LUIGI'S MANSION: DARK MOON | 3DS | 2013 | 4.10 |
| 9 | PROFESSOR LAYTON AND THE DIABOLICAL BOX | DS | 2007 | 3.92 |
| 10 | LEGO INDIANA JONES: THE ORIGINAL ADVENTURES | Xbox 360 | 2008 | 3.72 |

## PAC-MAN LEGACY

This iconic video game character has been featured in 89 different editions of video games spanning almost every platform, including the Atari 2600, NES, and PS3. Over 24 million sales later, Pac-Man continues to appear in new titles developed for smartphones and tablets.

THE MOVIE PIXELS FEATURING PAC-MAN WAS RELEASED

**JULY 22, 2015**

TOP 10...
# BIGGEST PUZZLE GAMES

Proving that a simple concept can still remain a popular puzzler, most of the titles in this chart are more than 20 years old...

| | NAME | PLATFORM | RELEASED | UNIT SALES (MILLIONS) |
|---|---|---|---|---|
| 1 | TETRIS | Game Boy | 1989 | 30.26 |
| 2 | PAC-MAN | Atari 2600 | 1982 | 7.81 |
| 3 | TETRIS | NES | 1988 | 5.58 |
| 4 | DR. MARIO | Game Boy | 1989 | 5.34 |
| 5 | DR. MARIO | NES | 1990 | 4.85 |
| 6 | PAC-MAN COLLECTION | GBA | 2001 | 2.94 |
| 7 | WARIOWARE: SMOOTH MOVES | Wii | 2006 | 2.87 |
| 8 | MARIO VS. DONKEY KONG: MINI-LAND MAYHEM! | DS | 2010 | 2.67 |
| 9 | TETRIS PLUS | PS | 1996 | 2.40 |
| 10 | WARIOWARE TOUCHED! | DS | 2004 | 2.29 |

## TETRIS

The most recognizable puzzle video game in the world was created by Russian programmer Alexey Pajitnov. The first version of Tetris was released on June 6, 1984. In 1996, Pajitnov formed The Tetris Company with Dutch game designer Henk Rogers, to facilitate and protect the license.

124

# SIM GRAPH

Here is how the top five's sales from the below chart compare visually...

**NINTENDOGS**
24.65

**ANIMAL CROSSING: WILD WORLD**
12.08

**COOKING MAMA**
5.60

**ANIMAL CROSSING: CITY FOLK**
4.60

**TOMODACHI LIFE**
3.89

## ◉ NINTENDOGS + CATS

This Nintendo franchise has sold more than 28 million copies worldwide.

THE ANIMAL CROSSING FRANCHISE (7 RELEASES) HAS SOLD
**27.61 MILLION** UNITS

**TOP 10...**

# BIGGEST **SIMULATION** GAMES

From traditional simulation experiences like fighter jets, to taking care of virtual pets, sim games still shift millions of copies...

| | NAME | PLATFORM | RELEASED | UNIT SALES (MILLIONS) |
|---|---|---|---|---|
| 1 | NINTENDOGS | DS | 2005 | 24.65 |
| 2 | ANIMAL CROSSING: WILD WORLD | DS | 2005 | 12.08 |
| 3 | COOKING MAMA | DS | 2006 | 5.60 |
| 4 | ANIMAL CROSSING: CITY FOLK | Wii | 2008 | 4.60 |
| 5 | TOMODACHI LIFE | 3DS | 2013 | 3.89 |
| 6 | MYSIMS | DS | 2007 | 3.65 |
| 7 | POKÉMON SNAP | N64 | 1999 | 3.63 |
| 8 | COOKING MAMA 2: DINNER WITH FRIENDS | DS | 2007 | 3.57 |
| 9 | NINTENDOGS + CATS | 3DS | 2011 | 3.52 |
| 10 | ACE COMBAT 04: SHATTERED SKIES | PS2 | 2001 | 3.17 |

Single!

Player 2nd AI3

AI - Pro 3rd AI4

SCORE 6904

LEVEL 3

SCORE 4420

## TEKKEN 3

This fighting game is the sixth best-selling PlayStation game of all time.

## STREET FIGHTER LEGACY

For almost 30 years, the *Street Fighter* franchise has seen multiple games, live-action and animated movies, comics, and merchandise. More than 90 playable characters populate the game series.

## TOP 10...
# BIGGEST FIGHTING GAMES

The graphics and attack combinations in fighting games get more complex with each new release. These are the 10 biggest hitters...

| | NAME | PLATFORM | RELEASED | UNIT SALES (MILLIONS) |
|---|---|---|---|---|
| 1 | SUPER SMASH BROS. BRAWL | Wii | 2008 | 12.55 |
| 2 | TEKKEN 3 | PS | 1998 | 7.16 |
| 3 | SUPER SMASH BROS. MELEE | GameCube | 2001 | 7.07 |
| 4 | STREET FIGHTER II: THE WORLD WARRIOR | SNES | 1992 | 6.30 |
| 5 | TEKKEN 2 | PS | 1996 | 5.74 |
| 6 | SUPER SMASH BROS. FOR WII U AND 3DS | 3DS | 2014 | 5.68 |
| 7 | SUPER SMASH BROS. | N64 | 1999 | 5.55 |
| 8 | STREET FIGHTER II TURBO | SNES | 1992 | 4.10 |
| 9 | STREET FIGHTER IV | PS3 | 2009 | 4.06 |
| 10 | TEKKEN TAG TOURNAMENT | PS2 | 2000 | 4.05 |

**TOP 10...**
# BIGGEST **ACTION GAMES**

One open world "sandbox" video game series is the king of the genre and this Top 10...

| | NAME | PLATFORM | RELEASED | UNIT SALES (MILLIONS) |
|---|---|---|---|---|
| 1 | GRAND THEFT AUTO: SAN ANDREAS | PS2 | 2004 | 20.81 |
| 2 | GRAND THEFT AUTO V | PS3 | 2013 | 19.34 |
| 3 | GRAND THEFT AUTO: VICE CITY | PS2 | 2002 | 16.15 |
| 4 | GRAND THEFT AUTO V | Xbox 360 | 2013 | 15.01 |
| 5 | GRAND THEFT AUTO III | PS2 | 2001 | 13.10 |
| 6 | GRAND THEFT AUTO IV | Xbox 360 | 2008 | 10.88 |
| 7 | GRAND THEFT AUTO IV | PS3 | 2008 | 10.35 |
| 8 | GRAND THEFT AUTO: LIBERTY CITY STORIES | PSP | 2005 | 7.65 |
| 9 | THE LEGEND OF ZELDA: OCARINA OF TIME | N64 | 1998 | 7.60 |
| 10 | THE LEGEND OF ZELDA: TWILIGHT PRINCESS | Wii | 2006 | 7.07 |

## ⌖ ZELDA

*The Legend Of Zelda: The Ocarina Of Time* was given a 3D makeover for the 3DS in 2011.

THE LEGEND OF ZELDA: TWILIGHT PRINCESS IS SET **100 YEARS** AFTER THE OCARINA OF TIME

## ⌖ GRAND THEFT AUTO SAN ANDREAS

Across the nine platforms it was released for, this *GTA* title sold 23.7 million copies.

## TWO-FRANCHISE RACE

This visual chart shows how much one gaming franchise dominates the action genre...

**GTA 8**

**Zelda 2**

## POKÉMON

2015 marked the 20th anniversary of the *Pokémon* franchise.

DUCK HUNT FIRST APPEARED ON THE NES ON **APRIL 21, 1984**

**TOP 10...**

# BIGGEST CONSOLE GAMES OF ALL TIME

Across every single gaming console ever made, these are the 10 games that have out-sold all the rest...

| | NAME | GENRE | RELEASED | PLATFORM | UNIT SALES (MILLIONS) |
|---|---|---|---|---|---|
| 1 | WII SPORTS | Sports | 2006 | Wii | 82.39 |
| 2 | SUPER MARIO BROS. | Platform | 1985 | NES | 40.24 |
| 3 | MARIO KART WII | Racing | 2008 | Wii | 35.11 |
| 4 | WII SPORTS RESORT | Sports | 2009 | Wii | 32.61 |
| 5 | POKÉMON RED/BLUE/GREEN | RPG | 1996 | Game Boy | 31.37 |
| 6 | TETRIS | Puzzle | 1989 | Game Boy | 30.26 |
| 7 | NEW SUPER MARIO BROS. | Platform | 2006 | DS | 29.65 |
| 8 | WII PLAY | Party | 2006 | Wii | 28.88 |
| 9 | DUCK HUNT | Shooter | 1984 | NES | 28.31 |
| 10 | NEW SUPER MARIO BROS. WII | Platform | 2009 | Wii | 27.92 |

## WII SPORTS

Nintendo's *Wii Sports* and *Wii Sports Resort*'s combined sales of 115 million copies mean the franchise is 107 million units ahead of its nearest competitor, which is another Nintendo title, *Wii Fit* (22.69 million units). Four of the five best-selling sports games of all time are *Wii Fit/Sports* titles.

## PARTY GAMES

2015's *Guitar Hero Live* reinvents the video game that became one of the most popular party games of the last decade. The new title uses a real-world gig setting and puts the player on a stage among a real band.

THE MARIO KART SERIES IS
**24**
YEARS OLD
IN 2016

TOP 10...

# GENRE LEADERS

This Top 10 reveals the best-selling games from each of the most popular gaming genres around...

| | GENRE | NAME | RELEASED | PLATFORM | UNIT SALES (MILLIONS) |
|---|---|---|---|---|---|
| 1 | SPORTS | Wii Sports | 2006 | Wii | 82.39 |
| 2 | PLATFORM | Super Mario Bros. | 1985 | NES | 40.24 |
| 3 | RACING | Mario Kart Wii | 2008 | Wii | 35.11 |
| 4 | RPG | Pokémon Red/Blue/Green | 1996 | Game Boy | 31.37 |
| 5 | PUZZLE | Tetris | 1989 | Game Boy | 30.26 |
| 6 | PARTY | Wii Play | 2006 | Wii | 28.88 |
| 7 | SHOOTER | Duck Hunt | 1984 | NES | 28.31 |
| 8 | SIMULATION | Nintendogs | 2005 | DS | 24.65 |
| 9 | ACTION | Grand Theft Auto: San Andreas | 2004 | PS2 | 20.81 |
| 10 | FIGHTING | Super Smash Bros. Brawl | 2008 | Wii | 12.55 |

## TETRIS

This puzzler has appeared in over 60 releases, amounting to more than 93 million unit sales.

TETRIS®

## CALL OF DUTY

...ranchise sees its 15th game, ...Of Duty: Black Ops III, released ...5, 2015.

THE NEED FOR SPEED MOVIE WAS RELEASED **MARCH 12, 2014**

TOP 10...

# BIGGEST GAME BRANDS

These 10 gaming franchises are the most financially lucrative of them all...

| | FRANCHISE | TOTAL UNIT SALES (MILLIONS) |
|---|---|---|
| 1 | SUPER MARIO BROS. | 557.47 |
| 2 | POKÉMON | 242.06 |
| 3 | CALL OF DUTY | 215.33 |
| 4 | WII FIT/SPORTS/PARTY | 199.80 |
| 5 | GRAND THEFT AUTO | 153.57 |
| 6 | FIFA | 145.19 |
| 7 | LEGO | 117.04 |
| 8 | SONIC THE HEDGEHOG | 110.41 |
| 9 | FINAL FANTASY | 107.68 |
| 10 | NEED FOR SPEED | 96.19 |

## ⦿ FINAL FANTASY

Since the first *Final Fantasy* was released in 1987 for the NES, over 108 million copies of the series' games have been sold.

## MARIO OVER THE DECADES

This chart shows how the most popular *Mario* games compare by their release date...

1990s
2

1980s
3

2000s
5

## TOP 10...

# BIGGEST **MARIO GAMES**

With this Nintendo franchise's total game sales approaching 600 million units, these are its 10 biggest sellers to date...

| | NAME | GENRE | PLATFORM | RELEASED | UNIT SALES (MILLIONS) |
|---|---|---|---|---|---|
| 1 | SUPER MARIO BROS. | Platform | NES | 1985 | 40.24 |
| 2 | MARIO KART WII | Racing | Wii | 2008 | 35.11 |
| 3 | NEW SUPER MARIO BROS. | Platform | DS | 2006 | 29.65 |
| 4 | NEW SUPER MARIO BROS. WII | Platform | Wii | 2009 | 27.92 |
| 5 | MARIO KART DS | Racing | DS | 2005 | 23.10 |
| 6 | SUPER MARIO WORLD | Platform | SNES | 1990 | 20.61 |
| 7 | SUPER MARIO LAND | Platform | Game Boy | 1989 | 18.14 |
| 8 | SUPER MARIO BROS. 3 | Platform | NES | 1988 | 17.28 |
| 9 | SUPER MARIO 64 | Platform | N64 | 1996 | 11.89 |
| 10 | SUPER MARIO GALAXY | Platform | Wii | 2007 | 11.22 |

## ⚲ SUPER MARIO GALAXY

This *Mario* adventure won 2008 Academy of Interactive Arts & Sciences Award for Adventure Game of the Year.

MARIO HAS APPEARED IN

# 269
GAMES

## ⚲ SUPER MARIO BROS.

More than 558 million copies of games featuring Mario and Luigi have been sold.

## BOND'S GAMING LEGACY

The world's most famous secret agent, created by Ian Fleming in 1952, has featured in 26 official *James Bond* video games since 1983's *James Bond 007*. To celebrate Bond's 50th anniversary, *007 Legends* was released in 2012. Its plot filled the six-year gap between the events of the films *Quantum of Solace* and *Skyfall* by combining plotlines from classic Bond films *Goldfinger*, *On Her Majesty's Secret Service*, *License to Kill*, *Die Another Day*, and *Moonraker*.

### TOP 10...
# BIGGEST MOVIE TIE-IN GAMES

Video game adaptations of movie franchises have been popular since the late '70s and early '80s. These are the best sellers...

| | NAME | GENRE | PLATFORM | RELEASED | UNIT SALES (MILLIONS) |
|---|---|---|---|---|---|
| 1 | GOLDENEYE 007 | Shooter | N64 | 1997 | 8.09 |
| 2 | LEGO STAR WARS: THE COMPLETE SAGA | Action | Wii | 2007 | 5.50 |
| 3 | LEGO STAR WARS: THE COMPLETE SAGA | Action | DS | 2007 | 4.70 |
| 4 | THE LORD OF THE RINGS: THE TWO TOWERS | Action | PS2 | 2002 | 4.67 |
| 5 | SPIDER-MAN: THE MOVIE | Action | PS2 | 2002 | 4.48 |
| 6 | HARRY POTTER & THE SORCERER'S STONE | Action | PS | 2001 | 3.73 |
| 7 | LEGO INDIANA JONES: THE ORIGINAL ADVENTURES | Adventure | Xbox360 | 2008 | 3.72 |
| 8 | STAR WARS BATTLEFRONT | Shooter | PS2 | 2004 | 3.61 |
| 9 | STAR WARS BATTLEFRONT II | Shooter | PS2 | 2005 | 3.59 |
| 10 | JAMES BOND 007: AGENT UNDER FIRE | Shooter | PS2 | 2001 | 3.53 |

JAMES BOND VIDEO GAMES HAVE SOLD
## 15.65 MILLION
UNITS WORLDWIDE

### BLOOD STONE

*James Bond 007: Blood Stone* (2010) featured the vocal talents of Daniel Craig and Judi Dench. This original Bond adventure sold 1.21 million copies across

### LEGO INDIANA JONES

The two LEGO video games based on Indiana Jones' four film adventures have sold 16.85 million copies. The 2009 sequel *LEGO Indiana Jones 2: The Adventure Continues* shifted 5.05 million units of this total.

# THE BIG THREE

Here is how the three most successful gaming publishers compare visually...

SONY COMPUTER ENTERTAINMENT
10

ACTIVISION
13

Nintendo
51

ELECTRONIC ARTS WERE FOUNDED
**33**
YEARS
AGO

# SHADOW OF MORDOR

he latest video game inspired by the niverse of J. R. R. Tolkien's *The Lord f the Rings* is 2014's *Middle-earth: hadow of Mordor*. It has sold more than million copies.

## TOP 10...
# BIGGEST GAMING PUBLISHERS

Looking at the 100 best-selling games, here are the publishers that appear the most...

| | PUBLISHER | NO. OF GAMES IN TOP 100 SELLERS |
|---|---|---|
| 1 | NINTENDO | 51 |
| 2 | ACTIVISION | 13 |
| 3 | SONY COMPUTER ENTERTAINMENT | 10 |
| 4 | TAKE-TWO INTERACTIVE | 8 |
| 5 | MICROSOFT GAME STUDIOS | 5 |
| = | ELECTRONIC ARTS | 5 |
| 7 | UBISOFT | 3 |
| 8 | BETHESDA SOFTWORKS | 1 |
| = | RED ORB | 1 |
| = | SQUARESOFT | 1 |

# ⚲ ACTIVISION & SPIDEY

This publisher's web-slinging video games, which have appeared on more than 15 different platforms since *Spider-Man* (2000), have notched up over 35 million sales.

## STAR WARS BATTLEFRONT

Aside from the *Battlefront II* sequel, this game also spawned 2007's *Star Wars: Renegade Squadron* and 2009's *Star Wars: Elite Squadron*.

### TOP 10...
# BIGGEST **STAR WARS** GAMES

Since 1979's Star Wars Electronic Battle Command Game, video games have become a key component of the expanded Star Wars universe...

| | NAME | GENRE | PLATFORM | RELEASED | UNIT SALES |
|---|---|---|---|---|---|
| 1 | LEGO STAR WARS: THE COMPLETE SAGA | Action | Wii | 2007 | 5.50 |
| 2 | LEGO STAR WARS: THE COMPLETE SAGA | Action | DS | 2007 | 4.70 |
| 3 | STAR WARS BATTLEFRONT | Shooter | PS2 | 2004 | 3.61 |
| 4 | STAR WARS BATTLEFRONT II | Shooter | PS2 | 2005 | 3.59 |
| 5 | LEGO STAR WARS: THE VIDEO GAMES | Action | PS2 | 2005 | 3.53 |
| 6 | STAR WARS: EPISODE III – REVENGE OF THE SITH | Action | PS2 | 2005 | 3.32 |
| 7 | STAR WARS: EPISODE I RACER | Racing | N64 | 1999 | 3.12 |
| 8 | LEGO STAR WARS II: THE ORIGINAL TRILOGY | Action | PS2 | 2006 | 2.69 |
| 9 | STAR WARS: THE FORCE UNLEASHED | Action | Xbox 360 | 2008 | 2.68 |
| 10 | STAR WARS: SHADOWS OF THE EMPIRE | Action | N64 | 1996 | 2.65 |

ACROSS ALL MAJOR GAMING PLATFORMS, STARS WARS: THE FORCE UNLEASHED HAS SOLD

# 13.63
MILLION UNITS

# STAR WARS

Hundreds of video games about the *Star Wars* films, TV series, and expanded universe have been made for over 30 years. Total unit sales of all the releases amounts to more than 113 million copies sold worldwide. Of this total, over 36 million of those sales are for *LEGO Star Wars* titles.

## TOP 10...
# BIGGEST LEGO GAMES

LEGO Island was the first ever LEGO video game, released Oct 2, 1997. More than 60 titles have been released since, including these...

| | NAME | GENRE | PLATFORM | RELEASED | UNIT SALES |
|---|---|---|---|---|---|
| 1 | LEGO STAR WARS: THE COMPLETE SAGA | Action | Wii | 2007 | 5.50 |
| 2 | LEGO STAR WARS: THE COMPLETE SAGA | Action | DS | 2007 | 4.70 |
| 3 | LEGO INDIANA JONES: THE ORIGINAL ADVENTURES | Adventure | Xbox360 | 2008 | 3.72 |
| 4 | LEGO STAR WARS: THE VIDEO GAMES | Action | PS2 | 2005 | 3.53 |
| 5 | LEGO BATMAN: THE VIDEOGAME | Adventure | Xbox 360 | 2008 | 3.29 |
| 6 | LEGO BATMAN: THE VIDEOGAME | Adventure | Wii | 2008 | 3.01 |
| = | LEGO BATMAN: THE VIDEOGAME | Adventure | DS | 2008 | 3.01 |
| 8 | LEGO STAR WARS II: THE ORIGINAL TRILOGY | Action | PS2 | 2006 | 2.69 |
| 9 | LEGO HARRY POTTER: YEARS 1-4 | Adventure | Wii | 2010 | 2.40 |
| 10 | LEGO STAR WARS: THE COMPLETE SAGA | Action | Xbox 360 | 2007 | 2.36 |

## ⊙ LEGO HARRY POTTER

Although the Nintendo Wii version of *LEGO Harry Potter: Years 1-4* was the biggest hit of all of this franchise's titles, when you combine the sales of all *LEGO Harry Potter* releases across all formats, the unit sales reach 12.5 million.

LEGO HARRY POTTER: YEARS 5-7 (2011) SOLD

**1.18 MILLION** COPIES FOR THE WII

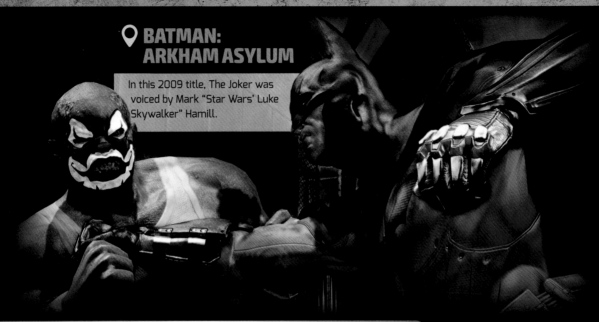

## BATMAN: ARKHAM ASYLUM

In this 2009 title, The Joker was voiced by Mark "Star Wars' Luke Skywalker" Hamill.

## TOP 10...
# BIGGEST **BATMAN GAMES**

One of DC Comics' most successful characters has also starred in countless movies, TV shows, and video games...

ALL BATMAN
VIDEO GAMES:
## 49.15
**MILLION**
UNITS SOLD

| | NAME | GENRE | PLATFORM | RELEASED | UNIT SALES (MILLIONS) |
|---|---|---|---|---|---|
| 1 | BATMAN: ARKHAM CITY | Action | PS3 | 2011 | 5.23 |
| 2 | BATMAN: ARKHAM CITY | Action | Xbox 360 | 2011 | 4.56 |
| 3 | BATMAN: ARKHAM ASYLUM | Action | PS3 | 2009 | 4.13 |
| 4 | BATMAN: ARKHAM ASYLUM | Action | Xbox 360 | 2009 | 3.39 |
| 5 | LEGO BATMAN: THE VIDEOGAME | Adventure | Xbox 360 | 2008 | 3.29 |
| 6 | LEGO BATMAN: THE VIDEOGAME | Adventure | Wii | 2008 | 3.01 |
| = | LEGO BATMAN: THE VIDEOGAME | Adventure | DS | 2008 | 3.01 |
| 8 | BATMAN: ARKHAM ORIGINS | Action | PS3 | 2013 | 2.13 |
| 9 | BATMAN: ARKHAM ORIGINS | Action | Xbox 360 | 2013 | 1.70 |
| 10 | LEGO BATMAN 2: DC HEROES | Action | Xbox 360 | 2012 | 1.58 |

## BATMAN

Ocean Software made the first ever Batman video game in 1986, and he has since featured in nearly 60 games across every format. The *Arkham* franchise has shifted more than 24 million units since *Batman: Arkham Asylum*.

## FINAL FANTASY XIII-2

This instalment of the almost 20-year-old franchise took one year and nine months from its start to its release date.

**TOP 10...**

# BIGGEST FINAL FANTASY GAMES

The Final Fantasy franchise has been around since 1987, and these are the most popular titles of the series...

| | NAME | GENRE | PLATFORM | RELEASED | UNIT SALES (MILLIONS) |
|---|---|---|---|---|---|
| 1 | FINAL FANTASY VII | RPG | PS | 1997 | 9.72 |
| 2 | FINAL FANTASY X | RPG | PS2 | 2001 | 8.05 |
| 3 | FINAL FANTASY VIII | RPG | PS | 1999 | 7.86 |
| 4 | FINAL FANTASY XII | RPG | PS2 | 2006 | 5.95 |
| 5 | FINAL FANTASY IX | RPG | PS | 2000 | 5.30 |
| 6 | FINAL FANTASY X-2 | RPG | PS2 | 2003 | 5.29 |
| 7 | FINAL FANTASY XIII | RPG | PS3 | 2009 | 5.25 |
| 8 | FINAL FANTASY III | RPG | SNES | 1994 | 3.42 |
| 9 | CRISIS CORE: FINAL FANTASY VII | RPG | PSP | 2007 | 3.14 |
| 10 | FINAL FANTASY XIII-2 | RPG | PS3 | 2011 | 2.65 |

FINAL FANTASY XV:
RELEASED
**DEC 31,**
**2015**
FOR PS4 AND
XBOX ONE

## FINAL FANTASY X

Of its total unit sales, 2.73 million were sold in Japan, and 2.91 million in the USA.

# FINAL FIVE

Here is how the top five best-selling *Final Fantasy* titles compare visually...

| FINAL FANTASY VII | FINAL FANTASY X | FINAL FANTASY VIII | FINAL FANTASY XII | FINAL FANTASY IX |
|---|---|---|---|---|
| 9.72 | 8.05 | 7.86 | 5.95 | 5.30 |

# PIXELS TO POPCORN

## ⦿ PRINCE OF PERSIA

The game franchise this movie was inspired by has sold 13.12 million copies.

### TOP 10...

# BIGGEST VIDEO GAME MOVIE ADAPTATIONS

The film world often adapts successful video game franchises into big-screen outings. These are the most successful...

| | MOVIE | RELEASED | BASED ON GAME/ FRANCHISE | BOX OFFICE (US $) |
|---|---|---|---|---|
| 1 | PRINCE OF PERSIA: THE SANDS OF TIME | 2010 | Prince Of Persia | 336,365,676 |
| 2 | RESIDENT EVIL: AFTERLIFE | 2010 | Resident Evil | 296,221,663 |
| 3 | LARA CROFT: TOMB RAIDER | 2001 | Tomb Raider | 274,703,340 |
| 4 | RESIDENT EVIL: RETRIBUTION | 2012 | Resident Evil | 240,159,255 |
| 5 | NEED FOR SPEED | 2014 | Need For Speed | 203,277,636 |
| 6 | POKÉMON: THE FIRST MOVIE | 1998 | Pokémon | 163,644,662 |
| 7 | LARA CROFT TOMB RAIDER: THE CRADLE OF LIFE | 2003 | Tomb Raider | 156,505,388 |
| 8 | RESIDENT EVIL: EXTINCTION | 2007 | Resident Evil | 147,717,833 |
| 9 | POKÉMON: THE MOVIE 2000 | 1999 | Pokémon | 133,949,270 |
| 10 | RESIDENT EVIL: APOCALYPSE | 2004 | Resident Evil | 129,394,835 |

## ⦿ RESIDENT EVIL

This film franchise's lead actress, Mila Jovovich, is married to its director/producer Paul W. S. Anderson.

RESIDENT EVIL MOVIE FRANCHISE MADE
**$915,934,664**
AT THE BOX OFFICE WORLDWIDE

WRECK-IT RALPH'S PRODUCTION BUDGET:
**$165 MILLION**

## TOP 10...
# BIGGEST MOVIES ABOUT **VIDEO GAMING**

There have also been original films made about the video game industry, which often feature games that have been created purely for the movie...

| | MOVIE | RELEASED | BOX OFFICE (US $) |
|---|---|---|---|
| 1 | WRECK-IT RALPH | 2012 | 471,222,889 |
| 2 | TRON LEGACY | 2010 | 400,062,763 |
| 3 | SPY KIDS 3D: GAME OVER | 2003 | 197,011,982 |
| 4 | WAR GAMES | 1983 | 79,567,667 |
| 5 | SCOTT PILGRIM VS. THE WORLD | 2010 | 47,664,559 |
| 6 | TRON | 1982 | 33,000,000 |
| 7 | THE LAST STARFIGHTER | 1984 | 28,733,290 |
| 8 | STAY ALIVE | 2006 | 27,105,095 |
| 9 | AVALON | 2001 | 15,740,796 |
| 10 | THE WIZARD | 1989 | 14,278,900 |

## ⦿ LARA CROFT: TOMB RAIDER

Angelina Jolie played Lara Croft in both movie adaptations. The game franchise has sold 36.91 million units.

## MORE ADAPTATIONS

Here are the box office takings of seven more movies that were inspired by video game franchises...

| | BOX OFFICE ($ WORLDWIDE) |
|---|---|
| MORTAL KOMBAT (1995) | $122,195,920 |
| RESIDENT EVIL (2002) | $102,441,078 |
| HITMAN (2007) | $99,965,792 |
| STREET FIGHTER (1994) | $99,423,521 |
| SILENT HILL (2006) | $97,607,453 |
| MAX PAYNE (2008) | $85,416,905 |
| FINAL FANTASY: THE SPIRITS WITHIN (2001) | $85,131,830 |

## ⦿ TRON LEGACY

This is a direct sequel to the 1982 original *Tron* movie.

THE FIRST EVER MARIO MOVIE (1986) RUNS FOR **60 MINS 50 SECS**

## 📍 MORTAL KOMBAT

Its director Paul W.S. Anderson went on to direct the first (and many) of the *Resident Evil* movies.

TOP 10...

# FIRST EVER MOVIES BASED ON VIDEO GAMES

Familiar gaming franchises appear here, but the release dates of these films pre-date more well-known adaptations such as Tomb Raider...

| | MOVIE | BASED ON GAME FRANCHISE | RELEASED |
|---|---|---|---|
| 1 | SUPER MARIO BROS.: THE GREAT MISSION TO RESCUE PRINCESS PEACH! | Super Mario Bros. | **July 20, 1986** |
| = | RUNNING BOY STAR SOLDIER | Star Soldier | **July 20, 1986** |
| 3 | SUPER MARIO BROS. | Super Mario Bros. | **May 28, 1993** |
| 4 | FATAL FURY: THE MOTION PICTURE | Fatal Fury | **July 16, 1994** |
| 5 | STREET FIGHTER II: THE ANIMATED MOVIE | Street Fighter II | **Aug 8, 1994** |
| 6 | DOUBLE DRAGON | Double Dragon | **Nov 4, 1994** |
| 7 | STREET FIGHTER | Street Fighter | **Dec 23, 1994** |
| 8 | MORTAL KOMBAT | Mortal Kombat | **Aug 18, 1995** |
| 9 | MORTAL KOMBAT: ANNIHILATION | Mortal Kombat | **Nov 21, 1997** |
| 10 | POKÉMON: THE FIRST MOVIE | Pokémon | **July 18, 1998** |

## FATAL FURY FRANCHISE

The 1994 movie was inspired by this fighting series that began in 1991 with *Fatal Fury: King of Fighters* (pictured here). Its Japanese game designer/producer Takashi Nishiyama was also the man behind the *Street Fighter* franchise.

📍 **DIGIMON**

As well as the TV series and video games, since 1999, there have been nine *Digimon* movies released.

📍 **KIRBY**

This inflatable hero first appeared on the Game Boy's *Kirby's Dream Land* in 1992.

TOP 10...

# LONGEST RUNNING TV SHOWS BASED ON VIDEO GAMES

Two Japanese franchises dominate this Top 10, which features several other familiar gaming titles...

| | TV SHOW | BASED ON GAME FRANCHISE | YEARS ON AIR | TOTAL EPS |
|---|---|---|---|---|
| 1 | POKÉMON | Pokémon | 18 (1997-present) | 850+ |
| 2 | DIGIMON | Digimon | 12 (1999-2011) | 332 |
| 3 | KIRBY: RIGHT BACK AT YA! | Kirby | 2 (2001-03) | 100 |
| 4 | SATURDAY SUPERCADE | Various | 2 (1983-85) | 97 |
| 5 | SONIC X | Sonic the Hedgehog | 2 (2003-05) | 78 |
| 6 | MEGA MAN STAR FORCE | Mega Man | 2 (2006-08) | 76 |
| 7 | MONSTER RANCHER | Monster Rancher | 2 (1999-2001) | 73 |
| 8 | ADVENTURES OF SONIC THE HEDGEHOG | Sonic the Hedgehog | 3 (1993-96) | 67 |
| 9 | THE SUPER MARIO BROS. SUPER SHOW! | Super Mario Bros. | 1 (1989) | 65 |
| 10 | BOMBERMAN JETTERS | Bomberman | 1 (2002-03) | 52 |

# GRAPH TOP FIVE

This visual chart illustrates how the five most successful shows compare...

**POKÉMON 850+**

**DIGIMON 332**

**KIRBY: RIGHT BACK AT YA! 100**

**SATURDAY SUPERCADE 97**

**SONIC X 78**

THE FIRST EVER DIGIMON WAS A
**1997**
NON-CONSOLE VIRTUAL PET

# HUMANKIND

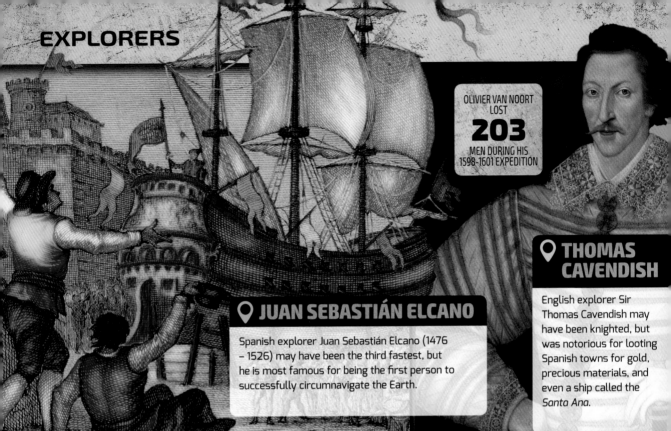

OLIVIER VAN NOORT LOST
## 203
MEN DURING HIS
1598-1601 EXPEDITION

📍 THOMAS CAVENDISH

English explorer Sir Thomas Cavendish may have been knighted, but was notorious for looting Spanish towns for gold, precious materials, and even a ship called the *Santa Ana*.

📍 JUAN SEBASTIÁN ELCANO

Spanish explorer Juan Sebastián Elcano (1476 – 1526) may have been the third fastest, but he is most famous for being the first person to successfully circumnavigate the Earth.

## TOP 10...
# FASTEST RENAISSANCE CIRCUMNAVIGATIONS

Numerous explorers tried to sail around the world in the 16th and early 17th century. Many perished, but these succeeded in the fastest times...

| | CAPTAIN | COUNTRY | VESSEL | YEARS TAKEN |
|---|---|---|---|---|
| 1 | THOMAS CAVENDISH | England | Desire | 2 (1586–1588) |
| = | WILLEM SCHOUTEN & JACOB LE MAIRE | Holland | Eendracht, Hoorn | 2 (1615–1617) |
| 3 | JUAN SEBASTIÁN ELCANO | Spain | Nao Victoria | 3 (1519–1522) |
| = | FRANCIS DRAKE | UK | The Golden Hind | 3 (1577–1580) |
| = | JACQUES MAHU | Holland | (Fleet of five ships) | 3 (1598–1601) |
| = | JORIS VAN SPILBERGEN | Holland | The Aeolus | 3 (1614–1617) |
| = | JACQUES L'HERMITE & JOHN HUGO SCHAPENHAM | Holland | (Fleet of 11 ships) | 3 (1623–1626) |
| = | OLIVIER VAN NOORT | Holland | The Mauritius | 3 (1598–1601) |
| 9 | MARTÍN IGNACIO DE LOYOLA* | Spain | Nuestra Señora de la Esperanza** | 4 (1580–1584/1585–1589) |
| 10 | ANDRÉS DE URDANETA | Spain | Santa María de la Victoria | 11 (1525–1536) |

*First person to circumnavigate the world twice in both directions. All other explorers listed only travelled westward.
**One of his galleons

## 📍 FRANCK CAMMAS

After pursuing careers in mathematics and music (studying the piano), Franck Cammas has won 24 international sailing competitions.

# FAST FIVE

Here is how the quickest five from the below chart compare visually...

| LOÏCK PEYRON 45D, 13H, 42M, 53S | FRANCK CAMMAS 48D, 7H, 44M, 52S | BRUNO PEYRON 50D, 16H, 20M, 4S | FRANCIS JOYON 57D, 13H, 34M, 6S | STEVE FOSSETT 58D, 9H, 32M, 45S |

### TOP 10...

# FASTEST AROUND THE WORLD BY SAILBOAT (EASTBOUND)

Over the decades, many people have attempted this difficult and treacherous journey. These are the 10 that have completed it the quickest...

| | SKIPPER/NO. OF CREW | COUNTRY | YACHT | DATE | TIME |
|---|---|---|---|---|---|
| 1 | LOÏCK PEYRON/14 | France | Banque Populaire | Jan 2012 | 45d, 13h, 42m, 53s |
| 2 | FRANCK CAMMAS/10 | France | Groupama 3 | Mar 2010 | 48d, 7h, 44m, 52s |
| 3 | BRUNO PEYRON/14 | France | Orange II | Mar 2005 | 50d, 16h, 20m, 4s |
| 4 | FRANCIS JOYON/1* | France | IDEC | Jan 2008 | 57d, 13h, 34m, 6s |
| 5 | STEVE FOSSETT/13 | USA | Cheyenne | Apr 2004 | 58d, 9h, 32m, 45s |
| 6 | BRUNO PEYRON/13 | France | Orange | May 2002 | 64d, 8h, 37m,24s |
| 7 | OLIVIER DE KERSAUSON/7 | France | Sport-Elec | Mar 1997 | 71d, 14h, 18m, 8s |
| 8 | ELLEN MACARTHUR/1* | UK | Castorama | Feb 2005 | 71d, 14h, 18m, 33s |
| 9 | FRANCIS JOYON/1* | France | IDEC | Feb 2004 | 72d, 22h, 54m, 22s |
| 10 | PETER BLAKE & ROBIN KNOX-JOHNSTON/2 | NZL, GB | Enza | Jan 1994 | 74d, 22h, 17m, 22s |

*Single-handed/solo

## 📍 ELLEN MACARTHUR

MacArthur retired from sailing on Feb 7, 2005. She founded the Ellen MacArthur Cancer Trust in 2003, which utilizes sailing to help young people who are recovering from cancer treatment regain confidence.

## 📍 LOÏCK PEYRON

Peyron's sailing wins include using this 39.6-m (130-ft)-long trimaran, *Banque Populaire V*.

DEEP-SEA VIDEO GAME FRANCHISE BIOSHOCK HAS SOLD

## 12.32 MILLION
COPIES OF ALL ITS TITLES

### ⦿ AUGUSTE PICCARD

Swiss explorer Auguste Piccard (Jan 28, 1884 – Mar 24, 1962) was also a famous inventor and physicist. His descendants include his grandson Bertrand, a famous balloonist.

## TOP 10...
# FIRST **MANNED DEEP-SEA** EXPLORATIONS

This list examines the first 10 times people have achieved a deep dive inside a mechanical device...

| | NAME | COUNTRY | EVENT | YEAR |
|---|---|---|---|---|
| 1 | WILLIAM BEEBE & OTIS BARTON | USA | First deep-sea divers inside the Bathysphere to 435 m (1,427 ft) | 1930 |
| 2 | WILLIAM BEEBE & OTIS BARTON | USA | Their Bathysphere gets to a depth of 923 m (3,028 ft) | 1934 |
| 3 | OTIS BARTON | USA | Bathysphere achieves a depth of 1,370 m (4,495 ft) | 1948 |
| = | AUGUSTE PICCARD | Switzerland | Inside his Bathyscaphe vessel, reached 1,402 m (4,600 ft) | 1948 |
| 5 | JACQUES PICCARD | Switzerland | Inside Trieste, he descends to 3,150 m (10,335 ft) | 1953 |
| 6 | AUGUSTE PICCARD | Switzerland | Piccard's Bathyscaphe vessel gets to 4,000 m (13,125 ft) | 1954 |
| 7 | JACQUES PICCARD & DON WALSH | Switzerland, USA | Inside Trieste, they descend to 10,915 m (35,810 ft) | 1960 |
| 8 | BILL RAINNIE & MARVIN MCCAMIS | USA | DSV (Deep-sea Submergible Vehicle) Alvin reaches 1,800 m (5,905 ft) | 1965 |
| 9 | US NAVY | USA | Alvin recovers a lost hydrogen bomb at 910 m (2,985 ft) | 1966 |
| 10 | WOODS HOLE OCEANOGRAPHIC INSTITUTE | USA | Alvin was attacked by a swordfish at 610 m (2,001 ft) | 1967 |

## THE BATHYSPHERE

This deep-sea device was designed by American engineer Otis Barton in the late 1920s. Together with American naturalist William Beebe, he went on many dives in the Bathysphere to study wildlife at great depths below the sea surface.

## AHMED GABR

Former Egyptian Army officer Gabr gained a scholarship to attend the U.S. Army Combat Diver Course. His number one position on this list is also a double world record.

## TOP 10...
# DEEPEST SOLO SEA DIVES

With just standard scuba equipment, these are the greatest depths divers have achieved...

| | NAME | COUNTRY | YEAR ACHIEVED | DIVE LOCATION | DEPTH (M) | (FT) |
|---|---|---|---|---|---|---|
| 1 | AHMED GABR | Egypt | 2014 | Red Sea | 332 | 1,090 |
| 2 | PASCAL BERNABÉ | France | 2005 | Mediterranean | 330 | 1,083 |
| 3 | NUNO GOMES | South Africa | 2005 | Red Sea | 318 | 1,044 |
| 4 | MARK ELLYATT | UK | 2003 | Andaman Sea | 313 | 1,026 |
| 5 | JOHN BENNETT | UK | 2001 | Philippines | 310 | 1,010 |
| 6 | WILL GOODMAN | UK | 2014 | Indonesia | 290 | 950 |
| 7 | KRZYSZTOF STARNAWSKI | Poland | 2011 | Red Sea | 283 | 928 |
| 8 | JIM BOWDEN | Mexico | 1994 | Mexico | 282 | 925 |
| 9 | GILBERTO M DE OLIVEIRA | Brazil | 2002 | Brazil | 274 | 898 |
| 10 | DAVID SHAW | Australia | 2004 | South Africa | 271 | 888 |

AUSTRIAN FREEDIVER HERBERT NITSCH HOLDS THE FREEDIVE RECORD:

**214 M**
(DEPTH)

# CHALLENGER

Filmmaker James Cameron (*Avatar*, *Aliens*, *The Terminator*) made history on March 26, 2012. Piloting the *Deepsea Challenger*, Cameron successfully travelled to the oceans' deepest point in the Mariana Trench, 10.99 km (6.83 miles) below the surface. This also marked the first time anyone had explored the very bottom of all oceans.

## ⊙ ALAN SHEPARD

During his NASA career, Alan Shepard (Nov 18, 1923 – July 21, 1998) completed two EVAs (spacewalks) totalling 9 hours and 23 minutes.

## ⊙ VLADIMÍR REMEK

This former cosmonaut is now the Czech Republic Ambassador to Russia. He served in the military and the space program between 1970–95.

## TOP 10...
# NATIONS' FIRST ASTRONAUTS

Most countries have launched a person into space, and these are each nations' firsts...

| | NATION | FIRST ASTRONAUT | LAUNCH DATE |
|---|---|---|---|
| 1 | SOVIET UNION (NOW RUSSIA) | Yuri Gagarin | Apr 12, 1961 |
| 2 | USA | Alan Shepard | May 5, 1961 |
| 3 | CZECH REPUBLIC | Vladimír Remek | Mar 2, 1978 |
| 4 | POLAND | Mirosław Hermaszewski | June 27, 1978 |
| 5 | EAST GERMANY (NOW GERMANY) | Sigmund Jähn | Aug 26, 1978 |
| 6 | BULGARIA | Georgi Ivanov | Apr 10, 1979 |
| 7 | HUNGARY | Bertalan Farkas | May 26, 1980 |
| 8 | VIETNAM | Phạm Tuân | July 23, 1980 |
| 9 | CUBA | Arnaldo Tamayo Méndez | Sep 18, 1980 |
| 10 | MONGOLIA | Jügderdemidiin Gürragchaa | Mar 22, 1981 |

PHẠM TUÂN SPENT **7 DAYS, 20 HOURS & 42 MINUTES** IN SPACE

# HELEN SHARMAN

This British chemist made history on May 18, 1991. As part of Project Juno, on board the Soyuz TM-12, she became the first British woman in space. During the mission, Sharman also became the first woman to visit the Russian Mir space station.

## ⬤ RUSSIA

This photo of (from left to right) USA's Barry Wilmore and Russia's Alexander Samokutyaev and Elena Serova was taken at a training session at Gagarin Cosmonauts' Training Centre in Star City, Moscow, Russia, on Aug 29, 2014.

RUSSIAN FEDERAL SPACE AGENCY WAS ESTABLISHED
**FEB 25, 1992**

**TOP 10...**

# NATIONS WITH THE MOST HUMAN SPACEFLIGHTS

This Top 10 shows which nations have invested the most time in spaceflight exploration...

| | COUNTRY | TOTAL TIME (DAYS) | ASTRONAUTS IN SPACE (YEARS) |
|---|---|---|---|
| 1 | RUSSIA (INCL. SOVIET UNION ERA) | 24,475.67 | 67.06 |
| 2 | USA | 17,369.43 | 47.6 |
| 3 | JAPAN | 929.77 | 2.55 |
| 4 | GERMANY | 658.97 | 1.81 |
| 5 | ITALY | 532.81 | 1.46 |
| 6 | CANADA | 506.15 | 1.39 |
| 7 | FRANCE | 432.19 | 1.18 |
| 8 | THE NETHERLANDS | 210.69 | 0.58 |
| 9 | BELGIUM | 207.66 | 0.57 |
| 10 | CHINA | 100.81 | 0.28 |

## THE ESA

The total human spaceflight for the ESA (European Space Agency) is 2,146.15 days, but this is made up of the collective of 18 different countries.

## MEXICO

Mexico's astronauts have currently spent the least amount of time in space, a total of 6.88 days.

# POWER STRUGGLE

## CHRISTIAN AUGUST

August was the Count Palatine of Sulzbach during 1632–1708, succeeding his father when he was just 10 years old. Sulzbach castle, situated in Bavaria, Germany, was home to August during his reign.

FRIEDRICH WAS JUST
**10**
YEARS OLD
WHEN HE BEGAN
HIS REIGN.

## SOBHUZA II

Firstly the Paramount Chief, and then the King of Swaziland, Sobhuza II (July 22, 1899 – Aug 21, 1982) received many honours during his lifetime, including Knight Commander of the Order of the British Empire, Civil Division (KBE).

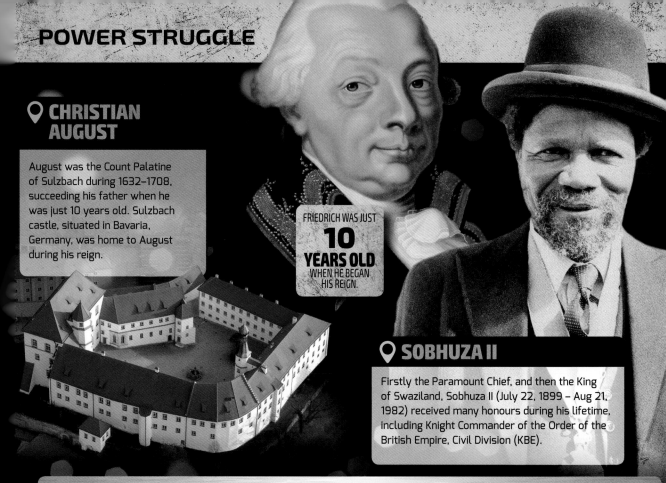

## TOP 10...
# LONGEST REIGNING MONARCHS OF ALL TIME

These people have served in their positions for more than the average lifetime...

| | NAME | DOMAIN | REIGN BEGAN | REIGN ENDED | TOTAL TIME |
|---|---|---|---|---|---|
| 1 | SOBHUZA II | Swaziland | Dec 10, 1899 | Aug 21, 1982 | 82 years, 254 days |
| 2 | BERNHARD VII | Lippe (Holy Roman Empire) | Aug 11, 1429 | Apr 2, 1511 | 81 years, 234 days |
| 3 | WILLIAM IV | Henneberg-Schleusingen | May 26, 1480 | Jan 24, 1559 | 78 years, 243 days |
| 4 | HEINRICH XI | Reuss-Obergreiz | Mar 17, 1723 | June 28, 1800 | 77 years, 103 days |
| 5 | IDRIS IBNI MUHAMMAD AL-QADRI | Malaysia | May 1, 1929 | Dec 26, 2005 | 76 years, 239 days |
| 6 | CHRISTIAN AUGUST | Palatinate-Sulzbach | Aug 14, 1632 | Apr 23, 1708 | 75 years, 253 days |
| 7 | MUDHOJI IV RAO NAIK NIMBALKAR | India | Dec 7, 1841 | Oct 17, 1916 | 74 years, 315 days |
| 8 | BHAGVATSINGH SAHIB | India | Dec 14, 1869 | Mar 10, 1944 | 74 years, 87 days |
| 9 | GEORG WILHELM | Schaumburg-Lippe | Feb 13, 1787 | Nov 21, 1860 | 73 years, 282 days |
| 10 | KARL FRIEDRICH | Baden | May 12, 1738 | June 10, 1811 | 73 years, 29 days |

CARL XVI GUSTAF OF SWEDEN'S ENTHRONEMENT
**SEP 19, 1973**

## ⦿ BHUMIBOL ADULYADEJ

This photo shows the current King of Thailand on the day of his coronation, May 5, 1950.

## ⦿ MARGRETHE II

When she ascended to the throne on Jan 14, 1972, she was the first female monarch Denmark had had for nearly 600 years. Margrethe I ruled Denmark and other Scandinavian countries between 1375–1412.

## TOP 10...
# LONGEST **REIGNING** MONARCHS ALIVE

Royal families often see a King or Queen in their position for several decades...

| NAME | COUNTRY | YEARS CURRENTLY REIGNED |
|------|---------|------------------------|
| 1 BHUMIBOL ADULYADEJ | Thailand | 68 |
| 2 ELIZABETH II | UK | 63 |
| 3 ABDUL HALIM | Malaysia | 56 |
| 4 SIKIRU KAYODE ADETONA | Nigeria | 55 |
| 5 HASSANAL BOLKIAH | Brunei | 47 |
| 6 GOODWILL ZWELITHINI KABHEKUZULU | South Africa | 46 |
| 7 QABOOS BIN SAID AL SAID | Oman | 44 |
| 8 MARGRETHE II | Denmark | 43 |
| = SULTAN BIN MOHAMMED AL-QASSIMI III | United Arab Emirates | 43 |
| 10 CARL XVI GUSTAF | Sweden | 41 |

## MOVIE MONARCH

The UK's Queen Elizabeth II has been portrayed several times in films and TV productions by a variety of different, award-winning actresses. Helen Mirren (pictured) won the Oscar for Best Actress for playing her in *The Queen* (2006).

VALENTINE STRASSER SERVED IN THE SIERRA LEONE ARMY FOR **11** YEARS

# YOUNGEST STATE LEADERS
## OF 20TH CENTURY

Some people in their late teens and twenties are completing a college course or getting into their career stride, and others become leaders of nations...

| | NAME | POSITION | YEAR ASSUMED OFFICE | AGE AT THIS TIME |
|---|---|---|---|---|
| 1 | JEAN-CLAUDE DUVALIER | President of Haiti | 1971 | 19 |
| 2 | VALENTINE STRASSER | President of Sierra Leone | 1992 | 25 |
| 3 | DOGSOMYN BODOO | Prime Minister of Mongolia | 1921 | 26 |
| = | MICHEL MICOMBERO | President of Burundi | 1966 | 26 |
| = | MARIA LEA PEDINI-ANGELINI | Captain Regent of San Marino | 1981 | 26 |
| 6 | AMET ZOGU | Prime Minister of Albania | 1922 | 27 |
| = | MUAMMAR GADDAFI | Guide of the Revolution | 1969 | 27 |
| = | GLORIANA RANOCCHINI | Captain Regent of San Marino | 1984 | 27 |
| = | GIOVANNI LONFERNINI | Captain Regent of San Marino | 2003 | 27 |
| = | ABDESSALAM JALLOUD | Prime Minister of Libya | 1972 | 27 |

## JEAN-CLAUDE DUVALIER

Known as "Baby Doc" (after his father's nickname of "Papa Doc"), this former President of Haiti died aged 63, on Oct 4, 2014.

## EMPEROR AKIHITO

As well as being the Reigning Emperor of Japan, he also has a strong interest in ichthyology, the study of fish. His published works include papers for the Japanese *Journal of Ichthyology*.

TOP 10...
# OLDEST STATE LEADERS
## CURRENTLY IN POWER

The phrase "age is but a number" is clearly something these people agree with, as they still hold important positions...

| | NAME | POSITION | DATE OF BIRTH | AGE (YEARS) |
|---|---|---|---|---|
| 1 | QUEEN ELIZABETH II | Queen of UK & Commonwealth | Apr 21, 1926 | 88 |
| 2 | BHUMIBOL ADULYADEJ | King of Thailand | Dec 5, 1927 | 87 |
| 3 | SABAH AL-AHMAD AL-JABER AL-SABAH | Emir of Kuwait | June 16, 1929 | 85 |
| 4 | ELLIOTT BELGRAVE | Governor-General of Barbados | Mar 16, 1931 | 84 |
| 5 | EDMUND LAWRENCE | Governor-General of Saint Kitts and Nevis | Feb 14, 1932 | 83 |
| 6 | MARGUERITE PINDLING | Governor-General of the Bahamas | June 26, 1932 | 82 |
| = | COLVILLE YOUNG | Governor-General of Belize | Nov 20, 1932 | 82 |
| 8 | AKIHITO | Emperor of Japan | Dec 23, 1933 | 81 |
| 9 | SALMAN BIN ABDULAZIZ AL SAUD | King of Saudi Arabia | Dec 31, 1935 | 79 |
| 10 | FREDERICK BALLANTYNE | Governor-General of Saint Vincent and the Grenadines | July 5, 1936 | 78 |

SIR COLVILLE NORBERT YOUNG WAS KNIGHTED IN
## 1994

## ⚲ MARGUERITE PINDLING

Before becoming Governor-General of the Bahamas on July 8, 2014, one of Marguerite Pindling's former jobs was working as a photographer's assistant.

## ⚲ AL-SABAH

The fourth son of Sheikh Ahmad Al-Jaber Al-Sabah, Sabah Al-Ahmad Al-Jaber Al-Sabah became the 5th Emir (and 15th Ruler) of Kuwait on 29 January 2006.

## SKIN

Our skin allows us to be aware of our surroundings as it communicates sensations, such as temperature. It also helps protect us from damaging our internal organs, working as a barrier against impacts.

SKIN HAS 3 LAYERS (OUTSIDE-IN: **THE EPIDERMIS, DERMIS, HYPODERMIS)**

## TOP 10...
# HEAVIEST HUMAN ORGANS

Your body is made up of many organs, and the heaviest will surprise you...

|  | NAME | AVERAGE WEIGHT IN ADULT (G) | (OZ) |
|---|---|---|---|
| 1 | SKIN | 10,750 | 379.2 |
| 2 | LIVER | 1500 | 52.9 |
| 3 | BRAIN | 1350 | 47.6 |
| 4 | LUNGS | 830 | 29.3 |
| 5 | HEART | 308 | 10.8 |
| 6 | KIDNEYS | 270 | 9.5 |
| 7 | SPLEEN | 170 | 6 |
| 8 | PANCREAS | 68 | 2.4 |
| 9 | THYROID | 40 | 1.4 |
| 10 | PROSTATE | 25 | 0.9 |

## LIVER

The liver is an incredibly important organ. Its functions include helping metabolism, the immune system, and how nutrients become stored within the body.

## TOP FIVE ORGANS

This pie chart shows just how much heavier skin is compared to other human organs...

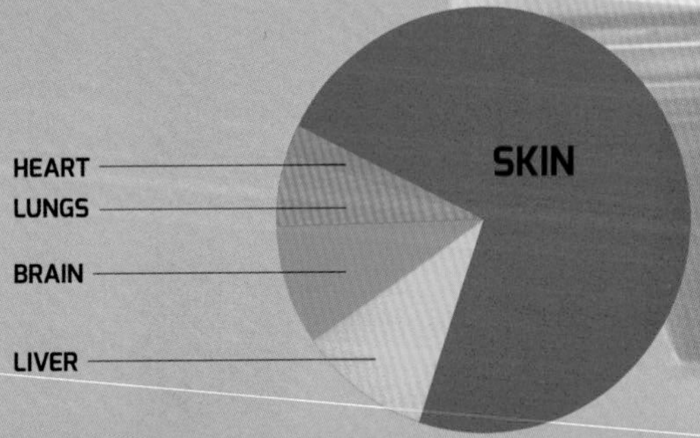

HEART
LUNGS
BRAIN
LIVER
SKIN

## ◉ USA

Here is the 2006 World's Strongest Man, USA's Phil Pfister, pulling a double-decker bus. Pfister is 1.98 m (6.5 ft) tall and weighs 170 kg (375 lb).

## ◉ LITHUANIA

Nicknamed "Big Z", Lithuanian Žydrūnas Savickas weighs 181.4 kg (400 lb).

THE WORLD'S STRONGEST MAN WAS ESTABLISHED IN
# 1977
FOR USA TV NETWORK CBS

## TOP 10...
# WORLD'S **STRONGEST MAN** WINNING NATION

This Top 10 gives a good indication of the countries that are home to people who enjoy gaining a huge amount of muscle mass...

| | | COUNTRY | TOTAL GOLD MEDALS | TOTAL SILVER MEDALS | TOTAL BRONZE MEDALS | TOTAL MEDALS |
|---|---|---|---|---|---|---|
| ⌀ | 1 | USA | 9 | 7 | 8 | 24 |
| | 2 | ICELAND | 8 | 5 | 3 | 16 |
| | 3 | UK | 4 | 2 | 7 | 13 |
| | 4 | FINLAND | 3 | 3 | 5 | 11 |
| ⌀ | 5 | LITHUANIA | 4 | 6 | 0 | 10 |
| | 6 | POLAND | 5 | 3 | 0 | 8 |
| | = | SWEDEN | 1 | 3 | 4 | 8 |
| | 8 | THE NETHERLANDS | 1 | 2 | 4 | 7 |
| | 9 | NORWAY | 1 | 1 | 1 | 3 |
| | 10 | UKRAINE | 1 | 0 | 1 | 2 |

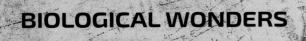

## ⊙ CHANDRA BAHADUR DANGI

This craftsman from Nepal, the world's shortest man, met India's Jyoti Amge (the world's smallest woman) in 2012 for a publicity event. On Nov 13, 2014, Bahadur met the world's tallest man, Turkish farmer Sultan Kösen.

DANGI IS
**1.96 M**
SHORTER THAN THE WORLD'S TALLEST MAN, SULTAN KÖSEN

## SIDE-BY-SIDE

Here, the shortest and tallest humans alive are compared...

## ⊙ JYOTI AMGE

The smallest woman in the world appeared on *Bigg Boss* in 2012, India's version of reality show franchise, *Big Brother*.

## TOP 10...
# SHORTEST HUMANS ALIVE

Human biology can produce extraordinary results, including these people...

| | NAME | COUNTRY | YEAR BORN | HEIGHT (CM) | (IN) |
|---|---|---|---|---|---|
| 1 | CHANDRA BAHADUR DANGI | Nepal | 1939 | 54.6 | 21.5 |
| 2 | JYOTI AMGE* | India | 1993 | 58.4 | 23 |
| 3 | JUNREY BALAWING | Philippines | 1993 | 60 | 23.6 |
| 4 | MADGE BESTER* | South Africa | 1963 | 65 | 25.6 |
| 5 | KHAGENDRA THAPA MAGAR | Nepal | 1992 | 67 | 26.4 |
| 6 | LIN YÜ-CHIH | Taiwan | 1972 | 67.5 | 26.6 |
| 7 | BRIDGETTE JORDAN* | USA | 1989 | 69 | 27.2 |
| 8 | EDWARD NIÑO HERNÁNDEZ | Colombia | 2010 | 70.2 | 27.6 |
| 9 | HATICE KOCAMAN* | Turkey | 1989 | 71 | 28 |
| 10 | AJAY KUMAR | India | 1976 | 76 | 29.9 |

*Female, the rest are male.

## SHAWN BRADLEY

Retired German basketball player Shawn Bradley missed out on this Top 10 with a height of 2.29 m (7.5 ft). During his NBA (National Basketball Association) career, he played with the New Jersey Nets, Dallas Mavericks, and the Philadelphia 76ers.

## ◉ SULTAN KÖSEN

Although very lean, Kösen's height puts his weight at 137 kg (320 lbs). His stature is not genetic, as his parents and siblings are of average height. A growth on Kösen's pituitary gland affected its function, leading to his extreme height.

BRAHIM TAKIOULLAH HAS THE LARGEST FEET IN THE WORLD:
**38.51 CM**

## ◉ BRENDEN ADAMS

During 2014, when Adams was 19 years old, he held the world record for the tallest teenager alive.

## TOP 10...
# TALLEST HUMANS ALIVE

Is the biggest person you know more than 1.83 m (6 ft) tall? Compare their height to the data in this Top 10...

| | NAME | COUNTRY | YEAR BORN | HEIGHT (M) | (FT) |
|---|---|---|---|---|---|
| 1 | SULTAN KÖSEN | Turkey | 1982 | 2.51 | 8.23 |
| 2 | BRAHIM TAKIOULLAH | Morocco | 1982 | 2.46 | 8.07 |
| = | MORTEZA MEHRZAD | Iran | 1987 | 2.46 | 8.07 |
| 4 | ZHANG JUNCAI | China | 1966 | 2.42 | 7.94 |
| 5 | NASEER SOOMRO | Pakistan | 1975 | 2.38 | 7.81 |
| 6 | SUN MING-MING | China | 1983 | 2.36 | 7.74 |
| = | BAO XISHUN | China | 1951 | 2.36 | 7.74 |
| 8 | RADHOUANE CHARBIB | Tunisia | 1968 | 2.35 | 7.71 |
| = | BRENDEN ADAMS | USA | 1995 | 2.35 | 7.71 |
| = | IGOR VOVKOVINSKIY | Ukraine | 1982 | 2.35 | 7.71 |

## JEANNE CALMENT

The longest-living person of all time, Jeanne Calment, outlived her daughter and her grandson by many decades. She took up fencing when she was 85, and only moved into a nursing home when she turned 110.

## TECHNOLOGICAL CHANGES

Everyone in the below Top 10 would have been witness to numerous, life-changing innovations in the way humans live and interact with one another, including these firsts: the pop-up toaster (1919), photocopier (1937), microwave (1946), video cassette recorder (1971) and, of course, the internet (1990).

## TOP 10...
# OLDEST PEOPLE OF ALL TIME

The ages that these people lived to is extraordinary, especially when you consider the changes they would have witnessed...

| | NAME | COUNTRY | DATE OF BIRTH | DATE OF DEATH | AGE |
|---|---|---|---|---|---|
| 1 | JEANNE CALMENT | France | Feb 21, 1875 | Aug 4, 1997 | 122 years, 164 days |
| 2 | SARAH KNAUSS | USA | Sep 24, 1880 | Dec 30, 1999 | 119 years, 97 days |
| 3 | LUCY HANNAH | USA | July 16, 1875 | Mar 21, 1993 | 117 years, 248 days |
| 4 | MARIE-LOUISE MEILLEUR | Canada | Aug 29,1880 | Apr 16, 1998 | 117 years, 230 days |
| 5 | MISAO OKAWA | Japan | Mar 5, 1898 | Apr 1, 2015 | 117 years, 27 days |
| 6 | MARÍA CAPOVILLA | Ecuador | Sep 14, 1889 | Aug 27, 2006 | 116 years, 347 days |
| 7 | GERTRUDE WEAVER | USA | July 4, 1898 | Apr 6, 2015 | 116 years 276 days |
| 8 | TANE IKAI | Japan | Jan 18, 1879 | July 12, 1995 | 116 years, 175 days |
| 9 | ELIZABETH BOLDEN | USA | Aug 15, 1890 | Dec 11, 2006 | 116 years, 118 days |
| 10 | BESSE COOPER | USA | Aug 16, 1896 | Dec 4, 2012 | 116 years, 100 days |

TOTAL YEARS OF TOP 10 OLDEST PEOPLE OF ALL TIME:

**1,176.9**

WORLDWIDE, THE AVERAGE LIFE EXPECTANCY OF A HUMAN IS **72.1 YEARS**

## TOP 10...
# OLDEST PEOPLE
## ALIVE TODAY

Many people all over the world are over 100 years old. These are the current record holders for age...

| | NAME | COUNTRY | DATE OF BIRTH | AGE (YEARS) |
|---|---|---|---|---|
| 1 | JERALEAN TALLEY | USA | 23 May, 1899 | 115 |
| 2 | SUSANNAH MUSHATT JONES | USA | 6 July, 1899 | 115 |
| 3 | EMMA MORANO-MARTINUZZI | Italy | Nov 29, 1899 | 115 |
| 4 | VIOLET BROWN | Jamaica | Mar 10, 1900 | 115 |
| 5 | ANTONIA GERENA RIVERA | Puerto Rico | May 19, 1900 | 114 |
| 6 | NABI TAJIMA | Japan | Aug 4, 1900 | 114 |
| 7 | GOLDIE STEINBERG | Russia | Oct 30, 1900 | 114 |
| 8 | KIYOKO ISHIGURO | Japan | Mar 4, 1901 | 114 |
| 9 | DOMINGA VELASCO | USA | May 12, 1901 | 114 |
| 10 | OLYMPE AMAURY | France | June 19, 1901 | 114 |

# THE WORLD AT WAR

World War I (July 28, 1914 – November 11, 1918) saw casualties total 37 million. These include more than 16 million fatalities. World War II (September 1, 1939 – September 2, 1945) saw the death toll increase to more than 60 million worldwide.

## ⦿ JERALEAN TALLEY

Far from slowing down, Talley still enjoys going fishing with her godson. She also enjoyed bowling at the age of 104.

## ⦿ SUSANNAH MUSHATT JONES

Currently living at Vandalia Senior Center in Brooklyn, New York, USA, Jones has more than 100 nieces and nephews.

LIBERIAN PEACE ACTIVIST LEYMAH GBOWEE WAS BORN ON

**FEB 1, 1972**

## ⚲ MALALA YOUSAFZAI & KAILASH SATYARTHI

The joint recipients of the 2014 Nobel Peace Prize – Yousafzai, from Pakistan, and Satyarthi, from India – were awarded for their work in helping prevent the suppression of young people, and for fighting for children to all have the right to an education.

TOP 10...

# MOST RECENT **NOBEL PEACE PRIZE** WINNERS (PEOPLE)

The award has been presented each year since its inception in 1901, honouring outstanding contributions to peace...

| | NAME | OCCUPATION | COUNTRY | YEAR |
|---|---|---|---|---|
| 1 | MALALA YOUSAFZAI | Human Rights Activist | **Pakistan** | 2014 |
| = | KAILASH SATYARTHI | Human Rights Activist | **India** | 2014 |
| 3 | LEYMAH GBOWEE | Peace Activist | **Liberia** | 2011 |
| = | TAWAKKUL KARMAN | Human Rights Activist, Journalist, Politician | **Yemen** | 2011 |
| = | ELLEN JOHNSON SIRLEAF | 24th President of Liberia | **Liberia** | 2011 |
| 6 | LIU XIAOBO | Human Rights Activist, Writer, Critic | **China** | 2010 |
| 7 | BARACK OBAMA | 44th President of USA | **USA** | 2009 |
| 8 | MARTTI AHTISAARI | 10th President of Finland | **Finland** | 2008 |
| 9 | AL GORE | 45th Vice President of USA, Philanthropist | **USA** | 2007 |
| 10 | MUHAMMAD YUNUS | Economist | **Bangladesh** | 2006 |

## ⚲ BARACK OBAMA

The 44th President of the United States was awarded the 2009 Nobel Peace Prize for his efforts and focus on strengthening international diplomacy.

## SINGAPORE

Singapore's Institute of Innovation and Entrepreneurship created 119 companies and raised the equivalent of U.S. $9.3 million in seed investment.

THE NETHERLANDS HAVE PIONEERED
**35**
INNOVATIONS IN THE USE AND QUALITY OF WATER

## DENMARK

The Innovation Centre Denmark (ICDK) is an important joint venture between Denmark's Ministry of Foreign Affairs and the country's Ministry of Higher Education and Science. The ICDK focuses on collaborations between Denmark's Innovation Centre and seven others all over the world.

## TOP 10...
# MOST INNOVATIVE COUNTRIES

The Global Innovation Index is a method of measuring countries' innovation, for example, their environmentally friendly advancements...

| | COUNTRY | GLOBAL INNOVATION INDEX |
|---|---|---|
| 1 | SWITZERLAND | 64.8 |
| 2 | UK | 62.4 |
| 3 | SWEDEN | 62.3 |
| 4 | FINLAND | 60.7 |
| 5 | NETHERLANDS | 60.6 |
| 6 | USA | 60.1 |
| 7 | SINGAPORE | 59.2 |
| 8 | DENMARK | 57.5 |
| 9 | LUXEMBOURG | 56.9 |
| 10 | CHINA | 56.8 |

## ALEXANDER ALEKHINE

By the young age of 22, Alekhine was already a world-class chess player. He reigned as world champion between the years 1927–35 and 1937–46.

## HISTORY OF CHESS

Originating from India in the 6th century, the earliest form of chess then spread to Persia. By the 19th century, its popularity had boomed enough for there to be the first ever world championship in 1886.

## EMANUEL LASKER

Aside from being the world chess champion for 27 consecutive years (1894 – 1921), Lasker also invented a variation of the game draughts which he called Lasca.

A GAME OF CHESS IS PLAYED ON A BOARD OF

**64**

CHECKED SQUARES WITH 16 PIECES FOR EACH PLAYER

TOP 10...

# GREATEST CHESS MINDS

This game requires the ability to plan many moves ahead, calculating multiple possible outcomes at once...

| | NAME | COUNTRY | TOTAL WORLD CHAMPIONSHIP TITLES |
|---|---|---|---|
| 1 | EMANUEL LASKER | Germany | 27 |
| 2 | ALEXANDER ALEKHINE | Russia | 17 |
| 3 | ANATOLY KARPOV | Russia | 16 |
| 4 | GARRY KASPAROV | Russia | 15 |
| 5 | MIKHAIL BOTVINNIK | Russia | 13 |
| 6 | VISWANATHAN ANAND | India | 8 |
| = | WILHELM STEINITZ | Austria | 8 |
| 8 | VLADIMIR KRAMNIK | Russia | 7 |
| 9 | JOSÉ RAÚL CAPABLANCA | Cuba | 6 |
| = | TIGRAN PETROSIAN | Russia | 6 |

## ⊙ MARTIN JACOBSON

This professional poker player was just 27 years old when he scored his record-breaking $14.8 million win in 2014. As part of the philanthropic community Raising for Effective Giving, Jacobson pledges to donate at least 2 percent of his tournament winnings.

## TOP 10...
# BEST BLUFFERS/ POKER FACES

The card game of Poker is a psychological battle between players who are desperate not to let their face convey the kind of hand they are holding...

| | NAME | COUNTRY | YEAR | TOTAL TOURNAMENT WIN (US $) |
|---|---|---|---|---|
| 1 | MARTIN JACOBSON | Sweden | 2014 | 14,833,732 |
| 2 | PHIL HELLMUTH | USA | 1989 | 12,189,531 |
| 3 | JAMIE GOLD | USA | 2006 | 12,067,292 |
| 4 | GREG MERSON | USA | 2012 | 9,781,483 |
| 5 | PETER EASTGATE | Denmark | 2008 | 9,152,416 |
| 6 | JONATHAN DUHAMEL | Canada | 2010 | 8,944,310 |
| 7 | PIUS HEINZ | Germany | 2011 | 8,798,924 |
| 8 | JOE CADA | USA | 2009 | 8,574,649 |
| 9 | CARLOS MORTENSEN | Spain | 2001 | 8,457,033 |
| 10 | RYAN RIESS | USA | 2013 | 8,359,531 |

# HISTORY OF CARD GAMES

The modern deck of playing cards is believed to have evolved from cards introduced from Arabic culture to Europe in the latter half of the 14th century.

TRADITIONALLY THERE ARE
## 52
PLAYING CARDS IN A FULL DECK

# EPIC
# STRUCTURES

## ONE WORLD TRADE CENTER

Opened on November 3, 2014, the formerly named "Freedom Tower" was designed by architects David Childs and Daniel Libeskind. It serves to honour those lost in the destruction of the World Trade Towers on September 11, 2001.

## TAIPEI 101

This building reigned as the tallest in the world between 2004–10. It received an award in 2011 for being one of the most environmentally friendly constructions ever built.

# MOST FLOORS

Here is a visual representation of the buildings with the most floors:

**ONE WORLD TRADE CENTER** 104

**WILLIS TOWER** 108

**INTERNATIONAL COMMERCE CENTRE** 108

**MAKKAH ROYAL CLOCK TOWER HOTEL** 120

**BURJ KHALIFA** 163

## TOP 10...
# TALLEST BUILDINGS

Comparing all of the man-made structures on Earth, these ten currently tower over all others...

| | BUILDING | COUNTRY | YEAR COMPLETED | FLOORS | HEIGHT (M) | (FT) |
|---|---|---|---|---|---|---|
| 1 | BURJ KHALIFA | United Arab Emirates | 2010 | 163 | 828 | 2,717 |
| 2 | MAKKAH ROYAL CLOCK TOWER HOTEL | Saudi Arabia | 2012 | 120 | 601 | 1,972 |
| 3 | ONE WORLD TRADE CENTER | USA | 2014 | 104 | 541 | 1,776 |
| 4 | TAIPEI 101 | Taiwan, China | 2004 | 101 | 508 | 1,666 |
| 5 | SHANGHAI WORLD FINANCIAL CENTER | China | 2008 | 101 | 492 | 1,614 |
| 6 | INTERNATIONAL COMMERCE CENTRE | China | 2010 | 108 | 484 | 1,588 |
| 7 | PETRONAS TWIN TOWERS | Malaysia | 1998 | 88 | 452 | 1,482 |
| 8 | ZIFENG TOWER | China | 2010 | 66 | 450 | 1,476 |
| 9 | WILLIS TOWER | USA | 1974 | 108 | 442.1 | 1,451 |
| 10 | KK100 | China | 2011 | 100 | 441.8 | 1,449 |

## FUJI-Q

Japan's Fuji-Q Highland has seven roller coasters. The longest and most popular is Fugiyama, operational since 1996. It just misses out on the Top 10 with a height of 79 m (259.2 ft).

SOUTH KOREA'S T EXPRESS IS **56 M** & THE TALLEST WOODEN ROLLER COASTER IN THE WORLD

TOP 10...

# TALLEST ROLLER COASTER DROPS

A thrilling theme park ride isn't just about the speed, it's about the height you plummet from...

| | ROLLER COASTER | LOCATION | HIGHEST DROP (M) | (FT) |
|---|---|---|---|---|
| 1 | KINGDA KA | Six Flags (USA) | 139 | 456 |
| 2 | TOP THRILL DRAGSTER | Cedar Point (USA) | 130 | 426.5 |
| 3 | SUPERMAN: ESCAPE FROM KRYPTON | Six Flags (USA) | 126.5 | 415 |
| 4 | TOWER OF TERROR II | Dreamworld (Australia) | 115 | 377.3 |
| 5 | FURY 325 | Carowinds (USA) | 99 | 324.8 |
| 6 | STEEL DRAGON 2000 | Nagashima Spa Land (Japan) | 97 | 318.2 |
| 7 | MILLENNIUM FORCE | Cedar Point (USA) | 94 | 308.4 |
| 8 | LEVIATHAN | Canada's Wonderland (Canada) | 93 | 305.1 |
| = | INTIMIDATOR 305 | King's Dominion (USA) | 93 | 305.1 |
| 10 | THUNDER DOLPHIN | Tokyo Dome City (Japan) | 80 | 262.5 |

## WHITE CYCLONE

Located in Japan's Nagashima Spa Land (also the theme park home to Steel Dragon 2000) White Cyclone is a 42 m (139 ft)-high wooden roller coaster. It has been open since 1994.

## ⦿ MILLAU VIADUCT

What began as a sketch in 1987 eventually became the tallest bridge in the world in December 2004. Its many engineering accolades include the 2006 Outstanding Structure Award by the International Association for Bridge and Structural Engineering.

### TOP 10...

# TALLEST **BRIDGES**

Encroaching on a third of a kilometre (a fifth of a mile) in height, these feats of engineering span great distances and carry countless vehicles across them every day...

| | NAME | COUNTRY | HEIGHT (M) | (FT) |
|---|---|---|---|---|
| 1 | MILLAU VIADUCT | France | 342 | 1,122 |
| 2 | RUSSKY BRIDGE | Russia | 320.9 | 1,053 |
| 3 | SUTONG BRIDGE | China | 306 | 1,004 |
| 4 | AKASHI-KAIKYO BRIDGE | Japan | 298.3 | 979 |
| 5 | STONECUTTERS BRIDGE | Hong Kong, China | 298 | 978 |
| 6 | YI SUN-SIN BRIDGE | South Korea | 270 | 890 |
| 7 | JINGYUE BRIDGE | China | 265 | 869 |
| 8 | GREAT BELT EAST BRIDGE | Denmark | 254 | 833 |
| 9 | ZHONGXIAN HUYU EXPRESSWAY BRIDGE | China | 247.5 | 812 |
| 10 | JIUJIANG FUYIN EXPRESSWAY BRIDGE | China | 244.3 | 802 |

DENMARK'S GREAT BELT EAST BRIDGE IS

## 31 M WIDE

## ⦿ STONECUTTERS BRIDGE

Completed in just five years, this toll-free bridge connects Hong Kong's Tsing Yi island and Stonecutters Island. It was officially opened for use on December 20, 2009.

## ⌖ CN TOWER

Located in Toronto, Canada, the
CN Tower (which stands for the rail
company that constructed the tower,
Canadian National) has 147 floors.
Open since October 1, 1976, it is still
used for telecommunications, but is
also a popular tourist attraction and
observation tower.

## ⌖ MILAD TOWER

Seven elevators serve the 12 floors which
exist in the top section of this tower in Tehran,
Iran. It is part of The Tehran International Trade and
Convention Centre.

**TOP 10...**

# TALLEST **COMMUNICATIONS** TOWERS

With their distinctive antenna and pod-like top sections, these communications
towers are some of the most distinctive structures on Earth...

| | BUILDING | COUNTRY | HEIGHT (M) | (FT) |
|---|---|---|---|---|
| 1 | TOKYO SKY TREE | Japan | 634 | 2,080 |
| 2 | CANTON TOWER | China | 600 | 1,969 |
| 3 | CN TOWER | Canada | 553.3 | 1,815 |
| 4 | OSTANKINO TOWER | Russia | 540 | 1,772 |
| 5 | ORIENTAL PEARL TELEVISION TOWER | China | 468 | 1,535 |
| 6 | MILAD TOWER | Iran | 435 | 1,427 |
| 7 | MENARA KUALA LUMPUR | Malaysia | 420.4 | 1,379 |
| 8 | TIANJIN RADIO & TV TOWER | China | 415.1 | 1,362 |
| 9 | HENAN PROVINCE RADIO & TV TOWER | China | 388 | 1,273 |
| 10 | CENTRAL RADIO & TV TOWER | China | 386.5 | 1,268 |

## ◉ SPRING TEMPLE BUDDHA

This towers above a Buddhist monastery in China's Fodushan Scenic Area in Lushan County, Henan. After 11 years of construction, the 1,000-tonne statue was completed in 2008.

## THE STATUE OF LIBERTY

With a height of 93 m (305.1 ft), New York, USA's monument of freedom is just off the Top 10 chart. Designed by Frédéric Auguste Bartholdi, Liberty Enlightening The World (its full name) was gifted from France to the USA on October 28, 1886.

## PETER THE GREAT

Off the chart (by just a few metres) is this 96 m (321.5 ft) monument to Pyotr "Peter the Great" Alexeyevich. Completed in 1997, it marked the 300th anniversary of the Russian Navy, which he founded.

## TOP 10...

# TALLEST HISTORICAL **STATUES**

Often representing religious figures, almost all of these man-made constructions and sculptures exceed 100m (328 ft) in height...

| | NAME | SUBJECT MATTER | LOCATION | HEIGHT (M) | (FT) |
|---|---|---|---|---|---|
| 1 | SPRING TEMPLE BUDDHA | Vairocana Buddha | Henan (China) | 153 | 502 |
| 2 | LAYKYUN SETKYAR | Buddha | Monywa (Myanmar) | 130 | 426.5 |
| 3 | USHIKU DAIBUTSU | Amitabha Buddha | Ushiku (Japan) | 120 | 393.7 |
| 4 | GUANYIN OF THE SOUTH SEA OF SANYA | Guanyin | Hainan (China) | 108 | 354.3 |
| 5 | EMPERORS YAN & HUANG | Emperors of China Yan & Huang | Henan (China) | 106 | 347.8 |
| 6 | CRISTO-REI | Jesus | Almada (Portugal) | 103 | 337.9 |
| 7 | MOTHER OF THE MOTHERLAND | Warrior statue war memorial | Kiev (Ukraine) | 102 | 334.7 |
| 8 | SENDAI DAIKANNON | Guanyin | Sendai (Japan) | 100 | 328.1 |
| = | AWAJI KANNON | Guanyin | Hyōgo Prefecture (Japan) | 100 | 328.1 |
| 10 | QIANSHOU QIANYAN GUANYIN OF WEISHAN | Guanyin | Hunan (China) | 99 | 324.8 |

PING AN FINANCE CENTRE WILL HAVE
# 76
ELEVATORS

## ◎ KINGDOM TOWER

Construction for the Kingdom Tower, located in Jeddah, Saudi Arabia, began on April 1, 2013. For a time, the project was named the Jeddah Tower. It will feature a range of residential and business spaces.

# MOST FUTURE FLOORS

Of the buildings of the future, these will have the most floors:

| LOTTE WORLD TOWER | WUHAN GREENLAND CENTER | GOLDIN FINANCE | SUZHOU ZHONGNAN CENTER | KINGDOM TOWER |
|---|---|---|---|---|
| **123** | **125** | **128** | **137** | **167** |

## TOP 10...
# TALLEST **FUTURE BUILDINGS** (UNDER CONSTRUCTION)

They're not open for business yet, but when these buildings are complete, the Top 10 Tallest Buildings In The World could feature some new entries...

| | BUILDING | COUNTRY | PLANNED COMPLETION | FLOORS | HEIGHT (M) | (FT) |
|---|---|---|---|---|---|---|
| 1 | KINGDOM TOWER | Saudi Arabia | 2018 | 167 | 1,000 | 3,281 |
| 2 | SUZHOU ZHONGNAN CENTER | China | 2020 | 137 | 729 | 2,392 |
| 3 | PING AN FINANCE CENTER | China | 2016 | 115 | 660 | 2,165 |
| 4 | WUHAN GREENLAND CENTER | China | 2017 | 125 | 636 | 2,087 |
| 5 | KL118 TOWER | Malaysia | 2019 | 118 | 610 | 2,001 |
| 6 | GOLDIN FINANCE | China | 2016 | 128 | 596.5 | 1,957 |
| 7 | PEARL OF THE NORTH | China | 2018 | 114 | 568 | 1,864 |
| 8 | LOTTE WORLD TOWER | South Korea | 2016 | 123 | 554.5 | 1,819 |
| 9 | NORDSTROM TOWER | USA | 2018 | 92 | 541 | 1,775 |
| 10 | TIANJIN CHOW TAI FOOK BINHAI CENTER | China | 2018 | 97 | 530 | 1,739 |

**TOP 10...**

# FASTEST ROLLER COASTERS

If you have visited any of the Disney or Universal Studios resorts, you may think you've been on fast rides, but look at the speed these 10 reach...

| | ROLLER COASTER | LOCATION | TOP SPEED (KPH) | (MPH) |
|---|---|---|---|---|
| 1 | FORMULA ROSSA | Ferrari World (United Arab Emirates) | 240 | 149.1 |
| 2 | KINGDA KA | Six Flags (USA) | 206 | 128 |
| 3 | TOP THRILL DRAGSTER | Cedar Point (USA) | 193.1 | 120 |
| 4 | DODONPA | Fuji-Q Highland (Japan) | 172 | 106.9 |
| 5 | SUPERMAN: ESCAPE FROM KRYPTON | Six Flags (USA) | 162.2 | 100.8 |
| 6 | TOWER OF TERROR II | Dreamworld (Australia) | 160.9 | 100 |
| 7 | STEEL DRAGON 2000 | Nagashima Spa Land (Japan) | 152.9 | 95 |
| = | FURY 325 | Carowinds (USA) | 152.9 | 95 |
| 9 | MILLENNIUM FORCE | Cedar Point (USA) | 149.7 | 93 |
| 10 | LEVIATHAN | Canada's Wonderland (Canada) | 148.1 | 92 |

## FORMULA ROSSA

Located in Abu Dhabi's Ferrari World park, Formula Rossa lasts 1 minute 32 seconds. The ride is intended to simulate what it's like to be in a Ferrari car during a F1 race. During development, it was originally called the F1 Coaster.

## DODONPA

Part of the Fuji-Q Highland Amusement Park in Fujiyoshida, Yamanashi, Japan, Dodonpa opened on December 21, 2001. It is 52 m (171 ft) high, and 1,000 people can experience the 55-second ride each hour.

## SHARK TANK SLIDE

Atlantis Paradise Island in the Bahamas features this, The Leap of Faith. After falling for one second from a nine-storey height, you slide through a clear tube surrounded by sharks and rays.

ATLANTIS PARADISE ISLAND'S AQUARIUM HAS

## 65,000 ANIMALS

**TOP 10...**

# FASTEST WATER SLIDES

Water parks often featured slides and flumes, but some include ones that make you go as fast as a sports car...

| | WATER RIDE | LOCATION | TOP SPEED (KPH) | (MPH) |
|---|---|---|---|---|
| 1 | VERRUCKT | USA | 125.5 | 78 |
| 2 | INSANO | Brazil | 105 | 65.2 |
| 3 | SPACEMAKER | Italy | 100 | 62.1 |
| 4 | KILIMANJARO | Brazil | 91 | 56.6 |
| 5 | SUMMIT PLUMMET | USA | 89 | 55.3 |
| 6 | JUMEIRAH SCEIRAH | United Arab Emirates | 80 | 49.7 |
| = | POWER TOWER | USA | 80 | 49.7 |
| 8 | CLIFFHANGER | USA | 56.3 | 35 |
| 9 | SCORPION'S TAIL | Canada | 54.9 | 34.1 |
| 10 | THE WILDEBEEST | USA | 39.5 | 24.5 |

## ⦿ INSANO

From a height of 41 m (134.5 ft), it takes four seconds to slide from the top of Insano to the splash pool at the bottom. It was built in 1989 and is part of Brazil's Beach Park resort, which receives over a million visitors each year.

## MELBOURNE CRICKET GROUND

Missing out on the Top 10 by fewer than 400 seats is Melbourne Cricket Ground in Victoria, Australia. The venue can hold 100,024 people, and is home to Australian Rules Football matches as well as cricket.

## TOP 10...
# BIGGEST STADIUMS

Sports and music concerts of all different varieties draw huge crowds. Often, the buildings we go to see them in have to be designed to cope with more than 100,000 attendees...

| | NAME | LOCATION | CAPACITY CROWD |
|---|---|---|---|
| 1 | Rungnado 1st of May Stadium | Pyongyang (North Korea) | 150,000 |
| 2 | Michigan Stadium | Michigan (USA) | 115,109 |
| 3 | Beaver Stadium | Pennsylvania (USA) | 107,282 |
| 4 | Kyle Field | Texas (USA) | 106,511 |
| 5 | Estadio Azteca | Mexico City (Mexico) | 105,000 |
| 6 | Ohio Stadium | Ohio (USA) | 104,944 |
| 7 | Neyland Stadium | Tennessee (USA) | 102,455 |
| 8 | Tiger Stadium | Louisiana (USA) | 102,321 |
| 9 | Bryant-Denny Stadium | Alabama (USA) | 101,821 |
| 10 | Bukit Jalil National Stadium | Kuala Lumpur (Malaysia) | 100,411 |

## SALT LAKE

In 2014, Salt Lake Stadium in Kolkata, India, reduced its capacity from 120,000 to 68,000 people, so it doesn't feature in this Top 10. This was done to increase the comfort and space for each attendee.

## STADIUM CAPACITIES

This is how the top 5 stadiums compare visually:

IN 1927, MICHIGAN STADIUM OPENED WITH A CAPACITY OF **72,000** PEOPLE

| ESTADIO AZTECA | KYLE FIELD | BEAVER STADIUM | MICHIGAN STADIUM | RUNGNADO 1ST OF MAY STADIUM |
|---|---|---|---|---|
| 105,000 | 106,511 | 107,282 | 115,109 | 150,000 |

## PHILIPPINE ARENA

This arena opened on July 21, 2014 in Santa Maria, Bulacan, Philippines. It has already hosted an eclectic range of events from religious sermons, through to stage plays and musical performances.

PHILIPPINE ARENA'S FIELD IS
**220 M**
IN LENGTH

## SMART ARANETA COLISEUM

Since 1960, this venue, also known as The Big Dome, has been home to basketball, boxing, and a variety of concerts. Taylor Swift, Kylie Minogue, and Incubus have all performed there.

## TOP 10...
# BIGGEST **INDOOR ARENAS**

Sports, music, dramas, and religious celebrations attract crowds in their thousands, and so indoor arenas need to be constructed to suit that demand...

| | NAME | LOCATION | CAPACITY CROWD |
|---|---|---|---|
| 1 | PHILIPPINE ARENA | Bocaue (Philippines) | 55,000 |
| 2 | SAITAMA SUPER ARENA | Saitama (Japan) | 37,000 |
| 3 | SC OLIMPIYSKIY | Moscow (Russia) | 35,000 |
| 4 | GWANGMYEONG VELODROME | Gwangmyeong (South Korea) | 30,000 |
| 5 | TELENOR ARENA | Bærum (Norway) | 26,000 |
| 6 | KOMBANK ARENA | Belgrade (Serbia) | 25,000 |
| = | MINEIRINHO | Belo Horizonte (Brazil) | 25,000 |
| = | SMART ARANETA COLISEUM | Quezon City (Philippines) | 25,000 |
| = | BAKU CRYSTAL HALL | Baku (Azerbaijan) | 25,000 |
| = | SCC PETERBURGSKIY | Saint Petersburg (Russia) | 25,000 |

## TOKYO DOME

This is Japan's first ever domed stadium. It officially opened on March 17, 1988 and can seat 55,000 people. For the Japan premiere of *Speed Racer* in 2008, a huge, temporary screen (made in the UK) was hoisted into the dome.

## TOP 10...
# BIGGEST CINEMA SCREENS EVER

Although IMAX provide movie theatres with gigantic screens, unexpected locations have served as even bigger cinemas...

| | CINEMA SCREEN | LOCATION | TOTAL AREA (SQ. M) | (SQ. FT) |
|---|---|---|---|---|
| 1 | LOVELL RADIO TELESCOPE* | Cheshire (UK) | 4,560.37 | 49,087 |
| 2 | NOKIA N8* | Malmö (Sweden) | 1,428 | 15,371 |
| 3 | PINEWOOD STUDIOS* | Middlesex (UK) | 1,337.73 | 14,399 |
| 4 | IMAX DARLING HARBOUR | Sydney (Australia) | 1,056.24 | 11,369 |
| 5 | IMAX MELBOURNE | Melbourne (Australia) | 736 | 7,922.2 |
| 6 | OSLO SPEKTRUM* | Oslo (Norway) | 676 | 7,276.4 |
| 7 | TOKYO DOME | Tokyo (Japan) | 647 | 6,964.2 |
| 8 | MEYDAN IMAX | Dubai (United Arab Emirates) | 638 | 6,840 |
| = | PRASADS IMAX | Hyderabad (India) | 638 | 6,840 |
| 10 | KRUNGSRI IMAX | Bangkok (Thailand) | 588 | 6,329.15 |

*Temporary screens erected for one-night events.

## LOVELL RADIO TELESCOPE

On October 5, 2007, this became a movie screen, showing footage of space exploration, to celebrate the 50th anniversary of the telescope.

## LONDON IMAX

This IMAX in England's capital city is owned by the BFI (British Film Institute). With a screen size of 520 m² (5,597.2 ft²), it narrowly misses out on this Top 10.

# CONSERVATION

Many aquariums are involved with vital conservation work to better understand and help the natural world. The USA's Georgia Aquarium has helped rehabilitate Loggerhead Sea Turtles and Southern Sea Otters since it opened in 2005, and was working closely with research and conservation groups for years before. Their other hands-on research includes helping Beluga Whales, Whale Sharks, and African Penguins.

AQUARIUM OF WESTERN AUSTRALIA HAS

## 400 SPECIES

TOP 10...

# BIGGEST **AQUARIUMS**

The largest aquariums in the world feature vast tanks so that their resident species can be as comfortable as possible while we learn important information to aid our water-dwelling neighbours...

| | AQUARIUM | LOCATION | TOTAL WATER (MILLIONS) (LTR) | (US GAL) |
|---|---|---|---|---|
| 1 | GEORGIA AQUARIUM | USA | 23.85 | 6.3 |
| 2 | DUBAI AQUARIUM & UNDERWATER ZOO | Dubai | 10 | 2.64 |
| 3 | OKINAWA CHURAUMI AQUARIUM | Japan | 7.5 | 1.98 |
| 4 | THE OCEANOGRÀFIC OF THE CITY OF ARTS AND SCIENCES | Spain | 7 | 1.85 |
| 5 | TURKUAZOO | Turkey | 5 | 1.32 |
| 6 | MONTEREY BAY AQUARIUM | USA | 4.54 | 1.2 |
| 7 | USHAKA MARINE WORLD | South Africa | 3.71 | 0.98 |
| 8 | SHANGHAI OCEAN AQUARIUM | China | 3.48 | 0.92 |
| 9 | AQUARIUM OF GENOA | Italy | 3.29 | 0.87 |
| 10 | AQUARIUM OF WESTERN AUSTRALIA | Australia | 3.03 | 0.8 |

## ⚲ GEORGIA AQUARIUM

This aquarium houses more than 500 different species, and up to 120,000 aquatic creatures. It also has webcams for its Whale Shark and Beluga Whale tanks, which can be viewed via www.georgiaaquarium.org

# BIGGEST BUILDS

**DUBAI'S POPULATION: 2.1 MILLION**

## ⦿ DUBAI

More than 100 buildings in Dubai measure more than 180 m (590 ft) tall. 18 of them exceed 300 m (984 ft). The Al Fahidi Fort (built in 1787) is the oldest man-made structure in Dubai. Its 23 m (75 ft) height made it the tallest building in the city for 179 years.

## TOP 10...
# CITIES WITH THE MOST 100 M+ BUILDINGS

This Top 10 gives a good indication of how built-up these cities are, and the sizes of their populations...

| | CITY | COUNTRY | TOTAL 100 M (328 FT)+ BUILDINGS |
|---|---|---|---|
| 1 | NEW YORK CITY | USA | 1,156 |
| 2 | HONG KONG | China | 503 |
| 3 | CHICAGO | USA | 406 |
| 4 | DUBAI | United Arab Emirates | 243 |
| 5 | HOUSTON | USA | 173 |
| 6 | TORONTO | Canada | 164 |
| 7 | SHANGHAI | China | 149 |
| = | PHILADELPHIA | USA | 149 |
| 9 | TOKYO | Japan | 136 |
| 10 | SEOUL | South Korea | 130 |

## LONDON

Of its 82 buildings that exceed 100 m, this financial building, "The Gherkin" (a.k.a. 30 St Mary Axe) is 180 m (591 ft) in height.

## LOS ANGELES

California's Los Angeles misses out on a place on this Top 10 with just 70 buildings more than 100 m (328 feet) high. Its tallest is the U.S. Bank Tower at 633 West Fifth Street. With 73 floors, it is 310 m (1,018 ft) tall.

# EPIC STRUCTURES

## 📍 PRINCESS TOWER

15 of the Top 30 largest residential buildings in the world are in United Arab Emirates. Open since 2012, the Princess Tower is an exclusively residential skyscraper and it is the second tallest building in Dubai.

## 📍 THE TORCH

This Dubai-based building is in the Marina district, which is built around a man-made canal. The Torch has 676 apartments.

UNITED ARAB EMIRATES IS HOME TO **8** OF THE **10** TALLEST RESIDENTIAL BUILDINGS IN THE WORLD

## TOP 10...
# LARGEST RESIDENTIAL BUILDINGS

Apartment blocks are becoming increasingly giddy places in which to live. The number one in this list is almost half a kilometre tall...

| | BUILDING | COUNTRY | YEAR COMPLETED | FLOORS | HEIGHT (M) | (FT) |
|---|---|---|---|---|---|---|
| 1 | PRINCESS TOWER | United Arab Emirates | 2012 | 101 | 413.4 | 1,356 |
| 2 | 23 MARINA | United Arab Emirates | 2012 | 90 | 392.8 | 1,289 |
| 3 | BURJ MOHAMMED BIN RASHID TOWER | United Arab Emirates | 2014 | 88 | 381.2 | 1,251 |
| 4 | ELITE RESIDENCE | United Arab Emirates | 2012 | 87 | 380.5 | 1,248 |
| 5 | THE TORCH | United Arab Emirates | 2011 | 86 | 352 | 1,155 |
| 6 | Q1 TOWER | Australia | 2005 | 78 | 322.5 | 1,058 |
| 7 | HHHR TOWER | United Arab Emirates | 2010 | 72 | 317.6 | 1,042 |
| 8 | OCEAN HEIGHTS | United Arab Emirates | 2010 | 83 | 310 | 1,017 |
| 9 | CAYAN TOWER | United Arab Emirates | 2013 | 73 | 306.4 | 1,005 |
| 10 | EAST PACIFIC CENTER TOWER A | China | 2013 | 85 | 306 | 1,004 |

## ⦿ ATLANTA INTERNATIONAL AIRPORT

Also known as the Hartsfield–Jackson Atlanta International Airport, this has been ranked as the most frequented airport in the world for 17 years. It has 207 gates and its own train system with no fewer than 38 stations.

### TOP 10...

# AIRPORTS WITH THE MOST PASSENGERS

Comparing the number of people that use airports around the world, these are the busiest...

| | AIRPORT | LOCATION | TOTAL PASSENGERS PER YEAR |
|---|---|---|---|
| 1 | HARTSFIELD–JACKSON ATLANTA INTERNATIONAL AIRPORT | Georgia (USA) | 72,199,400 |
| 2 | BEIJING CAPITAL INTERNATIONAL AIRPORT | Beijing (China) | 64,004,178 |
| 3 | HEATHROW AIRPORT | London (UK) | 55,687,927 |
| 4 | HANEDA AIRPORT | Tokyo (Japan) | 53,809,428 |
| 5 | LOS ANGELES INTERNATIONAL AIRPORT | California (USA) | 53,498,032 |
| 6 | O'HARE INTERNATIONAL AIRPORT | Chicago, Illinois (USA) | 52,434,527 |
| 7 | DUBAI INTERNATIONAL AIRPORT | Dubai (United Arab Emirates) | 52,422,547 |
| 8 | CHARLES DE GAULLE AIRPORT | Paris (France) | 48,482,940 |
| 9 | DALLAS/FORT WORTH INTERNATIONAL AIRPORT | Texas (USA) | 48,209,028 |
| 10 | HONG KONG INTERNATIONAL AIRPORT | Hong Kong (China) | 47,018,000 |

## ⦿ CHARLES DE GAULLE AIRPORT

Disneyland Resort Paris is 10 minutes away from this airport by TGV (France's high-speed rail service). Located North-east of Paris, the airport takes up 12.5 miles$^2$ (32.38 km$^2$). It has been operational since March 8, 1974.

PARIS' CHARLES DE GAULLE AIRPORT HANDLES **0.5 MILLION** AIRCRAFT MOVEMENTS ANNUALLY

# NUMBER OF STATIONS

Of the largest underground railways, these have the most stations:

| MADRID METRO | MÉTROPOLITAIN | BEIJING SUBWAY | SHANGHAI METRO | NEW YORK CITY SUBWAY |
|---|---|---|---|---|
| **300** | **303** | **318** | **337** | **421** |

LONDON UNDERGROUND SERVES **1.3 BILLION** TRAVELLERS EACH YEAR

**TOP 10...**

# LARGEST **UNDERGROUND** RAIL SYSTEMS

With railway tracks extending hundreds of miles, these subterranean transport systems have revolutionized how we travel...

| | NAME | LOCATION | STATIONS | TOTAL LENGTH (KM) | (MI) |
|---|---|---|---|---|---|
| 1 | SHANGHAI METRO | Shanghai (China) | 337 | 548 | 340.5 |
| 2 | BEIJING SUBWAY | Beijing (China) | 318 | 527 | 327 |
| 3 | LONDON UNDERGROUND | London (UK) | 270 | 402 | 249.8 |
| 4 | NEW YORK CITY SUBWAY | New York City (USA) | 421 | 373 | 231.8 |
| 5 | MOSCOW METRO | Moscow (Russia) | 196 | 327.5 | 203.5 |
| 6 | SEOUL SUBWAY (LINE 1–9) | Seoul (South Korea) | 296 | 327 | 203.2 |
| 7 | MADRID METRO | Madrid (Spain) | 300 | 293 | 182.1 |
| 8 | GUANGZHOU METRO | Guangzhou (China) | 130 | 240 | 150 |
| 9 | MEXICO CITY METRO | Mexico City (Mexico) | 195 | 226.5 | 140.7 |
| 10 | MÉTROPOLITAIN | Paris (France) | 303 | 214 | 133 |

## ⦿ NEW YORK

Since it opened in 1904, this subway system has grown to carry nearly two billion riders every year.

## ⦿ SEOUL

10 million people ride Seoul's subway each day. Several new lines and station developments are being carried out though to 2020.

# LONGEST DESIGNS

## THE BEAST

This ride lasts 4 minutes 10 seconds. A total of 36 people can ride The Beast each time. It is the longest wooden roller coaster in the world.

THE BEAST REACHES

# 104 KPH

## STEEL DRAGON

More than 1,000 people can ride the Steel Dragon in each hour. It opened on August 1, 2000.

**TOP 10...**

# LONGEST ROLLER COASTERS

Measuring the entire length of the track/ride, these are the roller coasters that cover the greatest distance...

| | ROLLER COASTER | LOCATION | LENGTH (M) | (FT) |
|---|---|---|---|---|
| 1 | STEEL DRAGON 2000 | Nagashima Spa Land (Japan) | 2,479 | 8,133 |
| 2 | THE ULTIMATE | Lightwater Valley (UK) | 2,268 | 7,442 |
| 3 | THE BEAST | Kings Island (USA) | 2,243 | 7,359 |
| 4 | FUJIYAMA | Fuji-Q Highland (Japan) | 2,045 | 6,709 |
| 5 | FURY 325 | Carowinds (USA) | 2,012 | 6,602 |
| 6 | MILLENNIUM FORCE | Cedar Point (USA) | 2,010 | 6,595 |
| 7 | FORMULA ROSA | Ferrari World (United Arab Emirates) | 2,000 | 6,562 |
| 8 | THE VOYAGE | Holiday World & Splashin' Safari | 1,964 | 6,442 |
| 9 | CALIFORNIA SCREAMIN' | Disney California Adventure | 1,851 | 6,072 |
| 10 | DESPERADO | Buffalo Bill's (USA) | 1,781 | 5,843 |

## CALIFORNIA SCREAMIN'

If you're 1.22 m (4 ft) or more in height, you can ride this 99.78 kph (62 mph) ride. The highest drop on this ride is 32.9 m (108 ft). It has been in operation since February 8, 2001.

PARADISE PIER

## GREAT WALL OF CHINA

Sections of this structure date back to 7th century BC. A common belief is that it can be seen from space. However, with the widest sections being only 9 m (30 ft) wide, this is considered false. No astronauts have ever reported seeing the Great Wall.

DUBAI INTERNATIONAL AIRPORT HOSTS
**127** AIRLINES

### TOP 10...
# LONGEST **BUILDINGS**

The longest construction in this list is nearly over 8,800 km (5,500 miles) in length, and dwarfs all of the other entries in this Top 10...

| | CONSTRUCTION | COUNTRY | LENGTH (M) | (FT) |
|---|---|---|---|---|
| 1 | GREAT WALL OF CHINA | China | 8,851,800 | 29,041,338.5 |
| 2 | RANIKOT FORT | Pakistan | 8,600 | 28215 |
| 3 | WALLS OF STON | Croatia | 5,500 | 18045 |
| 4 | KLYSTRON GALLERY | USA | 3,073.7 | 10084 |
| 5 | MODLIN FORTRESS | Poland | 2,250 | 7381.9 |
| 6 | MOSCOW KREMLIN WALL | Russia | 2,235 | 7332.7 |
| 7 | DUBAI INTERNATIONAL AIRPORT CARGO GATEWAY | United Arab Emirates | 1,774 | 5820.2 |
| 8 | SOBORNOSTI AVENUE/MOLODYOZHI STREET APARTMENT | Ukraine | 1,750 | 5741.5 |
| 9 | KANSAI INTERNATIONAL AIRPORT | Japan | 1,700 | 5577.4 |
| = | RED DOG MINE ENCLOSURE | USA | 1,700 | 5577.4 |

## KREMLIN WALL

This defensive structure surrounds the President's residence, the Kremlin (which means "fortress within a city") inside Russia's capital city, Moscow.

## MODLIN FORTRESS

This citadel has been in use for more than 200 years and has seen several battles. It is located 40 km (24.8 miles) North-west of Warsaw, Poland's capital city.

## ⦿ PONTCHARTRAIN CAUSEWAY

This is the longest bridge over a body of water. Over 9,000 concrete pilings support the bridge's panels over its 38.4 km (23.86 mile) span. The first version of the bridge was officially opened for public use on August 30, 1956.

HANGZHOU BAY BRIDGE WAS DESIGNED BY

**600 EXPERTS** OVER 9 YEARS

## TOP 10...
# LONGEST **BRIDGES**

With the longest of these nearly 165 km long, these feats of engineering cost billions of dollars and take years to construct...

| | NAME | COUNTRY | LENGTH (M) | (FT) |
|---|---|---|---|---|
| 1 | DANYANG-KUNSHAN GRAND BRIDGE | China | 164,800 | 540,700 |
| 2 | TIANJIN GRAND BRIDGE | China | 113,700 | 373,000 |
| 3 | WEINAN WEIHE GRAND BRIDGE | China | 79,732 | 261,588 |
| 4 | BANG NA EXPRESSWAY | Thailand | 54,000 | 177,000 |
| 5 | BEIJING GRAND BRIDGE | China | 48,153 | 157,982 |
| 6 | LAKE PONTCHARTRAIN CAUSEWAY | USA | 38,442 | 126,122 |
| 7 | MANCHAC SWAMP BRIDGE | USA | 36,710 | 120,440 |
| 8 | YANGCUN BRIDGE | China | 35,812 | 117,493 |
| 9 | HANGZHOU BAY BRIDGE | China | 35,673 | 117,037 |
| 10 | RUNYANG BRIDGE | China | 35,660 | 116,990 |

## ⦿ DANYANG-KUNSHAN GRAND BRIDGE

10,000 workers spent four years constructing this 164.8 km (102.4 mile)-long viaduct. It is the longest in the world by more than 48 km (30 miles), and it opened for use in 2011.

## FIVE LONGEST

Here is how the top 5 longest bridges compare graphically:

| | LENGTH (M) |
|---|---|
| DANYANG-KUNSHAN GRAND BRIDGE | 164,800 m |
| TIANJIN GRAND BRIDGE | 113,700 m |
| WEINAN WEIHE GRAND BRIDGE | 79,732 m |
| BANG NA EXPRESSWAY | 54,000 m |
| BEIJING GRAND BRIDGE | 48,153 m |

## POUGHKEEPSIE BRIDGE

Completed in 1889, this steel cantilever railroad bridge crosses the Hudson River, connecting New York (USA)'s Poughkeepsie and Highland. It became a footbridge in 2009.

## CAPILANO SUSPENSION BRIDGE

Over 80,000 people brave this footbridge in Vancouver, Canada each year. At 140.21 m (460 ft) long, it just misses out on a place in this Top 10.

## TOP 10...
# LONGEST **FOOTBRIDGES**

These record-breaking structures range from sturdy concrete and steel designs through to swaying, flexible footbridges suspended across vertigo-inducing chasms...

| | NAME | LOCATION | LENGTH (M) | (FT) |
|---|---|---|---|---|
| 1 | POUGHKEEPSIE BRIDGE | Poughkeepsie, New York (USA) | 2,060 | 6,767 |
| 2 | CHAIN OF ROCKS BRIDGE | Mississippi River (USA) | 1,632 | 5,353 |
| 3 | SHELBY STREET BRIDGE | Tennessee (USA) | 960 | 3,150 |
| 4 | HORAI BRIDGE | Shizuoka Prefecture (Japan) | 897.4 | 2,944 |
| 5 | NEWPORT SOUTHBANK BRIDGE | Ohio River (USA) | 813.8 | 2,670 |
| 6 | KURILPA BRIDGE | Brisbane (Australia) | 470 | 1,542 |
| 7 | MILLENNIUM BRIDGE | London (UK) | 370 | 1,214 |
| 8 | ESPLANADE RIEL | Red River (Canada) | 197 | 646.3 |
| 9 | WILLIMANTIC FOOTBRIDGE | Connecticut (USA) | 193.6 | 635 |
| 10 | DAVENPORT SKYBRIDGE | River Drive, Iowa (USA) | 175.3 | 575 |

## CHAIN OF ROCKS BRIDGE FOOTBRIDGE

This crosses the Mississippi River in Illinois, USA. Built in 1929, cars stopped using the bridge on February 25, 1970. Since then, it has been used as a footbridge and is also protected under the National Register of Historic Places.

## ANAHEIM

This area of California, USA is home to Disneyland Park, which opened its gates for the first time on July 17, 1955.

## TOKYO DISNEYLAND

Since April 15, 1983, Tokyo (Japan)'s Disneyland marked the first time a Disney resort had been constructed outside of the USA.

**TOP 10...**

# MOST POPULAR THEME PARKS

With attendees averaging over 10 million each year, theme parks remain as busy as ever...

| | NAME | LOCATION | ANNUAL ATTENDANCE |
|---|---|---|---|
| 1 | MAGIC KINGDOM (WALT DISNEY WORLD RESORT) | Lake Buena Vista, Florida (USA) | 18,588,000 |
| 2 | TOKYO DISNEYLAND | Tokyo (Japan) | 17,214,000 |
| 3 | DISNEYLAND (DISNEYLAND RESORT ANAHEIM) | California (USA) | 16,202,000 |
| 4 | TOKYO DISNEYSEA | Tokyo (Japan) | 14,084,000 |
| 5 | EPCOT (WALT DISNEY WORLD RESORT) | Lake Buena Vista, Florida (USA) | 11,229,000 |
| 6 | DISNEYLAND PARK (DISNEYLAND PARIS) | Marne-la-Vallée (France) | 10,430,000 |
| 7 | DISNEY'S ANIMAL KINGDOM (WALT DISNEY WORLD RESORT) | Lake Buena Vista, Florida (USA) | 10,198,000 |
| 8 | DISNEY'S HOLLYWOOD STUDIOS (WALT DISNEY WORLD RESORT) | Lake Buena Vista, Florida (USA) | 10,110,000 |
| 9 | UNIVERSAL STUDIOS JAPAN | Osaka (Japan) | 10,100,000 |
| 10 | DISNEY CALIFORNIA ADVENTURE (DISNEYLAND RESORT) | California (USA) | 8,514,000 |

## ISLANDS OF ADVENTURE

With 16 rides, this was built as part of Universal Studios Florida's expansion. From 2010, The Wizarding World of Harry Potter was an additional island in the Orlando resort.

DISNEYLAND HAS SEEN NEARLY

# 700 MILLION
PEOPLE VISIT SINCE 1955

## X-WING FIGHTER

32 experts in Kladno, Czech Republic's LEGO model shop spent 17,336 hours making this life-sized Star Wars spaceship. It was displayed in Times Square, New York City in May 2013.

**TOP 10...**

# BIGGEST **LEGO STRUCTURES** IN THE WORLD

If you enjoy creating things with LEGO bricks and pieces, these colossal constructions raise the bar considerably...

| | CONSTRUCTION | LOCATION | YEAR | NUMBER OF LEGO BRICKS |
|---|---|---|---|---|
| 1 | **AIRCRAFT:** X-WING FIGHTER (STAR WARS) | NYC, New York (USA) | 2013 | 5,335,200 |
| 2 | **PLACE:** AMOSKEAG MILLYARD | New Hampshire (USA) | 2006 | 3,000,000 |
| 3 | **INSECT:** MILLIPEDE MADE BY 20,000 CHILDREN | Bangkok (Thailand) | 2003 | 2,477,140 |
| 4 | **CHAIN:** LONG CHAIN OF LEGO | Prague (Czech Republic) | 1998 | 1,500,834 |
| 5 | **STATUE:** SITTING BULL | LEGOLAND Billund (Denmark) | 1974 | 1,500,000 |
| 6 | **CASTLE:** WITH 2,100 MINIFIGURE RESIDENTS | Museum in Ohio (USA) | 2008 | 1,400,000 |
| 7 | **FACADE:** SCHOOL/COMMUNITY CENTRE | London (UK) | 2010 | 1,263,801 |
| 8 | **PICTURE:** LEGO TRACTOR TRAILER PICTURE | Museum in Ohio (USA) | 2007 | 1,200,000 |
| 9 | **TOWER:** BUILT BY 1,800 VOLUNTEERS | Limmen (The Netherlands) | 2010 | 700,000+ |
| 10 | **CAR:** SUPER-SIZED LEGO MODEL CAR | Chicago (USA) | 1996 | 650,000 |

## CAR

LEGO employees spent more than 4,000 hours constructing this huge car in 1996. Weighing more than a ton, it measured 4.72 m (15.5 ft) long.

## SITTING BULL

Danish artist Bjørn Richter created this, along with a replica of Mount Rushmore, made from over a million bricks.

## BLIZZARD BEACH

Since it opened in 1995, this Bay Lake, Florida-based water park has been themed around the idea of a ski resort that is melting. The 27.4 m (90 ft)-high Mount Gushmore is one of its most popular attractions.

**AUSTRALIA'S WET'N'WILD HAS**

# 16 RIDES
**AND ATTRACTIONS**

## TYPHOON LAGOON

Along with the big drop water slides like Humunga Kowabunga, Florida's Typhoon Lagoon also offers surfing lessons. This is possible because of the state-of-the-art wave pool.

## TOP 10...

# MOST POPULAR WATER PARKS

For nearly 80 years, water parks have grown in popularity, size, and technological advancements. These are the most visited...

| | NAME | LOCATION | ANNUAL ATTENDANCE |
|---|---|---|---|
| 1 | CHIME-LONG WATER PARK | Guangzhou (China) | 2,710,000 |
| 2 | TYPHOON LAGOON (WALT DISNEY WORLD RESORT) | Florida (USA) | 2,142,000 |
| 3 | BLIZZARD BEACH (WALT DISNEY WORLD RESORT) | Florida (USA) | 1,968,000 |
| 4 | OCEAN WORLD | Gangwon-do (South Korea) | 1,700,000 |
| 5 | THERMAS DOS LARANJIAS | Olimpia (Brazil) | 1,650,000 |
| 6 | CARIBBEAN BAY (EVERLAND RESORT) | Gyeonggi-do (South Korea) | 1,623,000 |
| 7 | AQUATICA | Florida (USA) | 1,553,000 |
| 8 | WET 'N' WILD WATER WORLD | Queensland (Australia) | 1,409,000 |
| 9 | WET 'N WILD ORLANDO | Florida (USA) | 1,259,000 |
| 10 | AQUAVENTURE | Dubai (United Arab Emirates) | 1,200,000 |

# BUSIEST PARKS

These graphics provide an at-a-glance look at how the top three most popular water parks compare:

**BLIZZARD BEACH (WALT DISNEY WORLD RESORT)**
1,968,000

**TYPHOON LAGOON (WALT DISNEY WORLD RESORT)**
2,142,000

**CHIME-LONG WATER PARK**
2,710,000

## 📍 MAKKAH ROYAL CLOCK TOWER HOTEL

This hotel in Mecca, Saudi Arabia has the biggest clock face in the world at 43 m (141 ft) wide. It is part of a complex of six other smaller towers that range from 240 m (790 ft) to 260 m (850 ft).

## 📍 ZIFENG TOWER

Completed in 2010, after five years of construction, this tower in Nanjing, China also houses an observatory, restaurants, shops, and private offices. Its shape was designed to mirror the geometry of the neighbouring roads and buildings.

ZIFENG TOWER HAS
**1,200 PARKING** SPACES

### TOP 10...

# BIGGEST HOTELS

With the tallest almost a kilometre in height, these hotels scrape the sky more than any others in the world...

| | BUILDING | COUNTRY | YEAR COMPLETED | FLOORS | ROOMS | HEIGHT (M) | (FT) |
|---|---|---|---|---|---|---|---|
| **1** | BURJ KHALIFA | United Arab Emirates | 2010 | 163 | 304 | 828 | 2,717 |
| **2** | MAKKAH ROYAL CLOCK TOWER HOTEL | Saudi Arabia | 2012 | 120 | 858 | 601 | 1,972 |
| **3** | SHANGHAI WORLD FINANCIAL CENTER | China | 2008 | 101 | 174 | 492 | 1,614 |
| **4** | ZIFENG TOWER | China | 2010 | 66 | 450 | 450 | 1,476 |
| **5** | KK100 | China | 2011 | 100 | 249 | 441.8 | 1,499 |
| **6** | GUANGZHOU INTERNATIONAL FINANCE CENTER | China | 2010 | 103 | 374 | 438.6 | 1,439 |
| **7** | TRUMP INTERNATIONAL HOTEL & TOWER | USA | 2009 | 98 | 339 | 423.2 | 1,389 |
| **8** | JIN MAO TOWER | China | 1999 | 88 | 555 | 420.5 | 1,380 |
| **9** | JW MARRIOTT MARQUIS HOTEL DUBAI TOWERS | United Arab Emirates | 2012 & 2013 | 82 | 1,608* | 355.4 | 1,166 |
| **10** | TUNTEX SKY TOWER | Taiwan, China | 1997 | 85 | 150 | 347.5 | 1,140 |

*Split between the two towers.

## NUMBER OF ROOMS

By number of rooms, the table on the right has a different top five entirely:

GUANGZHOU INTERNATIONAL FINANCE CENTER — 374

ZIFENG TOWER — 450

JIN MAO TOWER — 555

1,608 — JW MARRIOTT MARQUIS HOTEL DUBAI TOWERS

858 — MAKKAH ROYAL CLOCK TOWER HOTEL

# SPORT

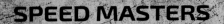

TYSON GAY'S GOLD-WINNING TIME

**37.38** SECS

AT THE 4x100M WORLD RELAY CHAMPIONSHIP

## 📍 USAIN BOLT

The 1.96 m (6.43 ft)-tall Jamaican runner has won a total of 16 gold medals. This includes six Olympic golds and eight at the World Championship.

2163

## FAST NATIONS

Here is how the quickest sprinters look by nation...

TYSON GAY

Jamaica 5

Trinidad & Tobago 1

USA 3

Canada 1

## TOP 10...
# FASTEST 100M MALE SPRINTERS

All of these sportsmen can run the 100m race in under 10 seconds, but it's the milliseconds that make all the difference when it comes to setting speed records...

| | NAME | COUNTRY | YEAR | TIME (SECS) | AVERAGE SPEED (KPH) | (MPH) |
|---|---|---|---|---|---|---|
| 1 | USAIN BOLT | Jamaica | 2009 | 9.58 | 37.58 | 23.35 |
| 2 | TYSON GAY | USA | 2009 | 9.69 | 37.14 | 23.08 |
| = | YOHAN BLAKE | Jamaica | 2012 | 9.69 | 37.14 | 23.08 |
| 4 | ASAFA POWELL | Jamaica | 2008 | 9.72 | 37.03 | 23.01 |
| 5 | JUSTIN GATLIN | USA | 2014 | 9.74 | 36.96 | 22.97 |
| 6 | NESTA CARTER | Jamaica | 2010 | 9.78 | 36.01 | 22.87 |
| 7 | MAURICE GREENE | USA | 1999 | 9.79 | 36.77 | 22.85 |
| 8 | STEVE MULLINGS | Jamaica | 2011 | 9.80 | 36.74 | 22.83 |
| 9 | RICHARD THOMPSON | Trinidad and Tobago | 2014 | 9.82 | 36.66 | 22.78 |
| 10 | DONOVAN BAILEY/BRUNY SURIN | Canada | 1996/1999 | 9.84 | 36.58 | 22.73 |

一汽 TOYOTA

GATLIN

## 📍 JUSTIN GATLIN

He improved his personal best 100m time by 0.03 secs on May 15, 2015 at the Qatar Athletic Super Grand Prix.

### ◉ SHELLY-ANN FRASER-PRYCE

The fastest female Jamaican in the world. At the 2008 Olympics in Beijing, China, she became the first Caribbean woman to win the Olympic 100m gold medal.

### ◉ FLORENCE GRIFFITH-JOYNER

Affectionately known all over the world as "Flo-Jo", her 100m record remains unbroken since 1988. In 1998, she tragically passed away in her sleep from an epileptic seizure.

CARMELITA JETER HAS WON
**13** MEDALS
INCLUDING 6 GOLD

## TOP 10...

# FASTEST 100M FEMALE SPRINTERS

The number one time on the chart hasn't been bested in nearly three decades, and half of the Top 10 speeds here were set between 20 and 30 years ago...

| | NAME | COUNTRY | YEAR | TIME (SECS) | AVERAGE SPEED (KPH) | (MPH) |
|---|---|---|---|---|---|---|
| 1 | Florence Griffith-Joyner | USA | 1988 | 10.49 | 34.31 | 21.32 |
| 2 | Carmelita Jeter | USA | 2009 | 10.64 | 33.83 | 21.02 |
| 3 | Marion Jones | USA | 1998 | 10.65 | 33.80 | 21.00 |
| 4 | Shelly-Ann Fraser-Pryce | Jamaica | 2012 | 10.70 | 33.65 | 20.91 |
| 5 | Christine Arron | France | 1998 | 10.73 | 33.56 | 20.85 |
| 6 | Merlene Ottey | Jamaica | 1996 | 10.74 | 33.52 | 20.83 |
| 7 | Kerron Stewart | Jamaica | 2009 | 10.75 | 33.49 | 20.81 |
| 8 | Evelyn Ashford | USA | 1984 | 10.76 | 33.46 | 20.79 |
| 9 | Veronica Campbell-Brown | Jamaica | 2011 | 10.76 | 33.46 | 20.79 |
| 10 | Irina Privalova/Ivet Lalova | Russia/Bulgaria | 1994/2004 | 10.77 | 33.43 | 20.77 |

## DAVID RUDISHA

Rudisha's world record 800m time was achieved in August at the 2012 Olympic Games held in London, England.

**TOP 10...**

# QUICKEST SPORTSMEN

Examining the sporting events that utilize the sprint muscles, these are the ten fastest men for each of those events...

| | SPORT | DISTANCE | FASTEST PERSON | COUNTRY | YEAR | TIME | AVERAGE SPEED (KPH) | (MPH) |
|---|---|---|---|---|---|---|---|---|
| 1 | Running | 100m | Usain Bolt | Jamaica | 2009 | 0:09.58 | 37.58 | 23.35 |
| 2 | Running | 200m | Usain Bolt | Jamaica | 2009 | 0:19.19 | 37.52 | 23.31 |
| 3 | Running | 400m | Michael Johnson | USA | 1999 | 0:43.18 | 33.35 | 20.72 |
| 4 | Running | 800m | David Rudisha | Kenya | 2012 | 1:40.91 | 28.54 | 17.73 |
| 5 | Swimming: Freestyle | 50m | Cesar Cielo | Brazil | 2009 | 0:20.91 | 8.61 | 5.35 |
| 6 | Swimming: Butterfly | 50m | Rafael Muñoz | Spain | 2009 | 0:22.43 | 8.02 | 4.99 |
| 7 | Swimming: Freestyle | 100m | Cesar Cielo | Brazil | 2009 | 0:46.91 | 7.67 | 4.77 |
| 8 | Swimming: Backstroke | 50m | Liam Tancock | UK | 2009 | 0:24.04 | 7.49 | 4.65 |
| 9 | Swimming: Butterfly | 100m | Michael Phelps | USA | 2009 | 0:49.82 | 7.23 | 4.49 |
| 10 | Swimming: Freestyle | 200m | Paul Biedermann | Germany | 2009 | 1:42.00 | 7.06 | 4.39 |

RAFAEL MUÑOZ WAS BORN IN

**1988**

ON MARCH 3RD

## CESAR CIELO

The fastest swimmer in the world (in two disciplines), Brazilian Cielo has amassed 20 gold medals since winning his first in 2007.

## ALAN FONTELES CARDOSO OLIVEIRA

Oliveira began competitive athletics aged eight, and first ran on carbon-fibre blades aged 15.

ZHANG LIXIN HAS WON **5 OLYMPIC** GOLD MEDALS

## BRAZIL POWER

Brazilian swimmer Andre Brasil's other 2009 records include:

| SPORT | DISTANCE | TIME |
|---|---|---|
| Backstroke | 100m | 0:57.29 |
| Ind. Medley | 100m | 0:57.68 |
| Freestyle | 400m | 3:54.57 |
| Ind. Medley | 200m | 2:04.05 |

TOP 10...

# QUICKEST MALE PARALYMPIANS

This list can never be a definitive Top 10 (as there are several different classes related to physical differences), but these are the fastest within each overall event...

| | SPORT | DISTANCE | FASTEST PERSON | CLASS | COUNTRY | YEAR | TIME | SPEED (KPH) | (MPH) |
|---|---|---|---|---|---|---|---|---|---|
| 1 | Running | 200m | Alan Fonteles Cardoso Oliveira | T43 | Brazil | 2013 | 0:20:66 | 34.85 | 21.65 |
| 2 | Running | 100m | Jason Smyth | T13 | Ireland | 2012 | 0:10.46 | 34.42 | 21.39 |
| 3 | Running | 400m | Zhang Lixin | T54 | China | 2008 | 0:45.07 | 31.95 | 19.85 |
| 4 | Running | 800m | Marcel Hug | T54 | Switzerland | 2010 | 1:31.12 | 31.61 | 19.64 |
| 5 | Swimming: Freestyle | 50m | Andre Brasil | S10 | Brazil | 2009 | 0:22.44 | 8.02 | 4.98 |
| 6 | Swimming: Freestyle | 100m | Andre Brasil | S10 | Brazil | 2009 | 0:48.70 | 7.39 | 4.59 |
| 7 | Swimming: Butterfly | 50m | Timothy Antalfy | S13 | Australia | 2014 | 0:24.60 | 7.32 | 4.55 |
| 8 | Swimming: Backstroke | 50m | Sean Russo | S13 | Australia | 2013 | 0:27.30 | 6.59 | 4.1 |
| 9 | Swimming: Butterfly | 100m | Andre Brasil | S10 | Brazil | 2009 | 0:54.76 | 6.57 | 4.08 |
| 10 | Swimming: Freestyle | 200m | Philippe Gagnon | S10 | Canada | 2002 | 1:52.83 | 6.38 | 3.97 |

SARAH SJÖSTRÖM IS
**1.8**
METRES
TALL

📍 **MARITA KOCH**

Not only has Koch's 400m time not been beaten in over 30 years, she also held 16 world records during her career.

## TOP 10...
# QUICKEST **SPORTSWOMEN**

Focusing on events that require a "sprint" explosion of power, these are the sportswomen who have achieved the fastest speeds...

| | SPORT | DISTANCE | FASTEST PERSON | COUNTRY | YEAR | TIME | AVERAGE SPEED (KPH) | (MPH) |
|---|---|---|---|---|---|---|---|---|
| 1 | Running | 100m | Florence Griffith Joyner | USA | 1988 | 0:10.49 | 34.32 | 21.32 |
| 2 | Running | 200m | Florence Griffith Joyner | USA | 1988 | 0:21.34 | 33.74 | 20.96 |
| 3 | Running | 400m | Marita Koch | Germany | 1985 | 0:47.60 | 30.25 | 18.8 |
| 4 | Running | 800m | Jarmila Kratochvílová | Czech Republic | 1983 | 1:53.28 | 25.42 | 15.8 |
| 5 | Swimming: Freestyle | 50m | Britta Steffen | Germany | 2009 | 0:23.73 | 7.59 | 4.71 |
| 6 | Swimming: Butterfly | 50m | Sarah Sjöström | Sweden | 2014 | 0:24.43 | 7.37 | 4.58 |
| 7 | Swimming: Freestyle | 100m | Britta Steffen | Germany | 2009 | 0:52.07 | 6.91 | 4.3 |
| 8 | Swimming: Backstroke | 50m | Jing Zhao | China | 2009 | 0:27.06 | 6.65 | 4.13 |
| 9 | Swimming: Butterfly | 100m | Dana Vollmer | USA | 2012 | 0:55.98 | 6.43 | 4 |
| 10 | Swimming: Freestyle | 200m | Federica Pellegrini | Italy | 2009 | 1:52.98 | 6.37 | 3.96 |

## RUTA MEILUTYTE

Just missing out on the above Top 10, in 2013 Lithuanian swimmer Ruta Meilutyte achieved a world record 50m breaststroke time of 0:29.48. This translates as an average speed of 6.11 kph (3.79 mph).

# TOP 10...
# QUICKEST FEMALE PARALYMPIANS

Although this is not an absolute Top 10 (as comparing the different classifications of physical differences is an unfair comparison), this data reveals the fastest speeds from each overall event...

| | SPORT | DISTANCE | FASTEST PERSON | CLASS | COUNTRY | YEAR | TIME | SPEED (KPH) | (MPH) |
|---|---|---|---|---|---|---|---|---|---|
| 1 | Running | 100m | Guohua Zhou | T12 | China | 2012 | 0:11.91 | 30.23 | 18.78 |
| 2 | Running | 200m | Omara Durand | T13 | Cuba | 2011 | 0:24.24 | 29.7 | 18.46 |
| 3 | Running | 400m | Chantal Petitclerc | T54 | Canada | 2004 | 0:51.91 | 27.74 | 17.24 |
| 4 | Running | 800m | Tatyana McFadden | T54 | USA | 2013 | 1:44.44 | 27. | 17.13 |
| 5 | Swimming: Freestyle | 50m | Oxana Savchenko | S12 | Russia | 2009 | 0:26.54 | 6.78 | 4.21 |
| 6 | Swimming: Butterfly | 50m | Sophie Pascoe | S10 | New Zealand | 2013 | 0:29.08 | 6.19 | 3.85 |
| 7 | Swimming: Freestyle | 100m | Oxana Savchenko | S12 | Russia | 2009 | 0:58.60 | 6.14 | 3.82 |
| 8 | Swimming: Backstroke | 50m | Sophie Pascoe | S10 | New Zealand | 2013 | 0:30.49 | 5.9 | 3.67 |
| 9 | Swimming: Freestyle | 200m | Valerie Grand-Maison | S13 | Canada | 2008 | 2:08.53 | 5.6 | 3.48 |
| 10 | Swimming: Butterfly | 100m | Joanna Mendak | S12 | Poland | 2009 | 1:05.10 | 5.53 | 3.44 |

VALERIE GRAND-
MAISON'S 2008 400M
MEDLEY TIME
**5:21:88**
SAW HER SWIM AT
**2.78 MPH**

## ⊙ OXANA SAVCHENKO

Russia's Oxana Savchenko swam the Individual Medley at a speed of 5.22 kph (3.25 mph) in the SM12 class.

## ⊙ OMARA DURAND

The Cuban runner won two gold medals at the 2012 London Paralympic Games, for the 100m and 400m, both in the T13 class.

## TOP 10...
# F1 LEGENDS

Since its foundation in 1946, Formula One racing has seen many drivers clock multiple race wins...

| | NAME | COUNTRY | TOTAL WINS |
|---|---|---|---|
| 1 | MICHAEL SCHUMACHER | Germany | 91 |
| 2 | ALAIN PROST | France | 51 |
| 3 | AYRTON SENNA | Brazil | 41 |
| 4 | SEBASTIAN VETTEL | Germany | 39 |
| 5 | LEWIS HAMILTON | UK | 34 |
| 6 | FERNANDO ALONSO | Spain | 32 |
| 7 | NIGEL MANSELL | UK | 31 |
| 8 | JACKIE STEWART | UK | 27 |
| 9 | JIM CLARK | UK | 25 |
| = | NIKI LAUDA | Austria | 25 |

MICHAEL SCHUMACHER ACHIEVED
**68 POLE POSITIONS**
IN HIS 308 RACES

## AYRTON SENNA

*Senna*, a film about the legendary driver, won the 2012 BAFTA (British Academy of Film and Television Arts) for Best Documentary Film.

## SEBASTIAN VETTEL

This racing driver even has a car named after him: the Sebastian Vettel Edition of the 2012 Infiniti FX-series SUV.

# F1 CAR SPEEDS

Initially referred to as "Formula A", the concept of Formula One racing came into its own in 1948. The first ever World Championship for Drivers debuted in 1950, and was a reaction to the World Motorcycle Championships being launched the previous year in 1949. From humble technological beginnings, the sport now has turbocharged, V6 engines, providing drivers with 600 bhp (brake horsepower).

RICHARD PETTY TOOK PART IN

**1,199**

RACES DURING HIS 37-YEAR CAREER

## 📍 DAVID PEARSON

The year he began his NASCAR career, Pearson won Rookie of the Year 1960.

TOP 10...

# NASCAR LEGENDS

Founded by Bill France, Sr. in 1948, NASCAR (National Association for Stock Car Auto Racing) is the USA's second most popular sport...

| | NAME | FROM | TOTAL NASCAR CHAMPIONSHIP WINS |
|---|---|---|---|
| 1 | RICHARD PETTY | North Carolina, USA | 201 |
| 2 | DAVID PEARSON | South Carolina, USA | 107 |
| 3 | JEFF GORDON | California, USA | 97 |
| = | DARRELL WALTRIP | Kentucky, USA | 97 |
| = | DALE EARNHARDT | North Carolina, USA | 97 |
| 6 | BOBBY ALLISON | Florida, USA | 92 |
| 7 | CALE YARBOROUGH | South Carolina, USA | 83 |
| 8 | JIMMIE JOHNSON | California, USA | 74 |
| 9 | RUSTY WALLACE | Missouri, USA | 55 |
| 10 | LEE PETTY | North Carolina, USA | 54 |

## NASCAR STATES

This chart shows how successful Carolina has been at producing NASCAR legends...

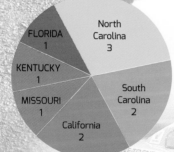

North Carolina 3

FLORIDA 1

KENTUCKY 1

MISSOURI 1

California 2

South Carolina 2

## 📍 JEFF GORDON

This champion NASCAR driver appears in the 2010 video game *Gran Turismo 5*.

## ◉ MICHAEL DOOHAN

The Australian achieved 58 pole positions during his ten-year career (1989-99).

## TOP 10...

# GRAND PRIX
# MOTORCYCLE
# MASTERS

Combining all of their career wins, here are the 10 most successful bikers...

| | NAME | COUNTRY | TOTAL WINS |
|---|---|---|---|
| 1 | GIACOMO AGOSTINI | Italy | 122 |
| 2 | VALENTINO ROSSI | Italy | 108 |
| 3 | ÁNGEL NIETO | Spain | 90 |
| 4 | MIKE HAILWOOD | UK | 76 |
| 5 | MICHAEL DOOHAN | Australia | 54 |
| = | JORGE LORENZO | Spain | 54 |
| 7 | PHIL READ | UK | 52 |
| 8 | DANI PEDROSA | Spain | 49 |
| 9 | MARC MÁRQUEZ | Spain | 45 |
| = | JIM REDMAN | Rhodesia | 45 |
| = | CASEY STONER | Australia | 45 |

## ◉ VALENTINO ROSSI

He has been world champion in 125cc, 250cc, 500cc, and MotoGP competitions.

JORGE LORENZO WAS BORN

**1987**
MAY 4TH

## CAMERON PILLEY

The Yamba, New South Wales-born squash player's highest world ranking is 11.

JUSTIN UPTON HAS HIT
**164**
HOME RUNS

## SAMUEL GROTH

Although his highest world ranking as a singles player is 68, Groth has achieved 24th Best Doubles Player in 2015.

**TOP 10...**

# SPORTS WITH **FASTEST SWING**

Examining all of the sports where a swinging arm motion is required, these are the top speeds...

| | SPORT | ATHLETE | NATIONALITY | YEAR | HEAD SPEED (KPH) | (MPH) |
|---|---|---|---|---|---|---|
| 1 | BADMINTON | Tan Boon Heong | **Malaysia** | 2013 | 493 | 306.34 |
| 2 | LONG DRIVE GOLF | Ryan Winther | **USA** | 2012 | 349.38 | 217.1 |
| 3 | RACQUETBALL | Egan Inoue | **USA** | 1990s | 307.39 | 191 |
| 4 | JAI ALAI | José Ramón Areitio | **Spain** | 1979 | 302 | 188 |
| 5 | SQUASH | Cameron Pilley | **Australia** | 2014 | 283.24 | 176 |
| 6 | TENNIS | Samuel Groth | **Australia** | 2012 | 263 | 163.4 |
| 7 | LACROSSE | Zak Dorn | **USA** | 2014 | 186.68 | 116 |
| 8 | ICE HOCKEY | Alexander Ryazantsev | **Russia** | 2012 | 183.7 | 114.1 |
| 9 | BASEBALL (BAT SWING) | Justin Upton | **USA** | 2012 | 171.4 | 106.5 |
| 10 | CRICKET (BOWL) | Shoaib Akhtar | **Pakistan** | 2003 | 161.3 | 100.2 |

## FURTHER FAST SWINGS

· In 2003, New Zealand table tennis player Lark Brandt achieved a world record serve of 112.5 kph (70 mph).
· Australian softball player Zara Mee pitched a ball at a world record speed of 111 kph (69 mph) in 2005.

## TOP 10...
# MOST DANGEROUS SPORTS

As this Top 10 reveals, it isn't just the fast sports that can prove fatal...

| | SPORT | TOTAL FATALITIES |
|---|---|---|
| 1 | MOTOR RACING | 379 |
| 2 | MOTORCYCLE RACING | 109 |
| 3 | SOCCER | 51 |
| 4 | BOXING | 48 |
| 5 | SKIING | 36 |
| 6 | SCUBA DIVING | 33 |
| 7 | CYCLING | 28 |
| 8 | HORSE RACING | 26 |
| 9 | PARACHUTING | 21 |
| 10 | CRICKET | 12 |

## SKIING

This popular sport and pastime was first practised competitively during the 18th century.

EARLY VERSIONS OF SOCCER DATE BACK NEARLY **2,500** YEARS

## MOTOR RACING

With speeds exceeding 250 kph (160 mph), and hairpin turns, it isn't surprising that professional motor car racing has such a high death toll.

## MORE DANGERS

· In Motorboat Racing, 11 people have died in competitive events.
· The sport of polo, played on horseback, has seen eight recorded deaths.

## NÜRBURGRING

Based in the German village of Nürburg in Rhineland-Palatinate, this circuit facility can hold 150,000 people.

# TOP 10...
# DEADLIEST CIRCUITS

Racing circuits all over the world have claimed the lives of drivers competing at high speed...

| | TRACK | FATALITIES (DRIVERS) | FATALITIES (MECHANICS/ SPECTATORS/WORKERS) | FATALITIES (TOTAL) |
|---|---|---|---|---|
| 1 | SNAEFELL MOUNTAIN COURSE | 245 | 14 | 269 |
| 2 | CIRCUIT DE LA SARTHE LE MANS | 22 | 83 | 105 |
| 3 | AUTODROMO NAZIONALE MONZA | 52 | 36 | 88 |
| 4 | NÜRBURGRING | 73 | 3 | 76* |
| 5 | INDIANAPOLIS MOTOR SPEEDWAY | 42 | 29 | 71 |
| 6 | CIRCUIT DE SPA-FRANCORCHAMPS | 48 | 4 | 52 |
| 7 | DAYTONA INTERNATIONAL SPEEDWAY | 35 | 1 | 36 |
| 8 | SUZUKA CIRCUIT | 17 | 1 | 18 |
| 9 | THOMPSON INTERNATIONAL SPEEDWAY | 8 | – | 8 |
| 10 | CIRCUIT DE MONACO | 4 | – | 4 |

*Allegedly more people are killed every year as the circuit is open to the public and deaths are kept private by the families/not made public.

THE LE MANS CAR RACE HAS BEEN HELD SINCE
**1923**

## AUTODROMO NAZIONALE MONZA

This Italian race circuit in Monza first opened on Sep 3, 1922. The most recent fatality was that of a marshal in 2000.

**RICARDO LÓPEZ HAS WON**

# 38

**OF HIS WINS**
BY KNOCK-OUT

## 📍 JOE CALZAGHE

Known as the "Italian Dragon" (echoing his Italian and Welsh heritage), with his 1.8-m (73-in) reach, Calzaghe won 32 of his 46 fights by knock-out.

## 📍 JACK MCAULIFFE

Born March 24, 1866 in Cork, Ireland, McAuliffe's career included five draws, no defeats, and 22 knock-outs. His name was immortalized when he was inducted into the International Boxing Hall of Fame in 1995.

**TOP 10...**

# GREATEST BOXERS WHO RETIRED UNDEFEATED

This Top 10 isn't about the number of championship wins, it's measured by the fighters who never lost a match during their career...

| | NAME | COUNTRY | YEARS | UNDEFEATED WINS |
|---|---|---|---|---|
| 1 | JIMMY BARRY | USA | 1894-99 | 59 |
| 2 | RICARDO LÓPEZ | Mexico | 1990-2002 | 51 |
| 3 | ROCKY MARCIANO | USA | 1952-56 | 49 |
| 4 | JOE CALZAGHE | Wales | 1997-2008 | 46 |
| 5 | SVEN OTTKE | Germany | 1998-2004 | 34 |
| 6 | JACK MCAULIFFE | USA | 1886-93 | 30 |
| 7 | HARRY SIMON | Namibia | 1998-2002 | 29 |
| 8 | MIHAI LEU | Romania | 1997 | 28 |
| 9 | EDWIN VALERO | Venezuela | 2006-10 | 27 |
| 10 | TERRY MARSH | England | 1987 | 26 |

## TOP 10...
# MOST SUCCESSFUL MMA FIGHTERS

Comparing all the Mixed Martial Art fighters around the world, these are the winning 10...

| | NAME | COUNTRY | WINS |
|---|---|---|---|
| 1 | TRAVIS FULTON | USA | 253 |
| 2 | DAN SEVERN | USA | 101 |
| 3 | JEREMY HORN | USA | 91 |
| 4 | TRAVIS WIUFF | USA | 73 |
| 5 | LUIS SANTOS | Brazil | 61 |
| = | IGOR VOVCHANCHYN | Ukraine | 61 |
| 7 | IKUHISA MINOWA | Japan | 59 |
| 8 | YUKI KONDO | Japan | 57 |
| 9 | ADRIAN SERRANO | USA | 56 |
| 10 | JEFF MONSON | USA | 55 |

DAN SEVERN WON
## 60
OF HIS MMA FIGHTS BY
**SUBMISSION**

# MMA TOP FIVE

**TRAVIS FULTON**
## 253

Here is how the top fighters' stats compare visually...

**DAN SEVERN**
## 101

**JEREMY HORN**
## 91

**TRAVIS WIUFF**
## 73

**LUIS SANTOS**
## 61

## ⦿ JEREMY HORN

The Omaha, Nebraska, USA-born MMA fighter made his pro debut in 1996.

RUNGRADO MAY
DAY STADIUM
FIRST OPENED
**MAY 1,
1989**

1963

## TOP 10...

# TEAMS WITH THE **LARGEST STADIUMS**

Oftentimes, a team's home stadium can become at least as famous as the team itself...

| | TEAM | SPORT | LOCATION | STADIUM | CAPACITY |
|---|---|---|---|---|---|
| 1 | KOREA DPR | Soccer | Pyongyang, North Korea | Rungrado May Day | 150,000 |
| 2 | INDIA AIFF (+ OTHERS) | Soccer | Kolkata, India | Salt Lake Stadium | 120,000 |
| 3 | MICHIGAN WOLVERINES | Football | Ann Arbor, USA | Michigan Stadium | 109,901 |
| 4 | PENN STATE NITTANY LIONS | Football | Pennsylvania, USA | Beaver Stadium | 107,282 |
| 5 | TEXAS A&M AGGIES | Football | Texas, USA | Kyle Field | 106,511 |
| 6 | CLUB AMÉRICA, MEXICO NATIONAL FOOTBALL | Soccer | Mexico City, Mexico | Estadio Azteca | 105,000 |
| 7 | OHIO STATE BUCKEYES | Football | Ohio, USA | Ohio Stadium | 104,944 |
| 8 | TENNESSEE VOLUNTEERS | Football | Tennessee, USA | Neyland Stadium | 102,455 |
| 9 | LSU TIGERS | Football | Louisiana, USA | Tiger Stadium | 102,321 |
| 10 | ALABAMA CRIMSON TIDE | Football | Alabama, USA | Bryant-Denny Stadium | 101,821 |

## 📍 PENN STATE NITTANY LIONS

Pennsylvania State University is the home of this collective of athletics teams. It includes the women's basketball team called the Lady Lions, which has 850 wins to its name.

## REAL MADRID C.F.

Real Madrid's Cristiano Ronaldo's official Facebook Page has more "Likes" than his team's... over 103 million.

LA LAKERS BEGAN LIFE IN

# 1947

### AS THE
MINNEAPOLIS LAKERS

TOP 10...

# MOST POPULAR
# TEAMS ON FACEBOOK

With all but one of these entries being soccer teams, it's a clear indication that it is the most popular sport in the world...

| | TEAM | SPORT | FACEBOOK "LIKES" |
|---|---|---|---|
| 1 | FC BARCELONA | Soccer | 80,691,653 |
| 2 | REAL MADRID C.F. | Soccer | 79,967,476 |
| 3 | MANCHESTER UNITED FC | Soccer | 63,462,398 |
| 4 | CHELSEA FC | Soccer | 40,893,080 |
| 5 | ARSENAL | Soccer | 31,860,902 |
| 6 | FC BAYERN MÜNCHEN | Soccer | 27,603,866 |
| 7 | LIVERPOOL FC | Soccer | 24,645,807 |
| 8 | A.C. MILAN | Soccer | 23,846,441 |
| 9 | LA LAKERS | Basketball | 20,994,567 |
| 10 | MANCHESTER CITY FC | Soccer | 18,416,382 |

## FC BARCELONA

Founded more than 115 years ago, this is the most popular soccer team in the world. They have won over 80 major competitions, including the UEFA Champions League four times.

📍 **SHAHID KHAN AFRIDI**

The retired cricketer, known by his nickname "Boom Boom Afridi", played 611 matches during his career.

## TOP 10...
# SPORTS THAT PROPEL
# THE BALL THE FURTHEST

If the sport features a ball being kicked, thrown, or struck, here is how they measure up with the record ball distances...

| | SPORT | CHAMPION | COUNTRY | YEAR | DISTANCE (M) | (FT) |
|---|---|---|---|---|---|---|
| 1 | LONG DRIVE GOLF | Mike Dobbyn | **USA** | **2007** | 503.83 | 1,653 |
| 2 | PGA GOLF | Mike Austin | **USA** | **1974** | 471 | 1,545.3 |
| 3 | BASEBALL (HOME RUN) | Mickey Mantle | **USA** | **1960** | 193.24 | 634 |
| 4 | CRICKET (HIT/SIX) | Shahid Khan Afridi | **Pakistan** | **2013** | 158 | 518.37 |
| 5 | BASEBALL (THROW) | Glen Gorbous | **Canada** | **1957** | 135.89 | 445.83 |
| 6 | CRICKET (THROW) | Roald Bradstock | **USA** | **2010** | 132.6 | 435.04 |
| 7 | SOCCER (GOAL) | Asmir Begović | **Bosnia** | **2014** | 91.9 | 301.5 |
| 8 | RUGBY | Gerry Brand | **South Africa** | **1932** | 77.7 | 254.92 |
| 9 | FOOTBALL (FIELD GOAL) | Ching Do Kim | **Hawaii** | **1944** | 71.32 | 234 |
| 10 | SOCCER (THROW IN) | Thomas Gronnemark | **Denmark** | **2010** | 51.33 | 168.4 |

## GOING THE DISTANCE

Here's a visual guide to how these ball distances compare...

| | |
|---|---|
| LONG DRIVE GOLF | **1,653 FT** |
| PGA GOLF | **1,545.3 FT** |
| BASEBALL (HOME RUN) | **634 FT** |
| BASEBALL (THROW) | **445.83 FT** |

📍 **MICKEY MANTLE**

Called "The Mick," the Dallas, Texas, USA-born star struck 536 home runs in his 17-year baseball career.

**JAVIER SOTOMAYOR**

Being 1.95 m (6.4 ft) is a useful height when mastering the high jump. It helped Sotomayor win 21 medals.

TOP 10...

# HIGHEST JUMPERS IN SPORT

Sports competitors who can jump extremely high aren't exclusively found in the discipline of gymnastics...

| | NAME | COUNTRY | SPORT | HEIGHT THEY CAN JUMP (CM) | (IN) |
|---|---|---|---|---|---|
| 1 | YAN ZHI CHENG | China | Acrobatics | 246 | 97 |
| 2 | JAVIER SOTOMAYOR | Cuba | High Jump | 245 | 96.5 |
| 3 | TONY JAA | Thailand | Martial Arts | 200 | 78.7 |
| 4 | KADOUR ZIANI | France | Basketball | 142.2 | 56 |
| 5 | HANUMAN | India | Parkour | 137.2 | 54 |
| 6 | LEONEL MARSHALL | Cuba | Volleyball | 127 | 50 |
| 7 | GERALD SENSABAUGH | USA | American Football | 117 | 46 |
| 8 | JARED BRENNAN | Australia | Australian Football | 102 | 40.2 |
| 9 | MAC BENNETT | USA | Ice Hockey | 86 | 34 |
| 10 | CRISTIANO RONALDO | Portugal | Soccer | 78 | 30.7 |

**JARED BRENNAN**

After retiring in 2013, Brennan had notched up 175 matches.

TONY JAA ALSO HAS

**14**

ACTING CREDITS

## WHEELS & WALKING

- If you'd like to attempt an "around the world" bike journey, you must complete a minimum of 40,075 km (24,901.5 miles). 28,970 km (18,001.1 miles) must be achieved on the bicycle, and the total time taken has to include any flights and other methods of travel.
- From June 20, 1970 to October 5, 1974, American David Kunst walked around the world. During his journey across four continents, Kunst traveled 23,258.2 km (14,452 miles).

ALL-ROUND SPORTSMAN AND ADVENTURER STEVE FOSSETT SET

**116**

RECORDS DURING HIS LIFETIME

## TOP 10...

# FASTEST AROUND THE **WORLD TRIPS**

Many people have completed an around the world challenge using various methods of transportation, and these achieved it in the quickest times...

| | VEHICLE/METHOD | DIRECTION | RECORD HOLDER | YEAR | TIME |
|---|---|---|---|---|---|
| 1 | CIVILIAN JET | Westbound | Tom Horne, Bud Ball, John McGrath, Ross Oetjen, Eric Parker | 2013 | 0d, 41h, 7m |
| 2 | SCHEDULED FLIGHTS | Westbound | David J. Springbett | 1980 | 0d, 44h, 6m |
| 3 | SCHEDULED FLIGHTS* | Westbound | Michael Quandt | 2004 | 0d, 66h, 31m |
| 4 | BALLOON (MIXED) | Westbound | Steve Fossett | 2002 | 13.5d |
| 5 | BALLOON (MIXED) | Westbound | Bertrand Piccard, Brian Jones | 1999 | 19d, 21h, 55m |
| 6 | TRIMARAN (CREWED) | Eastbound | Loïck Peyron (skipper of a crew of 13) | 2012 | 45d, 13h, 42m, 53s |
| 7 | TRIMARAN (SOLO) | Eastbound | Francis Joyon | 2008 | 57d, 13h, 34m, 6s |
| 8 | MONOHULL (SOLO) | Eastbound | François Gabart | 2013 | 78d, 2h, 16m |
| 9 | BICYCLE* | Eastbound | Alan Bate | 2010 | 106d, 10h, 33m |
| 10 | MONOHULL (SOLO) | Westbound | Jean-Luc Van Den Heede | 2003 | 122d, 14h, 3m, 49s |

*(6 continents)

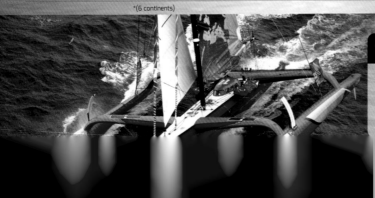

## 📍 FRANCIS JOYON

This vessel is the IDEC, a 28.9-m (95-ft)-long Trimaran in which Joyon achieved his solo world record.

THE TOUR DE FRANCE FIRST BEGAN IN **1903**

## TOP 10...
# LONGEST ENDURANCE SPORT EVENTS

Running a marathon (42.195 km / 26.219 miles) is a popular challenge of stamina and fitness, but there are events around the world that demand much more of the human body...

| | NAME | EVENTS INCLUDED | TOTAL DISTANCE COVERED (KM) | (MI) |
|---|---|---|---|---|
| 1 | **TOUR DE FRANCE^** | Cycling | 5,745*^ | 3,569.8*^ |
| 2 | **GREAT DIVIDE MOUNTAIN BIKE ROUTE** | Mountain biking | 4,418* | 2,745* |
| 3 | **FREEDOM TRAIL CHALLENGE** | Mountain biking | 2,350* | 1,460.2* |
| 4 | **ULTRAMARATHON** | Running and walking | 1,609+* | 1,000+* |
| 5 | **YUKON QUEST** | Dog sledding | 1,609 | 1,000* |
| 6 | **MONGOL DERBY** | Horse riding | 1,000** | 621.37** |
| 7 | **IRON MAN TRIATHALON** | Swimming (3.7 km), cycling (1.6 km), marathon (42.2 km) | 226.31 | 140.6 |
| 8 | **POWERMAN ZOFINGEN DUATHALON** | Hill run (9.9 km), hill cycle (150 km), hill run (29.9 km) | 190 | 118.06 |
| 9 | **QUADRATHALON** | Swimming (4 km), kayaking (20 km), cycling (100 km), running (21 km) | 145 | 90.1 |
| 10 | **CANADIAN SKI MARATHON** | Skiing | 160 | 99.42 |

^Longest ever Tour de France, staged in 1926
* Multi-day event
** Multiple horses used

## CANADIAN SKI MARATHON

Since 1967, this epic event has been held annually between Ottawa and Montreal. The difference between this marathon and most others is that it is not competitive. Those taking part simply challenge themselves.

## ⦿ ULTRAMARATHON

For those who love stamina-based challenges, the International Association of Ultrarunners (IAU) has held 100-km World Championships most years since 1987.

EXTRE
HEAT
DANG

## OLE EINAR BJØRNDALEN

Aptly known as "The King of the Biathlon", this Norwegian athlete has achieved 95 wins since his first professional win in 1992.

**TOP 10...**

# MOST SUCCESSFUL OLYMPIANS

Combining bronze, silver, and gold across all Olympic Games held so far, these are the competitors who have won the most medals...

| | NAME | DISCIPLINE | COUNTRY | YEARS | GOLD | SILVER | BRONZE | TOTAL |
|---|---|---|---|---|---|---|---|---|
| 1 | MICHAEL PHELPS | Swimming | USA | 2004-12 | 18 | 2 | 2 | 22 |
| 2 | LARISA LATYNINA | Gymnastics | Soviet Union (now Russia) | 1956-64 | 9 | 5 | 4 | 18 |
| 3 | NIKOLAI ANDRIANOV | Gymnastics | Soviet Union (now Russia) | 1972-80 | 7 | 5 | 3 | 15 |
| 4 | OLE EINAR BJØRNDALEN | Biathlon | Norway | 1998-2014 | 8 | 4 | 1 | 13 |
| = | BORIS SHAKHLIN | Gymnastics | Soviet Union (now Russia) | 1956-64 | 7 | 4 | 2 | 13 |
| = | EDOARDO MANGIAROTTI | Fencing | Italy | 1936-60 | 6 | 5 | 2 | 13 |
| = | TAKASHI ONO | Gymnastics | Japan | 1952-64 | 5 | 4 | 4 | 13 |
| 8 | PAAVO NURMI | Athletics | Finland | 1920-28 | 9 | 3 | 0 | 12 |
| = | BJØRN DÆHLIE | Cross-country Skiing | Norway | 1992-98 | 8 | 4 | 0 | 12 |
| = | BIRGIT FISCHER | Canoeing | Germany | 1980-2004 | 8 | 4 | 0 | 12 |

INCLUDING HIS 22 OLYMPIC MEDALS, MICHAEL PHELPS HAS WON

# 77

CAREER MEDALS

## LARISA LATYNINA

Latynina retired in 1966. She garnered a total of 46 championship-level medals.

## ⊘ BÉATRICE HESS

During the 2000 Paralympic Games, held in Sydney, Australia, Hess broke a total of nine world records during her events.

## ⊘ HEINZ FREI

His extraordinary career has seen him take part in every Summer Paralympics between 1984-2008.

CLAUDIA HENGST WAS INDUCTED INTO THE PARALYMPIC HALL OF FAME IN
# 2008

## TØP 10...
# MOST SUCCESSFUL PARALYMPIANS

Examining all of the Paralympic Games to date, these are the competitors who took home the most combined medals...

| | NAME | DISCIPLINE(S) | COUNTRY | YEARS | GOLD | SILVER | BRONZE | TOTAL |
|---|---|---|---|---|---|---|---|---|
| 1 | TRISCHA ZORN | Swimming | USA | 1980-2004 | 31 | 9 | 5 | 55 |
| 2 | HEINZ FREI | Athletics, Cycling, Cross-country Skiing | Switzerland | 1984-2000 | 14 | 6 | 11 | 31 |
| 3 | JONAS JACOBSSON | Shooting | Sweden | 1980-2012 | 17 | 4 | 9 | 30 |
| 4 | RAGNHILD MYKLEBUST | Biathlon, Cross-country Skiing, Ice sledge racing | Norway | 1988-2002 | 22 | 3 | 2 | 27 |
| 5 | ROBERTO MARSON | Athletics, Fencing | Italy | 1964-76 | 16 | 7 | 3 | 26 |
| 6 | BÉATRICE HESS | Swimming | France | 1984-2004 | 20 | 5 | 0 | 25 |
| = | CLAUDIA HENGST | Swimming | Germany | 1988-2004 | 13 | 4 | 8 | 25 |
| 8 | FRANK HÖFLE | Biathlon, Cross-country Skiing, Cycling | Germany | 1992-2002 | 14 | 5 | 5 | 24 |
| 9 | REINHILD MOELLER | Alpine Skiing, Athletics | Germany | 1980-2006 | 19 | 3 | 1 | 23 |
| = | MATTHEW COWDREY | Swimming | Australia | 2004-12 | 13 | 7 | 3 | 23 |

## GREAT BRITAIN

At the 2012 Summer Olympics and Paralympics (held in London, England), a total of 829 Team GB athletes and an additional 13 team members took part.

**TOP 10...**

# MOST SUCCESSFUL
# OLYMPIC NATIONS

Including both the Summer and Winter Olympic Games held over the decades to date, these countries triumphed the most...

| | COUNTRY/TEAM | TOTAL SUMMER GAMES' MEDALS | TOTAL WINTER GAMES' MEDALS | TOTAL MEDALS |
|---|---|---|---|---|
| 1 | USA | 2,400 | 281 | 2,681 |
| 2 | RUSSIA (+ SOVIET UNION ERA) | 1,407 | 318 | 1,725 |
| 3 | GERMANY (+ EAST & WEST ERA) | 1,186 | 358 | 1,544 |
| 4 | GREAT BRITAIN | 780 | 26 | 806 |
| 5 | FRANCE | 671 | 109 | 780 |
| 6 | ITALY | 549 | 114 | 663 |
| 7 | SWEDEN | 483 | 144 | 627 |
| 8 | CHINA | 473 | 53 | 526 |
| 9 | HUNGARY | 476 | 6 | 482 |
| 10 | AUSTRALIA | 468 | 12 | 480 |

**OF MO FARAH'S 22 MEDALS 14 ARE GOLD**

## RUSSIA

As different named nations, including the Soviet Union, Russia has competed in Olympic Games since 1900.

# FIRST OLYMPIC GAMES

The first modern Olympic Games took place in Athens, Greece in April 1896, to signify and honour the fact that Ancient Greece was where the first ever Olympic Games occurred.

## USA

This nation's total Paralympic medals includes an impressive 794 gold medals.

## TOP 10...
# MOST SUCCESSFUL
# PARALYMPIC NATIONS

Adding together all of the medals won across Summer and Winter Paralympic Games, here are the most successful countries...

| | COUNTRY/TEAM | TOTAL SUMMER GAMES' MEDALS | TOTAL WINTER GAMES' MEDALS | TOTAL MEDALS |
|---|---|---|---|---|
| 1 | USA | 1,939 | 277 | 2,216 |
| 2 | GREAT BRITAIN | 1,557 | 21 | 1,578 |
| 3 | GERMANY (+ EAST & WEST ERA) | 1,327 | 345 | 1,672 |
| 4 | FRANCE | 921 | 152 | 1,073 |
| 5 | CANADA | 947 | 135 | 1,082 |
| 6 | AUSTRALIA | 1,013 | 30 | 1,043 |
| 7 | CHINA | 794 | 0 | 794 |
| 8 | SPAIN | 630 | 43 | 673 |
| 9 | POLAND | 626 | 44 | 670 |
| 10 | SWEDEN | 564 | 99 | 663 |

CANADA HAS WON
# 390
**GOLD MEDALS**
AT THE
PARALYMPICS

# FIRST PARALYMPIC GAMES

The Paralympics is the second biggest sporting event on the planet. The first Summer Games were held in Rome, Italy in September 1960, with the first Winter Games established in Örnsköldsvik, Sweden in February 1976.

AT THE 2004 SUMMER OLYMPICS IN ATHENS, GREECE
## 201
NATIONS TOOK PART

## TOP 10...
# MOST EXPENSIVE OLYMPICS

Hosting the Olympic Games is no small feat, especially when it comes to the financial outlay required...

| | HOST CITY | COUNTRY | YEAR | EST. TOTAL COST ($) |
|---|---|---|---|---|
| 1 | SOCHI | Russia | 2014 | 51 billion |
| 2 | LONDON | UK | 2012 | 14.6 billion |
| 3 | BARCELONA | Spain | 1992 | 9.3 billion |
| 4 | ATHENS | Greece | 2004 | 9 billion |
| 5 | VANCOUVER | Canada | 2010 | 6.4 billion |
| 6 | MOSCOW | Soviet Union (now Russia) | 1980 | 1.35 billion |
| 7 | SALT LAKE CITY | USA | 2002 | 1.2 billion |
| 8 | MONTREAL | Canada | 1976 | 1.1 billion |
| 9 | CALGARY | Canada | 1988 | 718 million |
| 10 | LOS ANGELES | USA | 1984 | 413 million |

## 📍 SOCHI

2,873 athletes took part in the 2014 Winter Olympics, held in Sochi, Russia.

# TOP FIVE BUDGETS

Here is a visual representation of the most costly Olympics...

| SOCHI | LONDON | BARCELONA | ATHENS | VANCOUVER |
|---|---|---|---|---|
| 51 BILLION | 14.6 BILLION | 9.3 BILLION | 9 BILLION | 6.4 BILLION |

## 📍 LONDON

The specially constructed Olympic Stadium in Stratford, East London, took three years to build.

## TOP 10...
# MOST HOSTED OLYMPIC & PARALYMPIC NATIONS

These 10 countries have been home to Games more times than any others...

| | COUNTRY | TOTAL TIMES HOSTED OLYMPIC & PARALYMPIC GAMES |
|---|---|---|
| **1** | **USA** | **11** |
| **2** | **FRANCE** | **6** |
| **3** | **CANADA** | **5** |
| **=** | **ITALY** | **5** |
| **=** | **JAPAN** | **5** |
| **=** | **UK** | **5** |
| **7** | **AUSTRIA** | **4** |
| **=** | **GERMANY** | **4** |
| **=** | **GREECE** | **4** |
| **=** | **NORWAY** | **4** |

## ◉ JAPAN

The Japan Paralympic Committee was established in 1999. Its headquarters are in Tokyo, Japan's capital city.

## SOUTH KOREA

South Korea hosted two events, the Summer Olympics and Summer Paralympics in 1988.

FRANCE'S PARALYMPIC ATHLETES HAVE WON A TOTAL OF
# 354
GOLD MEDALS

## TOP 10...

# BIGGEST **BOXING** MOVIES

From Rocky to robots, these are the most successful boxing films of all time...

| | MOVIE | YEAR RELEASED | BOX OFFICE (WORLDWIDE $) |
|---|---|---|---|
| 1 | ROCKY IV | 1985 | 300,473,716 |
| 2 | REAL STEEL | 2011 | 299,268,508 |
| 3 | MILLION DOLLAR BABY | 2004 | 216,763,646 |
| 4 | ROCKY BALBOA | 2006 | 155,721,132 |
| 5 | THE FIGHTER | 2010 | 129,190,869 |
| 6 | ROCKY III | 1982 | 125,049,125 |
| 7 | ROCKY V | 1990 | 119,946,358 |
| 8 | ROCKY | 1976 | 117,235,147 |
| 9 | CINDERELLA MAN | 2005 | 108,539,911 |
| 10 | ALI | 2001 | 87,713,825 |

## MILLION DOLLAR BABY

This 2004 boxing drama, directed by Clint Eastwood, won four of its seven nominated Academy Awards, including Best Picture.

ROBOT BOXING MOVIE REAL STEEL IS

**127 MINS LONG**

# ROCKY

Here is how all of Sylvester Stallone's boxing dramas box office takings compare...

| ROCKY | ROCKY II | ROCKY III | ROCKY IV | ROCKY V | ROCKY BALBOA |
|---|---|---|---|---|---|
| $117,235,147 | $85,182,160 | $125,049,125 | $300,473,716 | $119,946,358 | $155,721,132 |

## THE FIGHTER

This multi-award-winning drama was actor Mark Wahlberg's 26th feature film.

## BLIND SIDE

Actor Quinton Aaron played the lead role of Michael Oher, and this film is based on Oher's life story.

THE LONGEST YARD ACTOR ADAM SANDLER HAS

**57**
ACTOR CREDITS

TOP 10...

# BIGGEST FOOTBALL MOVIES

Both dramas and comedies feature in this Top 10...

| | MOVIE | YEAR RELEASED | BOX OFFICE (WORLDWIDE $) |
|---|---|---|---|
| 1 | THE BLIND SIDE | 2009 | 309,208,309 |
| 2 | THE LONGEST YARD | 2005 | 190,320,568 |
| 3 | THE WATERBOY | 1998 | 185,991,646 |
| 4 | REMEMBERING THE TITANS | 2000 | 136,706,683 |
| 5 | ANY GIVEN SUNDAY | 1999 | 100,230,832 |
| 6 | FRIDAY NIGHT LIGHTS | 2004 | 61,950,770 |
| 7 | INVINCIBLE | 2006 | 58,480,828 |
| 8 | VARSITY BLUES | 1999 | 54,294,169 |
| 9 | RADIO | 2003 | 53,293,628 |
| 10 | THE REPLACEMENTS | 2000 | 50,054,511 |

## FRIDAY NIGHT LIGHTS

This is based on the real Texan town of Odessa and their inspiring high school team, The Permian High Panthers.

## ALL FAST & ALL FURIOUS

Here is how the box office figures compare for the first six F&F films...

| THE FAST & THE FURIOUS | 2 FAST 2 FURIOUS | THE FAST & THE FURIOUS: TOKYO DRIFT | FAST & FURIOUS 2009 | FAST FIVE | FAST & FURIOUS 6 |
|---|---|---|---|---|---|
| $207,283,925 | $236,350,661 | $158,468,292 | $363,164,265 | $626,137,675 | $788,679,850 |

## TOP 10...

# BIGGEST CAR RACING MOVIES

One film franchise almost dominates this entire Top 10 chart...

| | MOVIE | YEAR RELEASED | BOX OFFICE (WORLDWIDE $) |
|---|---|---|---|
| 1 | FURIOUS 7 | 2015 | 1,499,723,320 |
| 2 | FAST & FURIOUS 6 | 2013 | 788,679,850 |
| 3 | FAST FIVE | 2011 | 626,137,675 |
| 4 | CARS 2 | 2011 | 559,852,396 |
| 5 | CARS | 2006 | 461,983,149 |
| 6 | FAST & FURIOUS | 2009 | 363,164,265 |
| 7 | TURBO | 2013 | 282,570,682 |
| 8 | 2 FAST 2 FURIOUS | 2003 | 236,350,661 |
| 9 | THE FAST & THE FURIOUS | 2001 | 207,283,925 |
| 10 | NEED FOR SPEED | 2014 | 203,277,636 |

TURBO'S TIE-IN VIDEO GAME TURBO: SUPER STUNT SQUAD HAS SOLD

## 1,300 COPIES

## ⦿ CARS 2

*Cars 2*'s director (and Pixar co-founder) John Lasseter has helmed 18 animated productions since his 1979 short film *Lady And The Lamp*.

## THE ENDLESS SUMMER II

This iconic surfing documentary features music by The Sandals, and is directed and narrated by Bruce Brown.

### TOP 10...
# BIGGEST SPORTS DOCS

Covering every sport, these are the 10 most successful theatrically released sports documentaries...

| | DOCUMENTARY MOVIE | SPORT | YEAR OF RELEASE | BOX OFFICE ($ WORLDWIDE) |
|---|---|---|---|---|
| 1 | HOOP DREAMS | Basketball | 1994 | 11,830,611 |
| 2 | SENNA | F1 Racing | 2010 | 8,212,430 |
| 3 | THE ENDLESS SUMMER | Surfing | 1966 | 5,000,000 |
| 4 | RIDING GIANTS | Surfing | 2004 | 3,216,111 |
| 5 | WHEN WE WERE KINGS | Boxing | 1996 | 2,789,985 |
| 6 | FREERIDERS | Skiing, Snowboarding | 1998 | 2,750,064 |
| 7 | SNOWRIDERS 2 | Skiing, Snowboarding | 1997 | 2,287,639 |
| 8 | THE ENDLESS SUMMER II | Surfing | 1994 | 2,155,385 |
| 9 | SNOWRIDERS | Skiing, Snowboarding | 1996 | 2,068,490 |
| 10 | BEYOND THE MAT | Wrestling | 1999 | 2,053,648 |

## HOOP DREAMS

After five years of filming and 250 hours of footage, this project became a multi-award-winning basketball documentary.

## RIDING GIANTS

Successful surfer and pro-skater with the Z-Boys, Stacy Peralta, narrated and directed this celebration of surfing.

SNOWRIDERS DIRECTOR WARREN MILLER HAS MADE

# 55
DOCUMENTARIES

# MUSIC

## YEARS OF DOWNLOADS

This pie chart shows how the below data looks by each year...

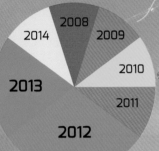

2008
2009
2014
2010
2013
2011
2012

## MUMFORD & SONS

The folk pop group from London, England were formed in late 2007.

AS A SOLO ARTIST, WILL.I.AM HAS RELEASED
**4** STUDIO ALBUMS

## TOP 10...

# MOST DOWNLOADED ALBUMS EVER

For more than a decade, the sales figures of digital music downloads have been logged. These are the 10 most-sold album downloads...

| | ARTIST(S) | ALBUM | YEAR RELEASED | TOTAL DOWNLOADS |
|---|---|---|---|---|
| 1 | ADELE | 21 | 2011 | 3,086,000 |
| 2 | MUMFORD & SONS | Sigh No More | 2009 | 1,729,000 |
| 3 | IMAGINE DRAGONS | Night Visions | 2012 | 1,485,000 |
| 4 | VARIOUS | Frozen (Original Soundtrack) | 2013 | 1,435,000 |
| 5 | TAYLOR SWIFT | 1989 | 2014 | 1,409,000 |
| 6 | MUMFORD & SONS | Babel | 2012 | 1,400,000 |
| 7 | BEYONCÉ | Beyoncé | 2013 | 1,394,000 |
| 8 | EMINEM | Recovery | 2010 | 1,357,000 |
| 9 | TAYLOR SWIFT | Red | 2012 | 1,200,000 |
| 10 | LADY GAGA | The Fame | 2008 | 1,104,000 |

## TAYLOR SWIFT

The American pop star was 16 years old when her self-titled debut album was released on Oct 24, 2006.

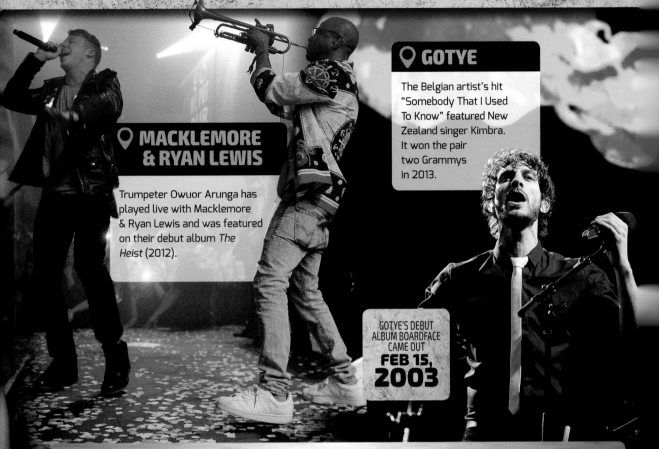

## MACKLEMORE & RYAN LEWIS

Trumpeter Owuor Arunga has played live with Macklemore & Ryan Lewis and was featured on their debut album *The Heist* (2012).

## GOTYE

The Belgian artist's hit "Somebody That I Used To Know" featured New Zealand singer Kimbra. It won the pair two Grammys in 2013.

GOTYE'S DEBUT ALBUM BOARDFACE CAME OUT
**FEB 15, 2003**

## TOP 10...
# MOST **DOWNLOADED SONGS** EVER

These days, the singles' chart is dominated by the digital download format, with millions of music fans choosing to purchase songs this way rather than on CD or vinyl...

| | ARTIST(S) | SONG | YEAR RELEASED | TOTAL DOWNLOADS |
|---|---|---|---|---|
| 1 | THE BLACK EYED PEAS | I Gotta Feeling | 2009 | 8,625,000 |
| 2 | ADELE | Rolling in the Deep | 2010 | 8,282,000 |
| 3 | LMFAO FT. LAUREN BENNETT & GOONROCK | Party Rock Anthem | 2001 | 7,997,000 |
| 4 | GOTYE FT. KIMBRA | Somebody That I Used To Know | 2011 | 7,789,000 |
| 5 | MACKLEMORE & RYAN LEWIS FT. WANZ | Thrift Shop | 2012 | 7,682,000 |
| 6 | CARLY RAE JEPSEN | Call Me Maybe | 2011 | 7,509,000 |
| 7 | IMAGINE DRAGONS | Radioactive | 2012 | 7,478,000 |
| 8 | ROBIN THICKE FT. T.I. & PHARRELL | Blurred Lines | 2013 | 7,285,000 |
| 9 | LADY GAGA | Poker Face | 2008 | 7,177,000 |
| 10 | FLORIDA GEORGIA LINE | Cruise | 2012 | 7,131,000 |

## TOP 10...
# BIGGEST SELLING
# DIGITAL ALBUMS 2014

Several music stars from all the different genres had huge releases in 2014, but these 10 outsold all the rest...

| | ARTIST(S) | ALBUM | TOTAL DOWNLOADS |
|---|---|---|---|
| 1 | TAYLOR SWIFT | 1989 | 1,409,000 |
| 2 | VARIOUS | Frozen (Soundtrack) | 1,261,000 |
| 3 | SAM SMITH | In the Lonely Hour | 573,000 |
| 4 | VARIOUS | Guardians of the Galaxy (Soundtrack) | 556,000 |
| 5 | ED SHEERAN | X | 455,000 |
| 6 | LORDE | Pure Heroine | 437,000 |
| 7 | COLDPLAY | Ghost Stories | 425,000 |
| 8 | BEYONCÉ | Beyoncé | 422,000 |
| 9 | PENTATONIX | That's Christmas to Me | 403,000 |
| 10 | J COLE | 2014 Forest Hills Drive | 366,000 |

## LORDE

Real name Ella Marija Lani Yelich-O'Connor, New Zealander Lorde's debut *The Love Club EP* was released Mar 8, 2013, when she was 15.

COLDPLAY CELEBRATE
## 20 YEARS
TOGETHER IN 2016

## GUARDIANS OF THE GALAXY

Groot first appeared in comics in 1960, with the other Guardians from the 2014 movie first showing up in comics in the '70s. The movie made $774,176,600 at the box office.

# DIGITAL TOP FIVE

This is how the best-selling digital albums compare visually...

| TAYLOR SWIFT | VARIOUS | SAM SMITH | VARIOUS | ED SHEERAN |
|---|---|---|---|---|
| 1,409,000 | 1,261,000 | 573,000 | 556,000 | 455,000 |

## LIL JON

The American rapper's 2013 collaboration with French artist DJ Snake, "Turn Down for What," was featured in a number of films and their promos, including 2014's *22 Jump Street.*

DJ SNAKE PRODUCED LADY GAGA'S **BORN THIS WAY** ALBUM IN 2011

TOP 10...

# BIGGEST SELLING DIGITAL SONGS 2014

Be they singles or just popular songs from an album, these 10 tunes were the best-sellers of 2014...

| | ARTIST(S) | SONG | TOTAL DOWNLOADS |
|---|---|---|---|
| 1 | PHARRELL WILLIAMS | Happy | 6,455,000 |
| 2 | JOHN LEGEND | All of Me | 4,674,000 |
| 3 | KATY PERRY FT. JUICY J | Dark Horse | 4,430,000 |
| 4 | MEGHAN TRAINOR | All About That Bass | 4,357,000 |
| 5 | IGGY AZALEA FT. CHARLI XCX | Fancy | 3,974,000 |
| 6 | JASON DERULO FT. 2 CHAINZ | Talk Dirty | 3,959,000 |
| 7 | DJ SNAKE & LIL JON | Turn Down for What | 3,449,000 |
| 8 | TAYLOR SWIFT | Shake It Off | 3,431,000 |
| 9 | IDINA MENZEL | Let It Go | 3,370,000 |
| 10 | SAM SMITH | Stay With Me | 3,340,000 |

## CHARLI XCX

This eclectic English pop artist provided the chorus vocals for Iggy Azalea's huge 2014 song, "Fancy."

## JOHN LEGEND

Aside from his five studio albums and five live records, the multi-award-winning American singer-songwriter has been featured on 54 records by other artists.

## IGGY AZALEA

Australian rapper Azalea collaborated with British vocalist Rita Ora for her 2014 single "Black Widow."

CHILDREN'S SONGS MADE UP

**0.3%**

OF THE MOST POPULAR SONG GENRE IN 2014

**TOP 10...**

# MOST POPULAR GENRE OF SONGS 2014

Pop artists had a great 2014, but rock stars still outsold them...

| | GENRE | % OF TOTAL SALES |
|---|---|---|
| 1 | ROCK | 21.3 |
| 2 | POP | 21.1 |
| 3 | R&B/HIP-HOP | 19.1 |
| 4 | COUNTRY | 12.0 |
| 5 | DANCE/ELECTRONIC | 4.6 |
| 6 | CHRISTIAN/GOSPEL | 2.8 |
| 7 | LATIN | 1.8 |
| 8 | HOLIDAY/SEASONAL | 0.9 |
| 9 | JAZZ | 0.6 |
| 10 | CLASSICAL | 0.5 |

## MUSIC FANS

In the US, 93 percent of the entire population spends more than 25 hours every week listening to music. Comparing the different locations where music is enjoyed, 25 percent of listening occurs in the car, and 41 percent of people use their smartphone to access music.

## TOP 10...
# MOST **STREAMED** ARTISTS 2014

These artists had the most successful albums of 2014 that were streamed in full this many times...

| | ARTIST(S) | TOTAL AUDIO STREAMS |
|---|---|---|
| 1 | SAM SMITH | 285,271,000 |
| 2 | ARIANA GRANDE | 260,176,000 |
| 3 | LORDE | 257,961,000 |
| 4 | VARIOUS (FROZEN SOUNDTRACK) | 218,997,000 |
| 5 | KATY PERRY | 216,535,000 |
| 6 | ED SHEERAN | 204,933,000 |
| 7 | BEYONCÉ | 162,408,000 |
| 8 | LUKE BRYAN | 125,736,000 |
| 9 | PHARRELL WILLIAMS | 111,198,000 |
| 10 | TAYLOR SWIFT | 26,143,000 |

### ◉ SAM SMITH

This British pop star was born May 19, 1992

### MAGIC!

This Canadian reggae rock group's 2013 debut single "Rude" reached number one in the singles chart in seven countries. The song itself had over 72 million audio streams, but the full album it came from *Don't Kill the Magic*, didn't clock enough streams to get into the above Top 10.

MUSIC FANS ENJOYED
**164** BILLION
STREAMS IN 2014

229

##  MARIAH CAREY

In 24 years, since her 1990 debut, Carey has released 14 studio albums.

## EMINEM

The American rapper's film *8 Mile* (2002) made $242,875,078 at the box office worldwide.

MARIAH CAREY HAS BEEN IN

**8**

**FEATURE** FILMS

### TOP 10...

# BIGGEST **SELLING** **ARTISTS** EVER

Counting every musical artist from every genre, these 10 have sold the most singles and albums...

| | ARTIST | TOTAL ALBUM SALES |
|---|---|---|
| 1 | GARTH BROOKS | 70,238,000 |
| 2 | THE BEATLES | 66,320,000 |
| 3 | METALLICA | 54,669,000 |
| 4 | MARIAH CAREY | 54,579,000 |
| 5 | CELINE DION | 52,349,000 |
| 6 | EMINEM | 45,868,000 |
| 7 | GEORGE STRAIT | 45,655,000 |
| 8 | TIM MCGRAW | 42,395,000 |
| 9 | ALAN JACKSON | 40,737,000 |
| 10 | PINK FLOYD | 39,433,000 |

# BIGGEST MUSIC STARS

Here is how the top five biggest selling artists compare visually...

**Celine Dion** 52,349,000

**Garth Brooks** 70,238,000

**Mariah Carey** 54,579,000

**The Beatles** 66,320,000

**Metallica** 54,669,000

## ALANIS MORISSETTE

The multi-award-winning Canadian artist has been making music since her 1991 debut *Alanis*. Her 25 international awards include 12 JUNO Awards, Canada's most prestigious music awards ceremony.

ALANIS MORISSETTE HAS MADE
**8**
STUDIO ALBUMS

## WHITNEY HOUSTON

The American singer tragically died on Feb 11 2012, aged 48. She had global success with s studio albums. Her soundtracks included *The Bodyguard*, which she also starred in. The film made $411,006,740 at the box office.

TOP 10...

# BIGGEST SELLING ALBUMS EVER

Since the SoundScan era began in 1991, when music sales were first properly tracked, these are the 10 best-selling albums of all time...

| | ARTIST | ALBUM | YEAR RELEASED | TOTAL SALES |
|---|---|---|---|---|
| 1 | METALLICA | Metallica | 1991 | 16,077,000 |
| 2 | SHANIA TWAIN | Come On Over | 1997 | 15,584,000 |
| 3 | ALANIS MORISSETTE | Jagged Little Pill | 1995 | 14,968,000 |
| 4 | THE BEATLES | Beatles 1 | 2000 | 12,438,000 |
| 5 | BACKSTREET BOYS | Millennium | 1999 | 12,252,000 |
| 6 | WHITNEY HOUSTON/VARIOUS | The Bodyguard Soundtrack | 1992 | 12,150,000 |
| 7 | SANTANA | Supernatural | 1999 | 11,861,000 |
| 8 | BOB MARLEY & THE WAILERS | Legend | 1984 | 11,715,000 |
| 9 | CREED | Human Clay | 1999 | 11,696,000 |
| 10 | NSYNC | No Strings Attached | 2000 | 11,159,000 |

## ANNEKE VAN GIERSBERGEN

The acclaimed Dutch artist has released six solo albums. She has also sung lead vocals on five releases by Devin Townsend, and has featured on over 20 other collaboration projects since 1995.

THE ROCK GENRE AMOUNTS TO
### 24.7%
OF ALL STREAMED MUSIC

## AMPLIFIED

The first ever electric guitar available to buy was the Rickenbacker Electro A-22 in 1932.

TOP 10...
# MOST POPULAR GENRES OF ALL TIME

Contrary to what you might expect, rock is the most successful genre by a long way...

| | GENRE | % OF TOTAL SALES |
|---|---|---|
| 1 | ROCK | 29.0 |
| 2 | R&B/HIP-HOP | 17.2 |
| 3 | POP | 14.9 |
| 4 | COUNTRY | 11.2 |
| 5 | DANCE/ELECTRONIC | 3.4 |
| 6 | CHRISTIAN/GOSPEL | 3.1 |
| 7 | LATIN | 2.6 |
| = | HOLIDAY/SEASONAL | 2.6 |
| 9 | JAZZ | 1.4 |
| = | CLASSICAL | 1.4 |

## DEVIN TOWNSEND

Eclectic Canadian artist Devin Townsend's 25-year career spans multiple bands, projects, and genres, including heavy rock, metal, folk, and ambient. He has released more than 20 studio albums under various monikers, including the Devin Townsend Project's 2014 double album $Z^2$, comprising the records "Sky Blue" and "Dark Matters."

ARIANA GRANDE
WAS BORN ON
**JUNE 26,**
**1993**

## ◉ ED SHEERAN

As well as his solo albums and soundtrack work, Sheeran has released a book *Ed Sheeran: A Visual Journey*. His lifelong friend (and album artist) Phillip Butah provided illustrations for the book.

**TOP 10...**
# BIGGEST
# SONG-SELLING
# ARTISTS 2014

When it comes to shifting individual songs and singles, these 10 were the best in 2014...

| | ARTIST(S) | TOTAL SINGLES/SONGS SOLD |
|---|---|---|
| 1 | ARIANA GRANDE | 8,313,000 |
| 2 | VARIOUS (FROZEN SOUNDTRACK) | 7,982,000 |
| 3 | KATY PERRY | 7,742,000 |
| 4 | PHARRELL WILLIAMS | 7,344,000 |
| 5 | TAYLOR SWIFT | 7,210,000 |
| 6 | SAM SMITH | 6,782,000 |
| 7 | BEYONCÉ | 4,829,000 |
| 8 | LORDE | 4,683,000 |
| 9 | LUKE BRYAN | 4,579,000 |
| 10 | ED SHEERAN | 4,493,000 |

## ◉ LUKE BRYAN

Country star Luke Bryan released a series of *Spring Break* EPs from 2009-present to coincide with the US holiday break period.

235

## TOP 10...
# BIGGEST SELLING
# ALBUM GENRES
# 2014

Rock fans are still buying more albums than the rest of the record-buying public...

| | GENRE | % OF TOTAL ALBUM SALES |
|---|---|---|
| 1 | ROCK | 33.2 |
| 2 | R&B/HIP-HOP | 13.9 |
| 3 | COUNTRY | 11.8 |
| 4 | POP | 10.8 |
| 5 | CHRISTIAN/GOSPEL | 3.6 |
| = | HOLIDAY/SEASONAL | 3.6 |
| 7 | LATIN | 2.4 |
| 8 | CLASSICAL | 2.1 |
| 9 | DANCE/ELECTRONIC | 2.0 |
| = | JAZZ | 2.0 |

SIA HAS RELEASED/
BEEN FEATURED ON
# 34
## SINGLES

## 📍 SIA

Australian singer-songwriter Sia has also written for several other artists, including Rihanna, Zero 7, Carly Rae Jepsen, and Katy Perry.

## 📍 MACHINE HEAD

The iconic heavy rock/metal outfit have released eight studio albums and two live albums since the highly influential 1994 debut album, *Burn My Eyes*.

# GENRE SPLIT

This is how the top five from the above chart compare visually...

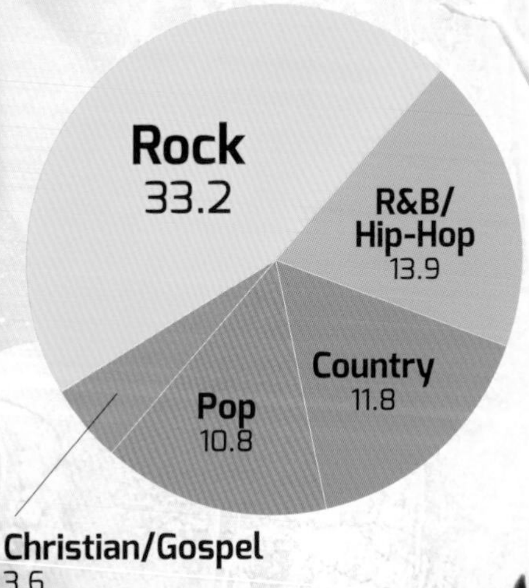

**Rock**
33.2

**R&B/Hip-Hop**
13.9

**Country**
11.8

**Pop**
10.8

**Christian/Gospel**
3.6

## PENTATONIX

The a capella group's seasonal record "That's Christmas to Me" was released Oct 21, 2014. They released a Christmas EP called *PTXmas* Nov 12, 2012.

PENTATONIX HAVE RELEASED

**7**

EPS AND ALBUMS SINCE 2012

TOP 10...

# BIGGEST SELLING ALBUMS (ALL FORMATS) 2014

When it comes to assessing individual album sales from 2014, pop stars had the biggest successes...

| | ARTIST(S) | ALBUM | TOTAL DOWNLOADS |
|---|---|---|---|
| 1 | TAYLOR SWIFT | 1989 | 3,661,000 |
| 2 | VARIOUS | Frozen (Soundtrack) | 3,527,000 |
| 3 | SAM SMITH | In the Lonely Hour | 1,207,000 |
| 4 | PENTATONIX | That's Christmas to Me | 1,139,000 |
| 5 | VARIOUS | Guardians of the Galaxy (Soundtrack) | 898,000 |
| 6 | BEYONCÉ | Beyoncé | 878,000 |
| 7 | BARBRA STREISAND | Partners | 856,000 |
| 8 | LORDE | Pure Heroine | 841,000 |
| 9 | ONE DIRECTION | Four | 814,000 |
| 10 | ERIC CHURCH | Outsiders | 811,000 |

## FROZEN

Disney's 2013 hit *Frozen* is the seventh biggest film of all time. Its soundtrack features 22 cues by the film's composer Christophe Beck, along with *Frozen*'s songs, including the Oscar-winning "Let It Go," performed by Idina Menzel.

GARTH BROOKS
HAS RELEASED
## 19
STUDIO AND
LIVE ALBUMS

## ◉ LANA DEL REY

Winner of 11 international
music awards, Del
Rey's 2015 album
*Honeymoon* is her
follow-up to 2014's
*Ultraviolence*.

## ◉ BRANTLEY GILBERT

His third album *Just As
I Am* was released May
19, 2014 and includes
"Bottoms Up," which
reached number one.

TOP 10...
# BIGGEST SELLING
# CD ALBUMS 2014 (USA)

With the popularity of streaming and the continued success of digital
downloads, the CD format popularity has declined since its 1990s boom...

| | ARTIST(S) | ALBUM | TOTAL SALES |
|---|---|---|---|
| **1** | **VARIOUS** | Frozen (Original Soundtrack) | **2,264,000** |
| **2** | **TAYLOR SWIFT** | 1989 | **2,228,000** |
| **3** | **PENTATONIX** | That's Christmas to Me | **736,000** |
| **4** | **BARBRA STREISAND** | Partners | **723,000** |
| **5** | **SAM SMITH** | In the Lonely Hour | **614,000** |
| **6** | **VARIOUS** | Now 50 | **585,000** |
| **7** | **GARTH BROOKS** | Man Against Machine | **518,000** |
| **8** | **LUKE BRYAN** | Crash My Party | **516,000** |
| **9** | **JASON ALDEAN** | Old Boots, New Dirt | **512,000** |
| **10** | **BRANTLEY GILBERT** | Just As I Am | **490,000** |

## PHYSICAL FORMATS

The purchasing trend for physical
versions of albums has changed
dramatically between 2013 and
2014. Although more than 150
million units of CDs, vinyl, and
cassettes were sold in the US
alone, this is a 21 million drop from
2013's total physical sales.

## AMY WINEHOUSE

Filmmaker Asif Kapadia directed the 2015 documentary about Winehouse's life called *Amy*.

## JACK WHITE

Since 1997, this American artist's bands have included The White Stripes (6 studio albums), The Raconteurs (2 studio albums), and The Dead Weather (2 studio albums).

THE BLACK KEYS HAVE RELEASED

# 8

STUDIO ALBUMS SINCE 2002

TOP 10...

# BIGGEST SELLING VINYL ALBUMS 2014 (USA)

The most popular vinyl releases were a mixture of new records and reissues of classics...

| | ARTIST(S) | ALBUM | YEAR RELEASED | TOTAL SALES |
|---|---|---|---|---|
| 1 | JACK WHITE | Lazaretto | 2014 | 86,700 |
| 2 | ARCTIC MONKEYS | AM | 2013 | 58,700 |
| 3 | LANA DEL REY | Born To Die | 2012 | 42,100 |
| 4 | THE BEATLES | Abbey Road | 1969 | 38,200 |
| 5 | BOB MARLEY & THE WAILERS | Legend | 1984 | 37,800 |
| 6 | THE BLACK KEYS | Turn Blue | 2014 | 34,200 |
| 7 | THE BEATLES | Sgt. Pepper's Lonely Hearts Club Band | 1967 | 33,600 |
| 8 | LANA DEL REY | Ultraviolence | 2014 | 31,800 |
| 9 | MILES DAVIS | Kind of Blue | 1959 | 31,700 |
| 10 | AMY WINEHOUSE | Back To Black | 2006 | 27,800 |

## TOP 10...
# MOST **PLAYED SONGS** OF 2014 (RADIO)

Radio airplay is still an important method of music reaching its audience, and these 10 artists received hundreds of thousands of spins...

| | ARTIST | SONG | TOTAL RADIO PLAYS |
|---|---|---|---|
| 1 | JOHN LEGEND | All of Me | 816,000 |
| 2 | PHARRELL WILLIAMS | Happy | 760,000 |
| 3 | KATY PERRY FT. JUICY J | Dark Horse | 738,000 |
| 4 | SAM SMITH | Stay With Me | 609,000 |
| 5 | NICO & VINZ | Am I Wrong | 604,000 |
| 6 | ONE REPUBLIC | Counting Stars | 589,000 |
| 7 | BASTILLE | Pompeii | 576,000 |
| 8 | MAGIC! | Rude | 569,000 |
| 9 | LORDE | Team | 565,000 |
| 10 | JASON DERULO FT. 2 CHAINZ | Talk Dirty | 496,000 |

## ⦿ ONE REPUBLIC

This band's 2007 debut album *Dreaming Out Loud* featured the hit "Apologize," produced by Timbaland, who also produced Chris Cornell's 2009 solo album *Scream*.

ONE REPUBLIC SINGER RYAN TEDDER HAS WRITTEN/CO-WRITTEN

# 192 SONGS

## ⦿ NICO & VINZ

Formerly known as Envy, this Norwegian duo officially became Nico & Vinz in 2014.

# RADIO GRAPHICS

Here is how the five most-played songs from the above chart compare visually...

| JOHN LEGEND 816,000 | PHARRELL WILLIAMS 760,000 | KATY PERRY FT. JUICY J 738,000 | SAM SMITH 609,000 | NICO & VINZ 604,000 |

## VINYL FIGHTS BACK

Although streaming increased in popularity by 54 percent in 2014 (with 164 billion streams) vinyl records are 52 percent more popular than they were in 2013. They now account for 6 percent of all physical format sales.

TOP 10...

# MOST ON-DEMAND STREAMS 2014 (AUDIO + VIDEO)

Combining music video and audio-only streams, here are the 10 songs that achieved on-demand greatness in 2014...

| | ARTIST | SONG<br>AUDIO & VIDEO STREAMS | TOTAL<br>ON-DEMAND |
|---|---|---|---|
| 1 | KATY PERRY FT. JUICY J | Dark Horse | 268,322,000 |
| 2 | IGGY AZALEA FT. CHARLI XCX | Fancy | 264,981,000 |
| 3 | MEGHAN TRAINOR | All About That Bass | 252,239,000 |
| 4 | JOHN LEGEND | All of Me | 236,105,000 |
| 5 | IDINA MENZEL | Let It Go | 234,536,000 |
| 6 | PHARRELL WILLIAMS | Happy | 230,098,000 |
| 7 | ARIANA GRANDE FT. IGGY AZALEA | Problem | 205,584,000 |
| 8 | TAYLOR SWIFT | Shake It Off | 193,502,000 |
| 9 | JASON DERULO FT. 2 CHAINZ | Talk Dirty | 188,410,000 |
| 10 | MAGIC! | Rude | 181,471,000 |

### ◉ JASON DERULO

His debut single "Whatcha Say" (2009) sampled Imogen Heap's 2005 hit "Hide And Seek."

MEGHAN TRAINOR'S DEBUT ALBUM TITLE (2014) FEATURES
**11** TRACKS

## TOVE LO

Singer Tove Lo won Artist of the Year and Song of the Year at the 2015 Grammis in her home country of Sweden.

TOP 10...

# MOST ON-DEMAND STREAMS (AUDIO) 2014

Streaming is becoming the most popular way of consuming music, as these tens-of-millions figures prove...

| | ARTIST | SONG AUDIO STREAMS | TOTAL ON-DEMAND |
|---|---|---|---|
| 1 | JOHN LEGEND | All of Me | 96,923,000 |
| 2 | IGGY AZALEA FT. CHARLI XCX | Fancy | 91,272,000 |
| 3 | KATY PERRY FT. JUICY J | Dark Horse | 87,051,000 |
| 4 | TOVE LO | Habits (Stay High) | 73,989,000 |
| 5 | PHARRELL WILLIAMS | Happy | 73,114,000 |
| 6 | MAGIC! | Rude | 72,975,000 |
| 7 | BASTILLE | Pompeii | 71,745,000 |
| 8 | ARIANA GRANDE FT. IGGY AZALEA | Problem | 70,583,000 |
| 9 | DISCLOSURE FT. SAM SMITH | Latch | 67,317,000 |
| 10 | SAM SMITH | Stay With Me | 65,199,000 |

BASTILLE HAVE WON 4 OF THEIR

**23**

INTERNATIONAL AWARD NOMINATIONS

## DISCLOSURE

British duo Disclosure's debut album *Settle* (2013) was nominated for a Best Dance/Electronic Award at the 2014 Grammys.

# VIDEO STARS

The viewership of online music videos increased 49.3 percent in 2014 from the previous year. 85.3 billion video streams were recorded in the US, compared to 57.1 billion in 2013. Audio streams increased by 60.5 percent, with nearly 79 billion accounted for in 2014.

SHAKE IT OFF WAS TAYLOR SWIFT'S
## 32ND SINGLE

⦿ NICKI MINAJ

The Trinidad and Tobago pop star's 2014 album *The Pinkprint* features the hit single "Anaconda," featured in the below Top 10.

⦿ PHARRELL WILLIAMS

The Virginia, USA-born artist's huge hit "Happy" was originally written and recorded for the 2013 *Despicable Me 2* soundtrack.

## TOP 10...
# MOST ON-DEMAND STREAMS (VIDEO) 2014

An engaging music video, especially one that goes viral, can lead to an artist's play-count reaching hundreds of millions, like these 10...

| | ARTIST | SONG VIDEO STREAMS | TOTAL ON-DEMAND |
|---|---|---|---|
| 1 | MEGHAN TRAINOR | All About That Bass | 188,749,000 |
| 2 | IDINA MENZEL | Let It Go | 183,918,000 |
| 3 | KATY PERRY FT. JUICY J | Dark Horse | 181,270,000 |
| 4 | IGGY AZALEA FT. CHARLI XCX | Fancy | 173,709,000 |
| 5 | TAYLOR SWIFT | Shake It Off | 167,360,000 |
| 6 | PSY | Gangnam Style | 166,043,000 |
| 7 | PHARRELL WILLIAMS | Happy | 156,984,000 |
| 8 | NICKI MINAJ | Anaconda | 143,183,000 |
| 9 | JOHN LEGEND | All of Me | 139,182,000 |
| 10 | ARIANA GRANDE FT. IGGY AZALEA | Problem | 135,001,000 |

## BOB MARLEY

The reggae legend's first major release was with The Wailers, entitled "The Wailing Wailers" (1965)

TOP 10...
# MOST FACEBOOK LIKES – SOLO

If you like the social network platform, you may like some of these "Likes"...

| | SOLO ARTISTS | "LIKES" |
|---|---|---|
| 1 | SHAKIRA | 100,236,949 |
| 2 | EMINEM | 91,952,626 |
| 3 | RIHANNA | 81,507,273 |
| 4 | MICHAEL JACKSON | 75,229,300 |
| 5 | BOB MARLEY | 73,288,764 |
| 6 | JUSTIN BIEBER | 72,536,731 |
| 7 | KATY PERRY | 72,008,262 |
| 8 | TAYLOR SWIFT | 71,038,836 |
| 9 | BEYONCÉ KNOWLES | 63,123,958 |
| 10 | LADY GAGA | 61,621,066 |

MICHAEL JACKSON RELEASED
# 27
STUDIO ALBUMS
(INCLUDING WITH THE JACKSONS & TWO POSTHUMOUS ALBUMS)

## SHAKIRA

This Colombian singer and producer has been a professional music artist since she was 13, when her debut album *Magia* was released in 1991.

## TOP 10...
# MOST **FACEBOOK** **LIKES** – BANDS/ GROUPS

This Top 10 is an extremely eclectic array of rock, pop, metal, and hip-hop...

| | | BAND/GROUP | "LIKES" |
|---|---|---|---|
| | 1 | LINKIN PARK | 62,992,958 |
| | 2 | THE BLACK EYED PEAS | 46,491,190 |
| | 3 | THE BEATLES | 41,477,956 |
| | 4 | MAROON 5 | 37,720,522 |
| | 5 | ONE DIRECTION | 37,500,906 |
| | 6 | COLDPLAY | 37,405,321 |
| | 7 | METALLICA | 36,954,593 |
| | 8 | LMFAO | 32,172,895 |
| | 9 | GREEN DAY | 31,986,182 |
| | 10 | AC/DC | 29,832,553 |

## ⊘ THE BLACK EYED PEAS

The hip-hop/pop/dance collective has made six studio albums. Their debut, *Behind the Front*, was released in June 1998.

THE BEATLES' PAUL MCCARTNEY HAS RELEASED
# 32
STUDIO AND LIVE ALBUMS (INCLUDING WITH WINGS)

## ⊘ LINKIN PARK

Aside from their six studio albums, five live albums and three remix records, Linkin Park have also released 14 fan-club exclusive albums.

# BAND & SOLO LIKES

**SHAKIRA**
100,236,949

**EMINEM**
91,952,626

Here is how the top 2 of each chart compare...

**LINKIN PARK**
62,992,958

**THE BLACK EYED PEAS**
46,491,190

# SOCIAL NETWORKING

## JAY Z

The American rapper and producer star has 3.19 million Twitter followers, and he doesn't follow anybody. His wife, Beyoncé, does have an official Twitter handle with 14 million followers, but she hasn't used it since August 2013. She prefers to use Instagram, where she has 36 million followers.

JUSTIN TIMBERLAKE'S WIFE JESSICA BIEL HAS **744,000** TWITTER FOLLOWERS

## ⊙ JUSTIN TIMBERLAKE

Including his time with boyband NSYNC, Timberlake has released eight studio records, including two Christmas albums.

**TOP 10...**

# MOST **TWITTER** FOLLOWERS – SOLO

When it comes to solo artists, it's wall-to-wall pop stars for the 10 most followed on Twitter...

| | ARTIST | TWITTER HANDLE | FOLLOWING | FOLLOWERS |
|---|---|---|---|---|
| 1 | KATY PERRY | @katyperry | 156 | 69,794,971 |
| 2 | JUSTIN BIEBER | @justinbieber | 210,893 | 63,903,692 |
| 3 | TAYLOR SWIFT | @taylorswift13 | 198 | 57,557,203 |
| 4 | LADY GAGA | @ladygaga | 132,638 | 46,621,837 |
| 5 | RIHANNA | @rihanna | 1,178 | 45,443,094 |
| 6 | JUSTIN TIMBERLAKE | @jtimberlake | 107 | 45,325,532 |
| 7 | BRITNEY SPEARS | @britneyspears | 398,920 | 41,842,626 |
| 8 | JENNIFER LOPEZ | @JLo | 1,485 | 32,064,421 |
| 9 | SHAKIRA | @shakira | 161 | 31,127,272 |
| 10 | SELENA GOMEZ | @selenagomez | 1,267 | 29,056,64 |

## ⊙ SELENA GOMEZ

The American actress/singer's debut feature film was 2003's *Spy Kids 3-D: Game Over*.

## ONE DIRECTION

This pop group have released four studio albums since 2011. Their 2013 documentary film *One Direction: This Is Us* was directed by *Super Size Me* director Morgan Spurlock.

## TOP 10...
# MOST **TWITTER** **FOLLOWERS** – GROUPS/BANDS

The 10 most popular bands/groups on Twitter here covers many more genres than the solo artists' chart opposite...

| | ARTIST | TWITTER HANDLE | FOLLOWING | FOLLOWERS |
|---|---|---|---|---|
| 1 | ONE DIRECTION | @onedirection | 3,901 | 23,557,249 |
| 2 | COLDPLAY | @coldplay | 1,474 | 14,674,990 |
| 3 | MAROON 5 | @maroon5 | 400 | 10,840,187 |
| 4 | LMFAO | @LMFAO | 1,564 | 8,587,852 |
| 5 | 5 SECONDS OF SUMMER | @5SOS | 33,141 | 6,659,937 |
| 6 | THE BLACK EYED PEAS | @bep | 48,019 | 5,307,622 |
| 7 | LINKIN PARK | @linkinpark | 43 | 4,730,286 |
| 8 | GREEN DAY | @greenday | 41 | 3,829,724 |
| 9 | PARAMORE | @paramore | 164 | 3,738,745 |
| 10 | ZOÉ | @zoetheband | 165 | 3,227,844 |

THE MUSIC VIDEO FOR HATE TO SEE YOUR HEART BREAK BY PARAMORE FT. JOY WILLIAMS:
**6.7 MILLION VIEWS**

## GREEN DAY

The core line-up of Billie Joe Armstrong (vocals/guitar), Mike Dirnt (bass) and Tré Cool (drums) has remained unchanged since 1990.

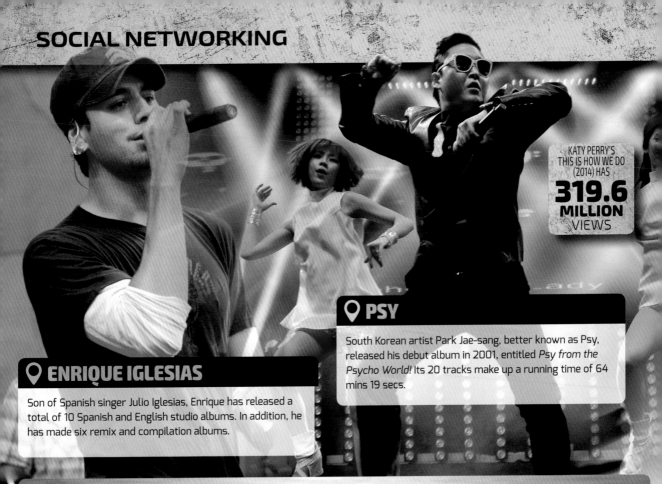

KATY PERRY'S
THIS IS HOW WE DO
(2014) HAS
**319.6**
MILLION
VIEWS

**⦿ PSY**

South Korean artist Park Jae-sang, better known as Psy, released his debut album in 2001, entitled *Psy from the Psycho World!* Its 20 tracks make up a running time of 64 mins 19 secs.

**⦿ ENRIQUE IGLESIAS**

Son of Spanish singer Julio Iglesias, Enrique has released a total of 10 Spanish and English studio albums. In addition, he has made six remix and compilation albums.

TOP 10...
# OFFICIAL MUSIC VIDEOS WITH THE MOST VIEWS

Katy Perry and PSY both appear twice in this Top 10, where the play-count for all music videos featured nears 11 billion...

| | SONG | ARTIST | DATE UPLOADED | VIEWS |
|---|---|---|---|---|
| 1 | GANGNAM STYLE | PSY | July 15, 2012 | 2,330,461,830 |
| 2 | BABY | Justin Bieber ft. Ludacris | Feb 19, 2010 | 1,165,682,469 |
| 3 | DARK HORSE | Katy Perry ft. Juicy J | Feb 20, 2014 | 946,616,794 |
| 4 | ROAR | Katy Perry | Sep 5, 2013 | 916,795,380 |
| 5 | PARTY ROCK ANTHEM | LMFAO ft. Lauren Bennett & GoonRock | Mar 8, 2011 | 868,132,367 |
| 6 | BAILANDO | Enrique Iglesias ft. Descemer Bueno & Gente De Zona | Apr 11, 2014 | 862,510,268 |
| 7 | LOVE THE WAY YOU LIE | Eminem ft. Rihanna | Aug 5, 2010 | 861,674,424 |
| 8 | WAKA WAKA (THIS TIME FOR AFRICA) | Shakira ft. Freshlyground | June 4, 2010 | 850,835,539 |
| 9 | BLANK SPACE | Taylor Swift | Nov 10, 2014 | 839,543,142 |
| 10 | GENTLEMAN | PSY | Apr 13, 2013 | 843,447,266 |

## TOP 10...
# MOST **STREAMED MUSIC GENRES**

Unlike the other genre charts in this zone, R&B/Hip-Hop comes out as the most popular...

| | GENRE | % OF TOTAL STREAMS |
|---|---|---|
| 1 | R&B/HIP-HOP | 28.5 |
| 2 | ROCK | 24.7 |
| 3 | POP | 21.1 |
| 4 | DANCE/ELECTRONIC | 6.8 |
| 5 | COUNTRY | 6.4 |
| 6 | LATIN | 5.0 |
| 7 | CHRISTIAN/GOSPEL | 1.6 |
| 8 | HOLIDAY/SEASONAL | 1.1 |
| 9 | CHILDREN'S | 0.4 |
| 10 | CLASSICAL | 0.3 |

## ROBYN

This Swedish pop/dance artist has made music for over two decades. Her latest, "Do It Again" (2014) is a collaboration with Norwegian duo Röyksopp.

## BIFFY CLYRO

Formed in 1995 in Kilmarnock, Scotland, rockers Biffy Clyro have released six studio albums since 2002, including 2013's double-album *Opposites*, comprised of 20 tracks.

SINCE 1999, BIFFY CLYRO HAVE RELEASED

**28 SINGLES**

## 📍 RIHANNA

Rihanna has released seven solo albums since her debut *Music of the Sun* (2005).

**TOP 10...**

# MOST SUBSCRIBED
# VEVO CHANNEL

Subscribing to an artist's channel means you get notifications of their new uploads...

| | ARTIST | SUBSCRIBERS |
|---|---|---|
| 1 | RIHANNA | 16,394,245 |
| 2 | ONE DIRECTION | 15,881,625 |
| 3 | KATY PERRY | 15,872,648 |
| 4 | EMINEM | 15,374,305 |
| 5 | TAYLOR SWIFT | 13,217,121 |
| 6 | JUSTIN BIEBER | 11,449,809 |
| 7 | NICKI MINAJ | 8,376,739 |
| 8 | DAVID GUETTA | 7,989,098 |
| 9 | BEYONCÉ | 7,532,524 |
| 10 | MILEY CYRUS | 7,330,657 |

RIHANNA WAS
BORN ON
**FEB 20,**
**1988**

## 📍 DAVID GUETTA

French producer Guetta has been a DJ and music-maker since 1984. His six solo albums include 2014's *Listen*, which features guest vocals from more than a dozen artists, including Sia and John Legend.

## HARRY STYLES

The British pop star's group One Direction has 8.9 million Instagram followers, giving Styles more than 21 million fans on that social media platform alone.

ARIANA GRANDE HAS APPEARED ON **41** RECORDED SONGS TO DATE

## ARIANA GRANDE

This Florida, USA-born singer had her first big break in the 2008 stage musical *13*. She played a cheerleader called Charlotte in the award-winning, all-teenage show.

## TOP 10...

# MOST INSTAGRAM FOLLOWERS

The social media platform for sharing photos and visuals attracts millions of fans...

| | ARTIST | HANDLE | FOLLOWERS (MILLIONS) |
|---|---|---|---|
| 1 | BEYONCÉ | @beyonce | 33.1 |
| 2 | ARIANA GRANDE | @arianagrande | 32.3 |
| 3 | SELENA GOMEZ | @selenagomez | 31.3 |
| 4 | TAYLOR SWIFT | @taylorswift | 30.5 |
| 5 | JUSTIN BIEBER | @justinbieber | 27.5 |
| 6 | NICKI MINAJ | @nickiminaj | 22.4 |
| 7 | KATY PERRY | @katyperry | 19.9 |
| 8 | MILEY CYRUS | @mileycyrus | 19.8 |
| 9 | RIHANNA | @badgalriri | 18.9 |
| 10 | HARRY STYLES | @harrystyles | 11.2 |

## BOYS VS. GIRLS

This visual shows just how far the girls tower over the boys in the Top 10 when it comes to attracting Instagram followers...

GIRLS **8**

BOYS **2**

TAYLOR SWIFT
WAS BORN
**DEC 13,
1989**

📍 **BEYONCÉ**

Including her time
with Destiny's Child,
Beyoncé has been
releasing hit singles
and albums for nearly
20 years.

📍 **KATY
PERRY**

Since 2001, American
solo artist Katy Perry
has released four
studio albums, an MTV
Unplugged album, and
19 singles.

TOP 10...

# TOTAL VOLUME (IN SALES, STREAMS, ON-DEMAND STREAMS) 2014

Ranking all artists by a volume value, these were 2014's most
significant across all platforms and formats...

| | ARTIST(S) | ALBUM | TOTAL VOLUME |
|---|---|---|---|
| **1** | **VARIOUS** | Frozen (Soundtrack) | **4,471,000** |
| **2** | **TAYLOR SWIFT** | 1989 | **4,399,000** |
| **3** | **SAM SMITH** | In the Lonely Hour | **2,075,000** |
| **4** | **ARIANA GRANDE** | My Everything | **1,514,000** |
| **5** | **KATY PERRY** | Prism | **1,503,000** |
| **6** | **LORDE** | Pure Heroine | **1,481,000** |
| **7** | **BEYONCÉ** | Beyoncé | **1,469,000** |
| **8** | **ED SHEERAN** | X | **1,396,000** |
| **9** | **PHARRELL WILLIAMS** | Girl | **1,390,000** |
| **10** | **LUKE BRYAN** | Crash My Party | **1,341,000** |

## TEGAN AND SARA

At the 2015 Oscars, the musical duo performed a live rendition of the award-nominated song "Everything Is Awesome" (from *The LEGO Movie*) with their collaborators, The Lonely Island.

### TOP 10...
# MOST POPULAR USA
# TV SPECIALS 2014

Aside from the 2014 State of the Union Address, the most watched TV specials were all related to the art form of music...

| | PROGRAM | NETWORK | VIEWERS |
|---|---|---|---|
| 1 | THE 56TH ANNUAL GRAMMY AWARDS | CBS | 13,779,000 |
| 2 | 2014 MTV VIDEO MUSIC AWARDS | MTV | 12,644,000 |
| 3 | THE OSCARS | ABC | 11,163,000 |
| 4 | THE BET AWARDS 2014 | BET | 10,891,000 |
| 5 | 2014 AMERICAN MUSIC AWARDS | ABC | 5,651,000 |
| 6 | 2014 BILLBOARD MUSIC AWARDS | ABC | 5,450,000 |
| 7 | 2014 MTV MOVIE AWARDS | MTV | 2,411,000 |
| 8 | THE 71ST ANNUAL GOLDEN GLOBE AWARDS | NBC | 2,359,000 |
| 9 | STATE OF THE UNION 2014 | All (TV Event) | 2,088,000 |
| 10 | THE 66TH PRIMETIME EMMY AWARDS | NBC | 1,102,000 |

THE FIRST VERSION OF THE GRAMMYS WAS HELD IN
# 1959

## MUSIC SPECIALS

Here is how the most popular TV Specials* compare according to network...

ABC 3
MTV 2
BET 1
NBC 2
CBS 1

*This pie chart totals 9 rather than 10 as all networks transmitted State of the Union.

## KRISTEN WIIG

For Sia's 2015 Grammy performance of "Chandelier," actress Kristen Wiig performed an artistic dance routine with Sia's regular collaborator Maddie Ziegler.

# MONEY MAKERS

## LA VIE EN ROSE

French actress Marion Cotillard won the 2008 Oscar for Best Leading Actress for playing iconic french singer Édith Piaf.

AS A SOLO ARTIST, TINA TURNER HAS RELEASED

**9 STUDIO ALBUMS**

## WHAT'S LOVE GOT TO DO WITH IT?

Actress Angela Bassett was nominated for the Best Leading Actress Oscar in 1994 for her portrayal of Tina Turner.

## OFF THE CHART BIOPICS

These two biopics just missed out on a place in this Top 10: 1996's Oscar-winning *Shine*, which told the story of Australian pianist David Helfgott, took $35,892,330 at the box office; and 1991's *The Doors*, which dramatised the life of the titular band made $34,416,893 from its theatrical release.

## TOP 10...
# MOST SUCCESSFUL MUSIC BIOPICS

Of all the narrative films made that have been inspired by real-life music artists, these are the 10 most popular of all time...

| | MOVIE | BIOPIC OF | YEAR OF RELEASE | BOX OFFICE ($ WORLDWIDE) |
|---|---|---|---|---|
| 1 | WALK THE LINE | Johnny Cash | 2005 | 186,438,883 |
| 2 | RAY | Ray Charles | 2004 | 124,731,534 |
| 3 | LA VIE EN ROSE | Edith Piaf | 2007 | 86,274,793 |
| 4 | JERSEY BOYS | The Four Seasons | 2014 | 67,347,013 |
| 5 | COAL MINER'S DAUGHTER | Loretta Lynn | 1980 | 67,182,787 |
| 6 | LA BAMBA | Richie Valens | 1987 | 54,215,416 |
| 7 | AMADEUS | Mozart | 1984 | 51,973,029 |
| 8 | NOTORIOUS | Notorious B.I.G. | 2009 | 44,371,751 |
| 9 | WHAT'S LOVE GOT TO DO WITH IT? | Tina Turner | 1993 | 39,100,956 |
| 10 | THE SOLOIST | Nathaniel Ayers | 2009 | 38,332,994 |

**20 FEET FROM STARDOM (2013) MADE**
# $4.945
**MILLION**
AT THE BOX OFFICE

## SIXTO RODRIGUEZ

This American artist was the subject of *Searching For Sugar Man* (2012), which took $3,696,196 at the box office.

**TOP 10...**
# MOST SUCCESSFUL
# MUSIC DOCUMENTARIES

From in-depth, behind-the-scenes films, to more concert-led pieces, these theatrically released music documentaries are the biggest ever...

| | NAME | YEAR RELEASED | BOX OFFICE (WORLDWIDE $) |
|---|---|---|---|
| 1 | MICHAEL JACKSON'S THIS IS IT | 2009 | 261,183,588 |
| 2 | JUSTIN BIEBER: NEVER SAY NEVER | 2011 | 99,036,827 |
| 3 | HANNAH MONTANA/MILEY CYRUS: BEST OF BOTH WORLDS CONCERT | 2008 | 70,642,036 |
| 4 | ONE DIRECTION: THIS IS US | 2013 | 68,532,898 |
| 5 | KATY PERRY: PART OF ME | 2012 | 32,726,956 |
| 6 | MADONNA: TRUTH OR DARE | 1991 | 29,012,935 |
| 7 | JONAS BROTHERS: THE 3D CONCERT EXPERIENCE | 2009 | 23,186,960 |
| 8 | U2 3D | 2008 | 22,730,842 |
| 9 | GLEE: THE 3D CONCERT MOVIE | 2011 | 18,663,238 |
| 10 | SHINE A LIGHT | 2008 | 15,773,351 |

## MUSIC AT THE MOVIES

**THIS IS IT**
$261,183,588

**WALK THE LINE**
$186,438,883

Here is how the top 2 entries from both these charts look combined...

**RAY**
$124,731,534

**NEVER SAY NEVER**
$99,036,827

## ⦿ JUSTIN BIEBER

His second feature documentary, *Believe* (2013) took $6.2 million at the box office, $93 million less than his first.

# OUTER
# SPACE

# MOST ASTRONAUTS LAUNCHED BY A NATION

Of all the countries on Earth, these have focused the most on space exploration...

| | COUNTRY | TOTAL PEOPLE SENT INTO SPACE |
|---|---|---|
| 1 | USA | 334 |
| 2 | RUSSIA | 120 |
| 3 | GERMANY | 11 |
| 4 | CHINA | 10 |
| 5 | CANADA | 9 |
| = | FRANCE | 9 |
| = | JAPAN | 9 |
| 8 | ITALY | 7 |
| 9 | BULGARIA | 2 |
| = | NETHERLANDS | 2 |

## OTHER COUNTRIES

24 countries have each sent one person on a mission into space: Afghanistan, Austria, Brazil, Cuba, Czech Republic, Hungary, India, Israel, Malaysia, Mexico, Mongolia, Poland, Romania, Saudi Arabia, Slovakia, South Africa, South Korea, Spain, Sweden, Switzerland, Syria, Ukraine, UK, and Vietnam.

## ISS

### INTERNATIONAL SPACE STATION

At 239 ft (72.8 m) long and 356 ft (108.5 m) wide, the ISS (International Space Station) is the largest man-made structure in space. It has been occupied for over 14 years by astronauts from 15 different countries. The first ever piece of the ISS was positioned in space in 1998. A maximum of six people can live inside the ISS.

TOTAL PEOPLE
THE ESA
HAS SENT INTO SPACE

**38**

## ⊙ VALERI POLYAKOV

Born in Tula, Russia on April 27, 1942, retired cosmonaut Valeri Polyakov's 1994-95 record for the longest consecutive time spent in space remains unbroken. He is Moscow's current Deputy Director of the Ministry of Public Health.

## THE ESA

The ESA (European Space Agency) includes 18 countries: Austria, Belgium, Czech Republic, Denmark, Finland, France, Germany, Greece, Ireland, Italy, Luxembourg, Netherlands, Norway, Portugal, Spain, Sweden, Switzerland, and UK.

## TOP 10...
# LONGEST HUMAN SPACE FLIGHTS

Some astronauts have completed missions that kept them among the stars for over a year...

| | NAME | COUNTRY | CONSECUTIVE DAYS IN SPACE |
|---|---|---|---|
| 1 | VALERI POLYAKOV | Russia | 437.7 |
| 2 | SERGEI AVDEYEV | Russia | 379.6 |
| 3 | VLADIMIR TITOV | Russia (Soviet Union era) | 365 |
| = | MUSA MANAROV | Russia (Soviet Union era) | 365 |
| 5 | YURI ROMANENKO | Russia (Soviet Union era) | 326.5 |
| 6 | SERGEI KRIKALEV | Russia (Soviet Union era) | 311.8 |
| 7 | VALERI POLYAKOV | Russia (Soviet Union era) | 240.9 |
| 8 | LEONID KIZIM | Russia (Soviet Union era) | 237 |
| = | VLADIMIR SOLOVYOV | Russia (Soviet Union era) | 237 |
| = | OLEG ATKOV | Russia (Soviet Union era) | 237 |

## TOP 10...

# LONGEST TOTAL
# SPACEWALK TIME

During space missions, EVA (Extra-Vehicular Activity) can refer to lunar-based moonwalks and spacewalks...

| | NAME | COUNTRY | TOTAL SPACE WALKING TIME |
|---|---|---|---|
| 1 | ANATOLY SOLOVYEV | Russia | 82:22 |
| 2 | MICHAEL LOPEZ-ALEGRIA | Spain/USA | 67:40 |
| 3 | JERRY L. ROSS | USA | 58:32 |
| 4 | JOHN M. GRUNSFELD | USA | 58:30 |
| 5 | RICHARD MASTRACCHIO | USA | 53:04 |
| 6 | FYODOR YURCHIKHIN | Russia | 51:53 |
| 7 | SUNITA WILLIAMS | USA | 50:40 |
| 8 | STEVEN L. SMITH | USA | 49:48 |
| 9 | MICHAEL FINCKE | USA | 48:37 |
| 10 | STEPHEN G. BOWEN | USA | 47:18 |

## ◉ MICHAEL LOPEZ-ALEGRIA

This Madrid-born astronaut was a crew member on three Space Shuttle missions and achieved ten separate spacewalks. He retired from NASA in 1992 and is now the President of the Commercial Spaceflight Federation. Find out more about its focus on the development of human spaceflight at www. commercialspaceflight.org.

NUMBER OF ARTIFICIAL
SATELLITES
ORBITING EARTH
**2,465**

## GPS EXPLAINED

The US Government began developing the Global Positioning System in 1973. The system now comprises 24 satellites orbiting our planet, the ground control network, and the software and hardware of the user. All three elements work together to provide information such as the exact global location of the user, the weather, and amount of traffic.

TOP 10...
# MOST **ISS VISITS** BY NATION

Since Expedition 1 arrived on November 2, 2000, these nations have sent astronauts to the International Space Station most often...

| | NATION | INDIVIDUAL(S) | ISS CREW MEMBER(S) |
|---|---|---|---|
| **1** | USA | 140 | 46 |
| **2** | RUSSIA | 44 | 37 |
| **3** | CANADA | 7 | 2 |
| **4** | JAPAN | 6 | 4 |
| **5** | ITALY | 5 | 3 |
| **6** | GERMANY | 3 | 2 |
| **7** | FRANCE | 3 | 1 |
| **8** | BELGIUM | 1 | 1 |
| **=** | NETHERLANDS | 1 | 1 |
| **10** | SWEDEN | 1 | 0 |

## ISS VISITS

Here is a graphic representation of how individual visits to the ISS measure up...

USA

BELGIUM/
NETHERLANDS/
SWEDEN

FRANCE
GERMANY
ITALY
JAPAN
CANADA

RUSSIA

## 📍 ANATOLY SOLOVYEV

Retired Russian astronaut Anatoly Solovyev was born in Riga, Latvia. His first mission was on June 7, 1988, visiting the Mir space station, which also marked Bulgarian astronaut Aleksandr Aleksandrov's first spaceflight. Solovyev carried out 16 spacewalks during his career—a world record.

# ASTRONAUTS

## HUBBLE SPACE TELESCOPE

2015 is the 25th anniversary of the Hubble Space Telescope (HST). Named after American astronomer Edwin Hubble, it is co-funded by NASA and ESA. Space Shuttle Discovery took off on April 24, 1990 to deploy HST into Earth's orbit.

## TOP 10...

# MOST EXPENSIVE FUTURE SPACE PROJECTS

Exploring the vacuum of outer space costs nations billions in research, development, construction, and maintenance...

| | PROJECT | FUTURE PLANS | COST ($ BILLIONS) |
|---|---|---|---|
| 1 | INTERNATIONAL SPACE STATION | Developed; could extend until 2028 | 150* |
| 2 | BEIDOU NAVIGATION SATELLITE SYSTEM | Continued development to 2020 | 65.3 |
| 3 | HUBBLE SPACE TELESCOPE | May continue usage until 2020 | 10 |
| 4 | JAMES WEBB SPACE TELESCOPE | Launch date 2018 | 4 |
| 5 | CASSINI–HUYGENS (SATURN EXPLORER) | Mission ends 2017 | 3.26 |
| 6 | ORION MULTI-PURPOSE CREW VEHICLE | First manned mission 2020 | 2.6 |
| 7 | MARS SCIENCE LABORATORY | Ongoing | 2.5 |
| 8 | ALPHA MAGNETIC SPECTROMETER | Continuing to at least 2021 | 2 |
| 9 | JUPITER ICY MOON EXPLORER | Launch date 2022 | 1.3 |
| 10 | JUNO (JUPITER EXPLORATORY CRAFT) | Will arrive at Jupiter 2016 | 1 |

*Including the necessary space shuttle flights/visits

## HERSCHEL SPACE OBSERVATORY

Herschel Space Observatory performed infrared telescopic duties between 2009 and 2013, seeing temperatures in space. The ESA project cost $1.44 billion.

TOP 10...

# BIGGEST
# ASTRONAUT
# MOVIES

Focusing on box office hits that strongly feature real-world human astronauts, these are the most successful...

| | MOVIE | YEAR OF RELEASE | BOX OFFICE ($ WORLDWIDE) |
|---|---|---|---|
| 1 | GRAVITY | 2013 | 716,392,705 |
| 2 | INTERSTELLAR | 2014 | 671,643,910 |
| 3 | ARMAGEDDON | 1998 | 553,709,788 |
| 4 | APOLLO 13 | 1995 | 355,237,933 |
| 5 | MOONRAKER | 1979 | 210,308,099 |
| 6 | 2001: A SPACE ODYSSEY | 1968 | 190,700,000 |
| 7 | SPACE COWBOYS | 2000 | 128,884,132 |
| 8 | MISSION TO MARS | 2000 | 110,983,407 |
| 9 | 2010 | 1984 | 40,400,657 |
| 10 | SUNSHINE | 2007 | 32,017,803 |

## GRAVITY

*Gravity* won seven of its ten Oscar nominations in 2014. London, England's visual effects company Framestore created the computer-generated images that make up 80 per cent of the film. Its director, Mexican filmmaker Alfonso Cuarón, used many long shots, resulting in the film only having 156 shots in total.

## APOLLO 18

Spanish filmmaker Gonzalo López-Gallego's 2011 shocker *Apollo 18* narrowly misses out on the the above Top 10, with box office takings of $25,562,924. This found-footage style horror posited that the cancelled titular mission landed on the moon in 1973 and discovered malevolent aliens.

HUBBLE 3D
(2010 DOCUMENTARY)
MADE

# $47.7
# MILLION

## FARTHEST FROM THE SUN

At a distance of 12 billion km (7.46 billion miles) from the Sun, the pink-coloured "2012 VP113" is the farthest planetoid away from the Sun. With its "VP" initials, some call it "Biden" as a nod to USA Vice President Joe Biden.

### TOP 10...

# PLANETS/ DWARF PLANETS
## NEAREST OUR SUN

These celestial bodies are closest to the giant star at the centre of our solar system...

OUR SOLAR SYSTEM HAS MORE THAN

## 200 BILLION STARS

| | MASS | AVERAGE DISTANCE FROM THE SUN (KM) | (MI) |
|---|---|---|---|
| 1 | MERCURY | 46-70 million | 28-43 million |
| 2 | VENUS | 108 million | 67 million |
| 3 | EARTH | 150 million | 93 million |
| 4 | MARS | 230 million | 142 million |
| 5 | CERES | 419 million | 260 million |
| 6 | JUPITER | 778 million | 483 million |
| 7 | SATURN | 1.4 billion | 0.9 billion |
| 8 | URANUS | 3 billion | 1.9 billion |
| 9 | NEPTUNE | 4.5 billion | 2.8 billion |
| 10 | PLUTO | 5.9 billion | 3.7 billion |

## VENUS DEBATE

*Since its discovery on November 11, 2002, the Earth orbit-crossing asteroid "2002 VE68" left experts perplexed for some time. It became known as Venus' quasi-moon, but it actually orbits the Sun.

## TOP 10...

# PLANETS/DWARF PLANETS WITH MOST MOONS

Our planet only has one moon, but we have discovered that other planets in our solar system have many more natural satellites...

| | PLANET/DWARF PLANET | MOON(S) | | | PLANET/DWARF PLANET | MOON(S) |
|---|---|---|---|---|---|---|
| **1** | **JUPITER** | **67** | | **6** | **MARS** | **2** |
| **2** | **SATURN** | **62** | | **7** | **HAUMEA** | **2** |
| **3** | **URANUS** | **27** | | **8** | **EARTH** | **1** |
| **4** | **NEPTUNE** | **14** | | **9** | **ERIS** | **1** |
| **5** | **PLUTO** | **5** | | **10** | **VENUS** | **1*** |

## THE SUN

At the very centre of our solar system is a giant star that we call the Sun. It is so colossal, it takes up 99.8 per cent of the mass of our entire solar system. Its surface temperature is 10,000 °F (5,500 °C).

**TOP 10...**

# PLANETS/ DWARF PLANETS WITH LONGEST DAYS

Midnight to midnight takes 24 hours on Earth, but on other planetary realms, an Earth day would feel very different...

| | PLANET/DWARF PLANET | EQUIVALENT EARTH TIME |
|---|---|---|
| 1 | VENUS | 243 days |
| 2 | MERCURY | 58.7 days |
| 3 | PLUTO | 6.4 days |
| 4 | ERIS | 25.9 hours |
| 5 | MARS | 24.6 hours |
| 6 | MAKEMAKE | 22.5 hours |
| 7 | URANUS | 17.2 hours |
| 8 | NEPTUNE | 16.1 hours |
| 9 | SATURN | 10.7 hours |
| 10 | JUPITER | 9.9 hours |

## ◉ PLUTO

Pluto was discovered by Clyde Tombaugh on Feb 18, 1930. It was classified as a planet until 2006 when the qualities of what defines a planet were changed. Launched on Jan 19, 2006, NASA's robotic spacecraft New Horizons had its closest approach to dwarf planet Pluto on July 14, 2015.

## ◉ MAKEMAKE

This dwarf planet, along with Haumea and Pluto, can be found in the Kuiper Belt, an area of space outside Neptune's orbit. Makemake takes 111,528.49 days to orbit the Sun.

## 📍 MARS

Named after the Roman god of war, the planet Mars has been a constant source of inspiration for art in all mediums, like *Flash Gordon's Trip To Mars*. This 15-part serial was released in cinemas in 1938.

**TOP 10...**

# FASTEST **PLANETS/ DWARF PLANETS** ORBITING OUR SUN

Using the measurement of an Earth day, these are the planets that complete a full orbit of the Sun in the shortest amount of time...

| | MASS | ONE ORBIT OF THE SUN (DAYS) | | MASS | ONE ORBIT OF THE SUN (DAYS) |
|---|---|---|---|---|---|
| 1 | MERCURY | 87.97 | 6 | JUPITER | 4,332.82 |
| 2 | VENUS | 224.7 | 7 | SATURN | 10,755.7 |
| 3 | EARTH | 365.26 | 8 | URANUS | 30,687.15 |
| 4 | MARS | 686.98 | 9 | NEPTUNE | 60,190.03 |
| 5 | CERES | 1,680.19 | 10 | PLUTO | 90,553.02 |

## TWO OF THE DWARVES

### HAUMEA
Named after the Hawaiian goddess of childbirth and fertility, Haumea takes 102,977.75 days to orbit the Sun. It was officially classified as a dwarf planet on Sep 17, 2008.

### ERIS
Discovered in 2003, Eris takes 205,046 days to orbit the Sun.

TOP 10...

# SMALLEST PLANETS /DWARF PLANETS IN OUR SOLAR SYSTEM

Compared to some of the other planets in our galaxy, Earth is by no means giant-sized, but there are many others that have a much smaller diameter...

| | PLANET/DWARF PLANET | (KM) | DIAMETER (MI) |
|---|---|---|---|
| 1 | CERES | 950 | 590 |
| 2 | MAKEMAKE | 1,422 | 883.59 |
| 3 | HAUMEA | 1,960 | 1,217 |
| 4 | ERIS | 2,326 | 1,445.3 |
| 5 | PLUTO | 2,368 | 1,471.4 |
| 6 | MERCURY | 4,878 | 3,031 |
| 7 | MARS | 6,792 | 4,220 |
| 8 | VENUS | 12,104 | 7,521 |
| 9 | EARTH | 12,720 | 7,904 |
| 10 | NEPTUNE | 49,528 | 30,775 |

TEMPERATURE ON MERCURY CAN REACH

# 801°F

# SATURN

Although the planet Saturn is regarded as a "gas giant", scientists hypothesize that its core is solid, surrounded by helium and hydrogen gas. Since 2004, NASA's unmanned, robot spaceship Cassini has been collecting and sending data back to Earth about Saturn and its neighbouring rings and moons.

## ITS MOONS

Of Saturn's 62 moons, 53 have been given official names. In the photo on the left, you can see a shadow cast by one of these moons. Some are believed to be able to support life. Saturn also has other smaller natural satellites colloquially called "moonlets." As many as 10 million of these mini-moons could be inside a single one of Saturn's seven rings.

## ○ CERES

In March 2015, after travelling through space for seven years, NASA's probe Dawn successfully achieved orbit around Ceres. This is the first time a man-made device has reached a dwarf planet. Its mission to collect data about Ceres will last approximately 14 months.

## ○ JUPITER

The giant gaseous planet has a diameter of 142,984 km (88,846.14 miles). Its mass is equal to 317.83 Earths. Being the largest planet in our solar system means that its name, taken from the Roman king of the gods, is very appropriate.

## ○ GANYMEDE

Scientists William McKinnon and Paul Schenk discovered a bulge as large as Ecuador on dwarf planet Ganymede. They presented the evidence at the 46th Lunar and Planetary Science Conference, held in Texas, USA, between March 16-20, 2015.

## TOP 10...

# BIGGEST MASSES IN OUR SOLAR SYSTEM

To get a greater understanding of how large our Sun is, compare the data of the planets that follow its number one position...

| | OBJECT | MASS (X 10 TO THE POWER OF 21 KG) |
|---|---|---|
| 1 | SUN | 1,989,100,000 |
| 2 | JUPITER | 1,898,130 |
| 3 | SATURN | 568,319 |
| 4 | NEPTUNE | 102,410 |
| 5 | URANUS | 86,810.3 |
| 6 | EARTH | 5,972.2 |
| 7 | VENUS | 4,867.3 |
| 8 | MARS | 641.69 |
| 9 | MERCURY | 330.1 |
| 10 | GANYMEDE (A JUPITER MOON) | 148.2 |

## SPUTNIK 1

Russia's (then the Soviet Union) Sputnik 1 was the first ever man-made satellite to successfully orbit Earth. It burned up on re-entry after 92 days.

**TOP 10…**

# FIRST COUNTRIES TO LAUNCH SATELLITES

The space race features many nations around the world, but these were the first satellites launched by each of those countries…

| | COUNTRY | SATELLITE | DATE |
|---|---|---|---|
| 1 | **SOVIET UNION** (NOW RUSSIA) | Sputnik 1 | **Oct 4, 1957** |
| 2 | **USA** | Explorer 1 | **Feb 1, 1958** |
| 3 | **UK** | Ariel 1 | **Apr 26, 1962** |
| 4 | **CANADA** | Alouette 1 | **Sep 29, 1962** |
| 5 | **ITALY** | San Marco 1 | **Dec 15, 1964** |
| 6 | **FRANCE** | Astérix | **Nov 26, 1965** |
| 7 | **AUSTRALIA** | WRESAT | **Nov 29, 1967** |
| 8 | **GERMANY** | Azur | **Nov 8, 1969** |
| 9 | **JAPAN** | Ōsumi | **Feb 11, 1970** |
| 10 | **CHINA** | Dong Fang Hong 1 | **Apr 24, 1970** |

SINCE 1948

**37**

MONKEYS AND APES HAVE GONE INTO SPACE

## EXPLORER 1

This, the first USA satellite, had a total mission time of 111 days. It provided vital information about cosmic radiation, especially the layer of charged particles that surrounds Earth called the Van Allen belt.

# ANIMALS IN SPACE

## LAIKA THE DOG

In 1957 we had limited knowledge about the effects of spaceflight on living tissue. Hours after mixed-breed dog Laika went into space, she died from overheating. On April 11, 2008, a statue in her honour was unveiled by the Moscow facility she trained at.

## FROGS

During a flight to the Mir space station on Dec 2, 1990, Japanese journalist Toyohiro Akiyama took tree frogs with him.

## GECKOS

To study the effects of reproduction in space, on July 19, 2014, Russia sent four females and one make gecko into low orbit. All five froze to death.

## TOP 10...
# FIRST LIVING THINGS IN SPACE

Long before rockets were piloted by humans, these organisms unwittingly went into space...

|    | ORGANISM | ROCKET | DATE |
|----|----------|--------|------|
| 1  | FRUIT FLIES | V2 | Feb 20, 1947 |
| 2  | MOSS | V2 | Various, 1947 |
| 3  | RHESUS MONKEY (ALBERT II) | V2 | June 14, 1949 |
| 4  | MOUSE | V2 | Aug 31, 1950 |
| 5  | DOG (LAIKA) | Sputnik 2 | Nov 3, 1957 |
| 6  | SQUIRREL MONKEY (GORDO) | Jupiter IRBM AM-13 | Dec 13, 1958 |
| 7  | RABBIT (MARFUSA) | R2 | July 2, 1959 |
| 8  | CHIMPANZEE (HAM) | Redstone | Jan 31, 1961 |
| 9  | GUINEA PIGS, FROGS & MICE | Vostok 3A | Mar 1961 |
| 10 | TORTOISE | Zond 5 | Sep 18, 1968 |

TOP 10...

# FIRST **V-2 ROCKETS** INTO SPACE

This particular kind of rocket became the model used by many to gather data from space, and these were the first to successfully reach the stars...

| | LAUNCHED BY (NATION) | HEIGHT ACHIEVED (KM) | (MI) | LAUNCH DATE |
|---|---|---|---|---|
| 1 | GERMANY | 176 | 109 | June 1944 |
| 2 | GERMANY | 189 | 117 | June 1944 |
| 3 | GERMANY | 176 | 109 | Sep 14, 1944 |
| 4 | GERMANY | 104 | 65 | Dec 7, 1944 |
| 5 | GERMANY | 106 | 66 | Dec 9, 1944 |
| 6 | USA | 112 | 70 | May 10, 1946 |
| 7 | USA | 189 | 117 | May 29, 1946 |
| 8 | USA | 117 | 73 | Jun 13, 1946 |
| 9 | USA | 108 | 67 | Jun 28, 1946 |
| 10 | USA | 134 | 83 | Jul 19, 1946 |

SPEED OF
V2 ROCKET

**5,633**
**KM/H**

## V-2

As well as being the first man-made object to be successfully launched into space, the V-2 began as a weapon. The "V" stands for *Vergeltungswaffen*, German for "retaliatory weapons." In 1944, the long-range missiles were launched at Britain, France, and Belgium.

# ROCKET HISTORY

American engineer Robert H. Goddard (Oct 5, 1882 – Aug 10, 1945) was responsible for the first ever rocket fuelled by a liquid propellant, successfully launched on Mar 16, 1926. Goddard's ideas regarding exploring outer space were decades ahead of their time, and were not taken very seriously. However, he patented hundreds of his inventions, which included a multi-stage rocket, something he came up with in 1914, 55 years before man would step foot on the Moon.

## JAXA

The Japan Aerospace Exploration Agency (JAXA) was founded in 2003 after National Aerospace Laboratory of Japan (NAL), the Institute of Space and Astronautical Science (ISAS), and the National Space Development Agency of Japan (NASDA) merged. In March 2014, astronaut Koichi Wakata became the first Asian commander of the ISS (International Space Station).

TOP 10...

# BIGGEST **SPACE PROGRAMS**

These are the organizations that are investing the most money and time into developing new technologies to explore the depth of space...

| | AGENCY | COUNTRY | BUDGET ($ MILLIONS) |
|---|---|---|---|
| 1 | **NASA** (NATIONAL AERONAUTICS & SPACE ADMINISTRATION) | USA | **17,800** |
| 2 | **ROSCOSMOS** (RUSSIAN FEDERAL SPACE AGENCY) | Russia | **5,600** |
| 3 | **ESA** (EUROPEAN SPACE AGENCY) | (European syndication) | **5,510** |
| 4 | **CNES** (NATIONAL CENTRE OF SPACE RESEARCH) | France | **2,500** |
| 5 | **JAXA** (JAPAN AEROSPACE EXPLORATION AGENCY) | Japan | **2,460** |
| 6 | **DLR** (GERMAN AEROSPACE CENTRE) | Germany | **2,000** |
| 7 | **ASI** (ITALIAN SPACE AGENCY) | Italy | **1,800** |
| 8 | **ISRO** (INDIAN SPACE RESEARCH ORGANIZATION) | India | **1,320** |
| 9 | **CNSA** (CHINA NATIONAL SPACE ADMINISTRATION) | China | **1,300** |
| 10 | **ISRO** (INDIAN SPACE RESEARCH ORGANIZATION) | India | **1,100** |

ASI (ITALIAN SPACE AGENCY) EMPLOYS

# 200 PEOPLE

## NASA

Established by President Dwight D. Eisenhower on July 29, 1958, NASA (National Aeronautics and Space Administration) is USA's space program. Its official vision statement is "To reach for new heights and reveal the unknown so that what we do and learn will benefit all humankind." Its headquarters are located in Washington, DC.

## SPACE SHUTTLES' FLIGHTS

Here is a graphic representation of each Space Shuttle's number of flights...

DISCOVERY
**39**

ATLANTIS
**33**

ENTERPRISE
**5**

COLUMBIA
**28**

CHALLENGER
**10**

ENDEAVOUR
**25**

# BIGGEST
# **MOUNTAINS**
# ON THE MOON

The more we have studied and explored our Moon, the greater understanding we have of its topography...

MOON'S LARGEST IMPACT CRATER, THE SOUTH POLE-AITKEN BASIN IS
**2,499 KM WIDE**

| | NAME | DIAMETER (KM) | (MI) |
|---|---|---|---|
| 1 | MONS RÜMKER | 70 | 43.5 |
| 2 | MONS ARGAEUS | 50 | 31.1 |
| 3 | MONS HUYGENS | 40 | 24.9 |
| 4 | MONS WOLFF | 35 | 21.7 |
| 5 | MONS AMPÈRE | 30 | 18.6 |
| = | MONS BRADLEY | 30 | 18.6 |
| = | MONS DELISLE | 30 | 18.6 |
| = | MONS HANSTEEN | 30 | 18.6 |
| = | MONS PENCK | 30 | 18.6 |
| 10 | MONS HADLEY | 25 | 15.5 |

MONTES TENERIF
MONTES JURA
MONS RÜMKER
MONS DELISLE
MONS BRADL
MONTES APENNINU
MONTES CARPATUS
MONS WOLFF
MONTES RIPHAEUS
MONS HANSTEEN
MONTES CORDILLERA
MONTES ROOK

EPICYCLVS II
LINEA MEDIA
EPICYCLVS II
RVM
LON

## GALILEO'S MOON NEWS

In 1610, Italian physicist, astronomer and philosopher Galileo Galilei was the first person to use a telescope to study the Earth's Moon. In his pamphlet *Sidereus Nuncius* (Italian for "Starry Messenger"), Galileo wrote down his telescopic observations, including that the Moon features craters and mountains.

MONTES ALPES

MONTES CAUCASUS

MONS HADLEY

MONTES HAEMUS

MONS HUYGENS
ONS AMPÈRE

MONS ARGAEUS

MONS PENCK

**TOP 10...**

# LONGEST **MOUNTAIN RANGES** ON THE MOON

The longest range on Earth is the Andes at 7,000 km (4,350 miles), but our Moon's still cover great distances...

| | NAME | LENGTH OF RANGE | |
|---|---|---|---|
| | | (KM) | (MI) |
| 1 | MONTES ROOK | 791 | 491.5 |
| 2 | MONTES CORDILLERA | 574 | 356.7 |
| 3 | MONTES HAEMUS | 560 | 348 |
| 4 | MONTES CAUCASUS | 445 | 276.5 |
| 5 | MONTES JURA | 422 | 262.2 |
| 6 | MONTES APENNINUS | 401 | 249.2 |
| 7 | MONTES CARPATUS | 361 | 224.3 |
| 8 | MONTES ALPES | 281 | 175 |
| 9 | MONTES RIPHAEUS | 189 | 117.4 |
| 10 | MONTES TENERIFFE | 182 | 113.1 |

## MOON LANDING

Prior to American astronaut Neil Armstrong being the first human to walk on the Moon, 1961-68 saw U.S. robot missions Ranger, Lunar Orbiter, and Surveyor capture visual intel of the Moon. Russia's 1959-76 robot missions included gathering samples from its surface.

## LUNAR MANIPULATION

Due to maltreatment, native Jamaicans refused Italian explorer Christopher Columbus and his crew any more food. Abusing his knowledge of an impending total lunar eclipse on March 1, 1504, Columbus terrified the natives into thinking the moon was "inflamed with wrath" because God was unhappy with their actions.

**TOP 10...**

# NEXT 10 LUNAR ECLIPSES

When the Sun, Earth and the Moon are in alignment, on the night of a full moon, a lunar eclipse occurs...

| | TIME | DATE |
|---|---|---|
| 1 | 11:47 | Mar. 23, 2016 |
| 2 | 09:42 | Aug. 18, 2016 |
| 3 | 18:54 | Sep. 16, 2016 |
| 4 | 00:44 | Feb. 11, 2017 |
| 5 | 18:20 | Aug. 7, 2017 |
| 6 | 13:30 | Jan. 31, 2018 |
| 7 | 20:22 | July 27, 2018 |
| 8 | 05:12 | Jan. 21, 2019 |
| 9 | 21:31 | July 16, 2019 |
| 10 | 19:10 | Jan. 10, 2020 |

## RAHU

In Hinduism it is believed that a decapitated head of an Asura (a spirit of nature) called Rahu creates eclipses by catching and eating the Sun or the Moon.

## TOP 10...
# NEXT 10 SOLAR ECLIPSES

A solar eclipse happens when the Moon passes directly in between Earth and the Sun...

| | TIME | DATE |
|---|---|---|
| 1 | 09:08:02 | Sep 1, 2016 |
| 2 | 14:54:33 | Feb 26, 2017 |
| 3 | 18:26:40 | Aug 21, 2017 |
| 4 | 20:52:33 | Feb 15, 2018 |
| 5 | 03:02:16 | Jul 13, 2018 |
| 6 | 09:47:28 | Aug 11, 2018 |
| 7 | 01:42:38 | Jan 6, 2019 |
| 8 | 19:24:08 | Jul 2, 2019 |
| 9 | 05:18:53 | Dec 26, 2019 |
| 10 | 06:41:15 | Jun 21, 2020 |

TOTAL NUMBER OF SOLAR & LUNAR ECLIPSES IN 2016

**4**

## 19TH CENTURY ECLIPSE

Austrian artist Johann Christian Schoeller (1782-1851) painted this depiction of the total eclipse of the sun which occurred in Vienna, Austria on July 8, 1842.

## PHOTOHELIOGRAPH

This illustration captures when the total solar eclipse in Rivabellosa, Spain was photographed on July 18, 1860. The photo was taken by British astronomer Warren de la Rue using a Kew Photoheliograph. This camera-telescope, designed by de la Rue, was constructed by Andrew Ross in 1857.

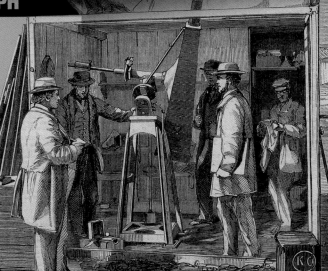

## RETURN OF THE FALCON

*Stars Wars: Episode VII – The Force Awakens* marks the return of Han Solo's starship, the Millennium Falcon. It featured strongly in previous episodes IV, V, and VI and was seen for a few seconds in Episode III.

## ⦿ STAR TREK LEGACY

Texas-born Gene Roddenberry created *Star Trek* in 1964. After development, its first episode "Where No Man Has Gone Before" aired on September 8, 1966.

6 DIFFERENT
STAR TREK SERIES =

## 725 EPISODES

### TOP 10...
# BIGGEST SPACE BATTLE MOVIES

Science fiction and fantasy films often see warring factions collide, and these are the ones that have made the most at the box office...

| | MOVIE | YEAR OF RELEASE | BOX OFFICE ($ WORLDWIDE) |
|---|---|---|---|
| 1 | STAR WARS: EPISODE I – THE PHANTOM MENACE | 1999 | 1,027,044,677 |
| 2 | STAR WARS: EPISODE III – REVENGE OF THE SITH | 2005 | 848,754,768 |
| 3 | INDEPENDENCE DAY | 1996 | 817,400,891 |
| 4 | STAR WARS: EPISODE IV – A NEW HOPE | 1977 | 775,398,007 |
| 5 | GUARDIANS OF THE GALAXY | 2014 | 774,176,600 |
| 6 | STAR WARS: EPISODE II – ATTACK OF THE CLONES | 2002 | 649,398,328 |
| 7 | STAR WARS: EPISODE V – THE EMPIRE STRIKES BACK | 1980 | 538,375,067 |
| 8 | STAR WARS: EPISODE VI – RETURN OF THE JEDI | 1983 | 475,106,177 |
| 9 | STAR TREK INTO DARKNESS | 2013 | 467,381,584 |
| 10 | STAR TREK | 2009 | 385,680,446 |

## 📍 DIGITAL WORLD

*Avatar* creator, three-time Oscar-winner James Cameron, utilized cutting edge motion-capture photography for the film. 900 people worked for Peter Jackson's Weta Digital to craft the film's computer-generated visuals.

## 📍 THE AVENGERS

*Avengers: Age of Ultron* (2015) featured the fan-favourite Iron Man suit, the "Hulkbuster." This colossal exo-suit works as an extra outer "skin" to Iron Man's armour. In the Marvel Comics world, it first appeared in May 1994 in *Iron Man* #304.

## TOP 10...
# BIGGEST **ALIEN/HUMAN** ENCOUNTER MOVIES

From benevolent travellers to aggressive monsters, aliens have interacted with humans in films for over 100 years. These are the most popular...

| | MOVIE | ALIENS ENCOUNTERED | YEAR OF RELEASE | BOX OFFICE ($ WORLDWIDE) |
|---|---|---|---|---|
| 1 | AVATAR | Pandorians | 2009 | 2,787,965,087 |
| 2 | THE AVENGERS | Chitauri | 2012 | 1,518,594,910 |
| 3 | TRANSFORMERS: DARK OF THE MOON | Autobots & Decepticons | 2011 | 1,123,794,079 |
| 4 | TRANSFORMERS: AGE OF EXTINCTION | Autobots & Decepticons | 2014 | 1,087,404,499 |
| 5 | TRANSFORMERS: REVENGE OF THE FALLEN | Autobots & Decepticons | 2009 | 836,303,693 |
| 6 | INDEPENDENCE DAY | Unnamed aliens | 1996 | 817,400,891 |
| 7 | E.T.: THE EXTRA TERRESTRIAL | E.T. | 1982 | 792,910,554 |
| 8 | GUARDIANS OF THE GALAXY | Several | 2014 | 774,176,600 |
| 9 | TRANSFORMERS | Autobots & Decepticons | 2007 | 709,709,780 |
| 10 | MAN OF STEEL | Kryptonians | 2013 | 662,845,518 |

## ALIEN VS. PREDATOR : REQUIEM

Composer Brian Tyler (*Avengers: Age Of Ultron, Sleepy Hollow, Iron Man 3*) wrote several nods to themes and sounds from *Predator* (1987) and *Aliens* (1986) for his *Aliens vs. Predator: Requiem* score.

## RIPLEY RETURNS

Sigourney Weaver reprises her Ellen Ripley role for director Neill Blomkamp's 2016 sequel to *Aliens* (1986).

**TOP 10...**
# MOST SUCCESSFUL
# SCARY MOVIE ALIENS

The Alien franchise's Xenomorph is one of the most terrifying creatures ever made, but there are many other sinister extra-terrestrials that have made their way onto the big screen...

## THE PREDATOR

Actor Kevin Peter Hall (May 9, 1955 – April 10, 1991) was the first to play the hunter creature in *Predator* (1987) and *Predator 2* (1990). He was 7.22 ft (2.2 m) tall.

| | MOVIE | ALIENS ENCOUNTERED | YEAR OF RELEASE | BOX OFFICE ($ WORLDWIDE) |
|---|---|---|---|---|
| 1 | WAR OF THE WORLDS | Martians in Tripods | 2005 | 591,745,540 |
| 2 | SIGNS | Greys | 2002 | 408,247,917 |
| 3 | PROMETHEUS | Parasitic creatures | 2012 | 403,354,354 |
| 4 | SUPER 8 | Unknown burrowing alien | 2011 | 260,095,986 |
| 5 | BATTLE: LOS ANGELES | Colonizing aliens | 2011 | 211,819,354 |
| 6 | ALIEN VS. PREDATOR | Xenomorphs, Predators | 2004 | 172,544,654 |
| 7 | ALIEN RESURRECTION | Xenomorphs | 1997 | 161,376,068 |
| 8 | ALIEN 3 | Xenomorph | 1992 | 159,814,498 |
| 9 | ALIENS | Xenomorphs | 1986 | 131,060,248 |
| 10 | ALIEN VS.PREDATOR: REQUIEM | Xenomorphs, Predators | 2007 | 128,884,494 |

TOP 10...

# LONGEST **RUNNING TV SERIES** SET IN SPACE

It's not just the world of movies which has tapped into our fascination with outer space. The medium of television has seen many successful series craft more than 100 episodes of galactic storytelling...

| | NAME | YEARS ON AIR | TOTAL EPISODES |
|---|---|---|---|
| 1 | SPACE PATROL | 1950–55 | **1,110** |
| 2 | DOCTOR WHO | 1963–84; 1985–89; 2005–present | **813** |
| 3 | STARGATE SG-1 | 1997–2007 | **214** |
| 4 | MYSTERY SCIENCE THEATER 3000 | 1988–99 | **197** |
| 5 | STAR TREK: THE NEXT GENERATION | 1987–94 | **178** |
| 6 | STAR TREK: DEEP SPACE NINE | 1993–99 | **176** |
| 7 | STAR TREK: VOYAGER | 1995–2001 | **172** |
| 8 | THUNDERCATS | 1985–89; 2011 | **156** |
| 9 | FUTURAMA | 1999–2003; 2008–13 | **141** |
| 10 | VOLTRON | 1984-85 | **124** |

MYSTERY SCIENCE THEATER 3000 RAN FOR

# 11 YEARS

## ◉ DR WHO

The Daleks have been the most famous antagonists for The Doctor to deal with since they first appeared in TV series *The Daleks* (Dec 21, 1963 – Feb 1, 1964). Set on their planet of Skaro, *The Daleks* followed directly on from the very first incarnation of *Doctor Who* (Nov 23, 1963 – Dec 14, 1964).

## DEFENDER

During the 1980s, the Atari 2600 version of Defender sold more than 1 million copies worldwide.

## ASTEROIDS

Since the arcade classic *Asteroids* came to home consoles, it has sold more than 5.5 million copies across multiple platforms including Atari 2600, PlayStation, Game Boy Advance, and N64. 2011 saw *Asteroids: Gunner* released for Apple iPhone's iOS system.

## TOP 10...
# OLDEST ARCADE GAMES SET IN SPACE

The origins of modern video gaming lie in arcade machines, and one of the most popular kinds to write gaming code for was surviving perils in space...

| | NAME | DEVELOPED BY | RELEASE DATE |
|---|---|---|---|
| 1 | GALAXY GAME | Bill Pitts and Hugh Tuck | **Sep 1971** |
| 2 | COMPUTER SPACE | Nolan Bushnell and Ted Dabney | **Nov 1971** |
| 3 | ASTRO RACE | Taito | **Jul 1973** |
| 4 | SPACE WARS | Cinematronics | **Oct 1977** |
| 5 | SPACE INVADERS | Taito | **Jul 1978** |
| 6 | GALAXIAN | Namco | **Oct 1979** |
| 7 | ASTEROIDS | Atari | **Nov 1979** |
| = | TAIL GUNNER | Vectorbeam | **Nov 1979** |
| 9 | DEFENDER | Williams Electronics | **Feb 1981** |
| 10 | ELIMINATOR | Sega | **Dec 1981** |

LEGO STAR WARS REBEL
SNOWSPEEDER
**1,457**
PIECES

TOP 10...

# BIGGEST **STAR WARS** LEGO SPACESHIPS (PER PIECES)

Of all the commercially released LEGO Star Wars sets, these ones contain the most pieces...

| | NAME | YEAR RELEASED | NUMBER OF LEGO PIECES |
|---|---|---|---|
| 1 | MILLENNIUM FALCON | 2007 | 5,195 |
| 2 | DEATH STAR | 2008 | 3,803 |
| 3 | DEATH STAR II | 2005 | 3,449 |
| 4 | SANDCRAWLER | 2014 | 3,296 |
| 5 | SUPER STAR DESTROYER | 2011 | 3,152 |
| 6 | IMPERIAL STAR DESTROYER | 2002 | 3,104 |
| 7 | IMPERIAL SHUTTLE | 2010 | 2,503 |
| 8 | R2-D2 | 2012 | 2,127 |
| 9 | SLAVE I | 2015 | 1,996 |
| 10 | EWOK VILLAGE | 2013 | 1,990 |

## LEGO DARTH

Darth Vader has been a popular LEGO Star Wars minifigure since its first release in 1999. There have been nine different versions since then. Luke Skywalker (pictured below in his Return Of The Jedi design) has appeared as a minifigure 29 times since it first appeared in a LEGO set in 1999.

LEGO'S
DEATH STAR
**3,803**
PIECES

# MOVIES

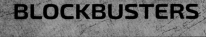

# BLOCKBUSTERS

**ALL 6 TOLKIEN ADAPTATIONS BETWEEN 2001-14:**

# $5.87 BILLION

AT THE BOX OFFICE WORLDWIDE

## THE DARK KNIGHT RISES

Just missing out on a place in the Top 10 Biggest Movies Of All Time is *The Dark Knight Rises* (2012). Filmmaker Christopher Nolan's third and final part of his Christian Bale-starring Dark Knight Trilogy took $1,084,439,099 at the box office, making it the 11th biggest film ever.

## TOP 10...
# BIGGEST MOVIES OF ALL TIME

Covering all genres, and every film that had a theatrical release, these 10 took the most money at box offices around the world...

| | MOVIE | YEAR OF RELEASE | BOX OFFICE ($ WORLDWIDE) |
|---|---|---|---|
| 1 | AVATAR | 2009 | 2,787,965,087 |
| 2 | TITANIC | 1997 | 2,186,772,302 |
| 3 | THE AVENGERS | 2012 | 1,518,594,910 |
| 4 | FURIOUS 7 | 2015 | 1,499,723,320 |
| 5 | AVENGERS: AGE OF ULTRON | 2015 | 1,371,528,000 |
| 6 | HARRY POTTER AND THE DEATHLY HALLOWS PART 2 | 2011 | 1,341,511,219 |
| 7 | FROZEN | 2013 | 1,274,219,009 |
| 8 | IRON MAN 3 | 2013 | 1,215,439,994 |
| 9 | TRANSFORMERS: DARK OF THE MOON | 2011 | 1,123,794,079 |
| 10 | THE LORD OF THE RINGS: THE RETURN OF THE KING | 2003 | 1,119,929,521 |

## TRANSFORMING THE BOX OFFICE

Since the 1986 animated movie, here is how the Transformers' cinematic stories compare:

**TRANSFORMERS: THE MOVIE (1986)** $5,849,647

**TRANSFORMERS (2007)** $709,709,780

**TRANSFORMERS: REVENGE OF THE FALLEN (2009)** $836,303,693

**TRANSFORMERS: DARK OF THE MOON (2011)** $1,123,794,079

**TRANSFORMERS: AGE OF EXTINCTION (2014)** $1,091,405,097

STARS WARS
FRANCHISE
(1977-2015) =
## $5.66 BILLION
TOTAL BOX OFFICE TAKINGS

## TOP 10...
# BIGGEST STAR WARS MOVIES

Before 2015's The Force Awakens release, this is how the Star Wars saga's box office success looks...

| | MOVIE | YEAR OF RELEASE | BOX OFFICE ($ WORLDWIDE) |
|---|---|---|---|
| 1 | STAR WARS: EPISODE I – THE PHANTOM MENACE | 2009 | 1,027,044,677 |
| 2 | STAR WARS: EPISODE III – REVENGE OF THE SITH | 2005 | 848,754,768 |
| 3 | STAR WARS: EPISODE IV – A NEW HOPE | 1977 | 775,398,007 |
| 4 | STAR WARS: EPISODE II – ATTACK OF THE CLONES | 2002 | 649,398,328 |
| 5 | STAR WARS: EPISODE IV – A NEW HOPE (SPECIAL EDITION) | 1997 | 579,646,015 |
| 6 | STAR WARS: EPISODE V – THE EMPIRE STRIKES BACK | 1980 | 538,375,067 |
| 7 | STAR WARS: EPISODE VI – RETURN OF THE JEDI | 1983 | 475,106,177 |
| 8 | STAR WARS: EPISODE VI – RETURN OF THE JEDI (SPECIAL EDITION) | 1997 | 353,096,720 |
| 9 | STAR WARS: EPISODE V – THE EMPIRE STRIKES BACK (SPECIAL EDITION) | 1997 | 347,689,833 |
| 10 | STAR WARS: THE CLONE WARS | 2008 | 68,282,844 |

# STAR WARS EP VII

The latest film is set 30 years after *Return Of The Jedi*. Emmy award-winning J.J. Abrams directs, with several *Star Wars Episode IV-VI* actors returning, including Harrison Ford, Mark Hamill, Carrie Fisher, and Peter Mayhew.

## FELICITY JONES

Released Dec 16, 2016, *Star Wars: Rogue One* stars Oscar-nominated British actress Felicity Jones (*A Monster Calls*, *The Theory Of Everything*). Its director is a fellow Brit, Gareth Edwards, the director of *Monsters* (2010) and *Godzilla* (2014). John Knoll, an Oscar-winning Visual Effects Supervisor and the Chief Creative Officer of Industrial Light & Magic (Star Wars creator George Lucas' visual effects company) came up with the story for *Rogue One*.

BASIL RATHBONE
PLAYED SHERLOCK
HOLMES IN

## 14 FILMS

## TOP 10...

# MOST MOVIES BASED ON A CHARACTER/ FRANCHISE

Creating a franchise around recurring characters can lead to multiple movies...

| | FRANCHISE | TOTAL MOVIES |
|---|---|---|
| 1 | MARVEL COMICS | 48 |
| 2 | SHERLOCK HOLMES | 37 |
| 3 | DC COMICS | 34 |
| 4 | JAMES BOND | 26 |
| 5 | POKÉMON | 18 |
| 6 | STAR TREK | 12 |
| = | FRIDAY 13TH | 12 |
| 8 | INSPECTOR CLOUSEAU | 11 |
| 9 | HALLOWEEN | 10 |
| 10 | BATMAN | 9 |

## ⌖ STAR TREK

Including animation voice-overs, Leonard Nimoy (Mar 26, 1931 – Feb 27, 2015) played *Star Trek*'s Spock 110 times. He appeared in 53 films and 46 different TV series.

## ⌖ INSPECTOR CLOUSEAU

British actor Peter Sellers (Sep 8, 1925 – July 24, 1980) played Inspector Jacques Clouseau in six films, including 1978's *Revenge Of The Pink Panther* which took $49,579,269 at the box office worldwide.

# TOP 10...
# BIGGEST **3D MOVIES** OF ALL TIME

3D films have been around since 1915. Out of all of those that received a theatrical released, these 10 attracted more people to cinemas than any others...

| | MOVIE | YEAR OF RELEASE | BOX OFFICE ($ WORLDWIDE) |
|---|---|---|---|
| **1** | AVATAR | **2009** | **2,787,965,087** |
| **2** | THE AVENGERS | **2012** | **1,518,594,910** |
| **3** | AVENGERS: AGE OF ULTRON | **2015** | **1,371,528,000** |
| **4** | HARRY POTTER AND THE DEATHLY HALLOWS PART 2 | **2011** | **1,341,511,219** |
| **5** | FROZEN | **2013** | **1,274,219,009** |
| **6** | IRON MAN 3 | **2013** | **1,215,439,994** |
| **7** | TRANSFORMERS: DARK OF THE MOON | **2011** | **1,123,794,079** |
| **8** | TRANSFORMERS: AGE OF EXTINCTION | **2014** | **1,091,405,097** |
| **9** | JURASSIC WORLD | **2015** | **1,084,500,000** |
| **10** | TOY STORY 3 | **2010** | **1,063,171,911** |

## GRAVITY

Although missing a Top 10 spot with a box office total of $716,392,705, *Gravity* was featured on 93 film critics' top ten Best Films of 2013 lists. 22 of those called it the number one film of the year.

## THE AMAZING SPIDER-MAN

Narrowly missing out on appearing in the above Top 10, *The Amazing Spider-Man* (2012) took $757,930,663. It was the first of two Spidey films to be directed by Marc Webb and star Andrew Garfield and Emma Stone.

## TOP 10...
# BIGGEST **BEST PICTURE** OSCAR WINNERS

Of all of the films that won the coveted Best Picture Oscar, these were the most financially successful...

| | MOVIE | YEAR WON ACADEMY AWARD FOR BEST PICTURE | BOX OFFICE ($ WORLDWIDE) |
|---|---|---|---|
| 1 | TITANIC | 1997 | 2,186,772,302 |
| 2 | THE LORD OF THE RINGS: THE RETURN OF THE KING | 2003 | 1,119,929,521 |
| 3 | FORREST GUMP | 1994 | 677,945,399 |
| 4 | GLADIATOR | 2000 | 457,640,427 |
| 5 | DANCES WITH WOLVES | 1990 | 424,208,848 |
| 6 | THE KING'S SPEECH | 2010 | 414,211,549 |
| 7 | SLUMDOG MILLIONAIRE | 2008 | 377,910,544 |
| 8 | AMERICAN BEAUTY | 1999 | 356,296,601 |
| 9 | RAIN MAN | 1988 | 354,825,435 |
| 10 | SCHINDLER'S LIST | 1993 | 321,306,305 |

## BIRDMAN

*Birdman* was edited to appear as one continuous shot, with no changes of camera/angle. It won four of its eight awards at the 2015 Oscars, bringing its global award wins to 122 of 275 nominations.

## ⚲ RETUN OF THE KING

The final part of filmmaker Peter Jackson's adaptations of J. R. R. Tolkien's *The Lord of The Rings* reaped the most global awards. Aside from its Oscar accolades, it won a further 105 awards from an additional 161 nominations. Overall, the trilogy (released 2001–03) won 247 international awards from 453 nominations and made $3,139,088,654 at the box office.

# HISTORY OF THE OSCARS

The first Academy Awards ceremony took place at the Hollywood Roosevelt Hotel on May 16, 1929. A mere 270 people attended. Although there are several conflicting explanations as to where the term "Oscar" came from, many believe it was first uttered in 1939 by the Academy Executive Secretary Margaret Herrick. She likened the statue to her cousin Oscar Pierce.

**INCLUDING THE 2015 OSCARS, CAST AND CREW HAVE BEEN AWARDED**
## 2,947 OSCARS

## TOP 10...
# MOVIES WITH THE MOST OSCAR WINS & NOMINATIONS

The drama genre clearly gets the most attention from the Academy Awards, but there is one smash-hit fantasy movie in this list as well...

| | MOVIE | YEAR | NOMINATIONS | WON |
|---|---|---|---|---|
| 1 | TITANIC | 1997 | 14 | 11 |
| 2 | THE LORD OF THE RINGS: THE RETURN OF THE KING | 2003 | 12 | 11 |
| 3 | BEN-HUR | 1959 | 11 | 11 |
| 4 | WEST SIDE STORY | 1961 | 11 | 10 |
| 5 | THE ENGLISH PATIENT | 1996 | 12 | 9 |
| 6 | GIGI | 1958 | 9 | 9 |
| = | THE LAST EMPEROR | 1987 | 9 | 9 |
| 8 | AMADEUS | 1984 | 11 | 8 |
| 9 | GONE WITH THE WIND | 1939 | 13 | 8 (+2 Hon.)* |
| 10 | FROM HERE TO ETERNITY | 1953 | 13 | 8 |

*2 posthumous honorary wins

## 12 YEARS A SLAVE

British filmmaker Steve McQueen brought Solomon Northup's 1853 memoirs *12 Years A Slave* to the big screen. Its 206 award wins from 375 nominations included Best Picture, Best Supporting Actress, and Best Adapted Screenplay at the 2015 Oscars.

# BLACK WIDOW

Since her debut role in Rob Reiner's *North* (1994), American actress and musician Scarlett Johansson has more than 50 acting credits, including playing Natasha "Black Widow" Romanoff five times in *Iron Man 2*, *The Avengers*, *Captain America: The Winter Soldier*, *Avengers: Age Of Ultron*, and 2016's *Captain America: Civil War*.

## TOP 10...
# BIGGEST **SUPERHERO** MOVIES

Comic book superheroes continue to rule the box office, especially Marvel Comics', whose characters are in eight of the 10 here...

| | MOVIE | YEAR OF RELEASE | BOX OFFICE ($ WORLDWIDE) |
|---|---|---|---|
| 1 | THE AVENGERS | 2012 | 1,518,594,910 |
| 2 | AVENGERS: AGE OF ULTRON | 2015 | 1,371,528,000 |
| 3 | IRON MAN 3 | 2013 | 1,215,439,994 |
| 4 | THE DARK KNIGHT RISES | 2012 | 1,084,439,099 |
| 5 | THE DARK KNIGHT | 2008 | 1,004,558,444 |
| 6 | SPIDER-MAN 3 | 2007 | 890,871,626 |
| 7 | SPIDER-MAN | 2002 | 821,708,551 |
| 8 | SPIDER-MAN 2 | 2004 | 783,766,341 |
| 9 | GUARDIANS OF THE GALAXY | 2014 | 774,176,600 |
| 10 | THE AMAZING SPIDER-MAN | 2012 | 757,930,663 |

## IRON MAN

Robert Downey Jr. has played Tony Stark/Iron Man five times since 2008. The character was created from a collaboration between Marvel's Stan Lee, Larry Lieber, Don Heck, and Jack Kirby.

## TOP 10...
# BIGGEST SUPERHERO FRANCHISES

Movie sequels and spin-offs increase the popularity of comic book characters, and none more so than these characters/franchises...

| | CHARACTER/FRANCHISE | NO. OF MOVIE APPEARANCES | BOX OFFICE ($ WORLDWIDE) |
|---|---|---|---|
| 1 | IRON MAN | 5 | 5,314,670,457 |
| 2 | CAPTAIN AMERICA | 4 | 3,975,459,256 |
| 3 | THOR | 4 | 3,969,912,528 |
| 4 | SPIDER-MAN | 5 | 3,963,259,504 |
| 5 | BATMAN | 9 | 3,723,441,151 |
| 6 | HULK | 4 | 3,398,910,941 |
| 7 | WOLVERINE/X-MEN | 7 | 3,053,047,399 |
| 8 | SUPERMAN | 7 | 1,489,206,516 |
| 9 | TEENAGE MUTANT NINJA TURTLES | 5 | 902,310,086 |
| 10 | GUARDIANS OF THE GALAXY | 1 | 774,176,600 |

## STARK POWER

This graph shows the number of Iron Man suits that were featured in his movies:

| IRON MAN | IRON MAN 2 | THE AVENGERS |
|---|---|---|
| **3** | **3** | **2** |
| (MK 1-3) | (MK 4-6) | (MK 6-7) |

IRON MAN 3
**36**
(MK7-42)

## GUARDIANS OF THE GALAXY

*Guardians Of The Galaxy* scooped 21 wins from 65 international nominations, including 2015 Oscar nominations for Best Achievement in Visual Effects and Best Achievement in Makeup and Hairstyling. Its Production Designer Charles Wood won a 2015 Art Directors' Guild Award for Excellence. A sequel is confirmed for May 5, 2017.

ROCKET RACCOON FIRST APPEARED IN MARVEL PREVIEW #7 IN
# 1976

## BLADE

Based on Marvel Comics' human-vampire hybrid character, *Blade* (1998) made $131,183,530 at the box office.

MARVEL FILM
THOR: THE DARK WORLD
(2013)
**$644.8 MILLION**
AT THE BOX OFFICE

## TOP 10...

# BIGGEST MARVEL COMIC BOOK MOVIES

Since the 1986 film adaptation of Marvel's Howard The Duck, these are the most successful movie versions of the publisher's comics...

| | MOVIE | YEAR OF RELEASE | BOX OFFICE ($ WORLDWIDE) |
|---|---|---|---|
| 1 | THE AVENGERS | 2012 | 1,518,594,910 |
| 2 | AVENGERS: AGE OF ULTRON | 2015 | 1,371,528,000 |
| 3 | IRON MAN 3 | 2013 | 1,215,439,994 |
| 4 | SPIDER-MAN 3 | 2007 | 890,871,626 |
| 5 | SPIDER-MAN | 2002 | 821,708,551 |
| 6 | SPIDER-MAN 2 | 2004 | 783,766,341 |
| 7 | GUARDIANS OF THE GALAXY | 2014 | 774,176,600 |
| 8 | THE AMAZING SPIDER-MAN | 2012 | 757,930,663 |
| 9 | X-MEN: DAYS OF FUTURE PAST | 2014 | 748,121,534 |
| 10 | CAPTAIN AMERICA: THE WINTER SOLDIER | 2014 | 714,766,572 |

## AGENT CARTER

British actress Hayley Atwell debuted as Peggy Carter in *Captain America: The First Avenger* (2008). She has played the character in seven Marvel productions. They include four 2015 projects: TV series *Agent Carter* and *Agents of S.H.I.E.L.D.*, plus *Avengers: Age Of Ultron* and *Ant-Man*. After the 2013 Marvel One-shot short film *Agent Carter*, she appeared (with prosthetic makeup) as an elderly Peggy in *Captain America: The Winter Soldier* (2014).

## CONSTANTINE

Actor Keanu Reeves' 58th role was as John Constantine in this 2005 movie adaptation of *Hellblazer*, created by Alan Moore and Stephen R. Bissette and published by DC Comics/Vertigo. Constantine missed out on this top 10 as it took $230,884,728 at the box office. October 2014 saw a TV series begin, inspired by the same comic, and also called *Constantine*, with Matt Ryan in the title role.

## TOP 10...

# BIGGEST DC COMIC BOOK MOVIES

1951 saw Superman and the Mole Men hit the big screen. 65 years on, these are DC Comics' box office winners...

| | MOVIE | YEAR OF RELEASE | BOX OFFICE ($ WORLDWIDE) |
|---|---|---|---|
| 1 | THE DARK KNIGHT RISES | 2012 | 1,084,439,099 |
| 2 | THE DARK KNIGHT | 2008 | 1,004,558,444 |
| 3 | MAN OF STEEL | 2013 | 668,045,518 |
| 4 | BATMAN | 1989 | 411,348,924 |
| 5 | SUPERMAN RETURNS | 2006 | 391,081,192 |
| 6 | BATMAN BEGINS | 2005 | 374,218,673 |
| 7 | BATMAN FOREVER | 1995 | 336,529,144 |
| 8 | SUPERMAN | 1978 | 300,218,018 |
| 9 | BATMAN RETURNS | 1992 | 266,822,354 |
| 10 | BATMAN AND ROBIN | 1997 | 238,207,122 |

## MARVEL vs DC

### TOP 10 BOX OFFICE TOTAL:

DC COMICS
**$5,1 BILLION**

MARVEL COMICS
**$8,9 BILLION**

### TOTAL ADAPTATIONS:

DC COMICS
**34**

MARVEL COMICS
**48**

## BANE

BAFTA-winning British actor Tom Hardy played the brutal League of Shadows affiliate Bane in *The Dark Knight Rises* (2012). As its director Christopher Nolan wanted "a very physical monster," Hardy gained 31 lbs (14 kg) of muscles for the role.

## HELLBOY

American comic book artist and writer Mike Mignola created *Hellboy* in 1993. Ron Perlman played the heroic demon agent twice in *Hellboy* (2004) and *Hellboy: The Golden Army* (2008).

**TOP 10...**

# BIGGEST CREATOR-OWNED COMIC BOOK MOVIES

It's not just Marvel and DC properties that get movie adaptations. These independent publishers' characters have had great success...

| | MOVIE | PUBLISHER | YEAR OF RELEASE | BOX OFFICE ($ WORLDWIDE) |
|---|---|---|---|---|
| 1 | TEENAGE MUTANT NINJA TURTLES | Mirage Studios/IDW | 2014 | 483,804,754 |
| 2 | THE MASK | Dark Horse | 1994 | 351,583,407 |
| 3 | WANTED | Top Cow | 2008 | 341,433,252 |
| 4 | THE GREEN HORNET | Dynamite | 2011 | 227,817,248 |
| 5 | TEENAGE MUTANT NINJA TURTLES | Mirage Studios/IDW | 1990 | 201,965,915 |
| 6 | HELLBOY II: THE GOLDEN ARMY | Dark Horse | 2008 | 160,388,063 |
| 7 | JUDGE DREDD | Fleetway/Rebellion | 1995 | 113,493,481 |
| 8 | HELLBOY | Dark Horse | 2004 | 99,318,987 |
| 9 | TMNT | Mirage Studios/IDW | 2007 | 95,608,995 |
| 10 | SPAWN | Image | 1997 | 87,840,042 |

## ROCKETEER

1991's film version of Dave Stevens' *The Rocketeer* (starring Bill Campbell and Jennifer Connelly) missed out on this top 10 with $46,704,056 at the box office.

TOP 10...

# BIGGEST SUPERHERO FRANCHISES' LONGEST RUNNING COMICS

Many characters you've seen at the movies have been in comic books for several decades...

| | MOVIE | FIRST APPEARANCE | YEARS IN PRINT |
|---|---|---|---|
| 1 | SUPERMAN | Apr 1938 | 77 |
| 2 | BATMAN | May 1939 | 76 |
| 3 | CAPTAIN AMERICA | Mar 1941 | 74 |
| 4 | FANTASTIC FOUR | Nov 1961 | 54 |
| 5 | HULK | May 1962 | 53 |
| = | SPIDER-MAN | Aug 1962 | 53 |
| = | THOR | Aug 1962 | 53 |
| 8 | IRON MAN | Mar 1963 | 52 |
| 9 | X-MEN | Sep 1963 | 52 |
| 10 | WOLVERINE | Oct 1974 | 41 |

## SNOWPIERCER

Chris Evans also played Curtis in *Snowpiercer* (2013), Korean filmmaker Bong Joon-ho's adaptation of the 1982 French graphic novel *Le Transperceneige* by Jacques Lob and Jean-Marc Rochette. The film took $86,758,912 at the box office.

## CHRIS EVANS' HEROES

The Boston-born actor has played more than one Marvel Comics' character. He also starred as *Fantastic Four*'s Johnny Storm. Here are the box office stats for those roles:

| | BOX OFFICE ($ WORLWIDE) |
|---|---|
| FANTASTIC FOUR (2005) | $330,579,719 |
| FANTASTIC FOUR: RISE OF THE SILVER SURFER (2007) | $289,047,763 |
| CAPTAIN AMERICA: THE FIRST AVENGER (2011) | $370,569,774 |
| THE AVENGERS (2012) | $1,518,594,910 |
| CAPTAIN AMERICA: THE WINTER SOLDIER (2014) | $714,766,572 |

## TOP 10...
# BIGGEST
# ANIMATED MOVIES

Including stop-motion, hand-drawn cell, and CG (computer-generated), these are the world's biggest animated hits...

| | MOVIE | YEAR OF RELEASE | BOX OFFICE ($ WORLDWIDE) |
|---|---|---|---|
| 1 | FROZEN | 2013 | 1,274,219,009 |
| 2 | TOY STORY 3 | 2010 | 1,063,171,911 |
| 3 | THE LION KING | 1994 | 987,483,777 |
| 4 | DESPICABLE ME 2 | 2013 | 970,761,885 |
| 5 | FINDING NEMO | 2003 | 936,743,261 |
| 6 | SHREK 2 | 2004 | 919,838,758 |
| 7 | ICE AGE: DAWN OF THE DINOSAURS | 2009 | 886,686,817 |
| 8 | ICE AGE: CONTINENTAL DRIFT | 2012 | 877,244,782 |
| 9 | SHREK THE THIRD | 2007 | 798,958,162 |
| 10 | SHREK FOREVER AFTER | 2010 | 752,600,867 |

# ICE AGE

With *Ice Age 5* out in 2016, here is an at-a-glance chart showing how successful each film has been :

**BOX OFFICE ($ WORLDWIDE)**

**ICE AGE: THE MELTDOWN (2006)**
$660,940,780

**ICE AGE: DAWN OF THE DINOSAURS (2009)**
$886,686,817

**ICE AGE: CONTINENTAL DRIFT (2012)**
$877,244,782

**ICE AGE (2002)**
$383,257,136

## 📍 THE LION KING

Disney's *The Lion King* is the only film in the above Top 10 that features traditional, hand-drawn cell animation.

THE FIRST 3 TOY STORY MOVIES MADE

## $1.9 BILLION
AT THE BOX OFFICE

## 📍 TOY STORY 3

Although Lee Unkrich has been at Pixar since 1994, and has co-directed projects, *Toy Story 3* (2010) was his directorial debut. Beyond their box office, Blu-ray, and DVD success, the Toy Story franchise has also spawned video games sales of 10.44 million units.

## TOP 10...
# BIGGEST DISNEY PIXAR MOVIES

When Pixar made the 100 percent CG (computer-generated) Toy Story in 1995, animation was changed forever...

| | MOVIE | YEAR OF RELEASE | BOX OFFICE ($ WORLDWIDE) |
|---|---|---|---|
| 1 | TOY STORY 3 | 2010 | 1,063,171,911 |
| 2 | FINDING NEMO | 2003 | 936,743,261 |
| 3 | MONSTERS UNIVERSITY | 2013 | 743,559,607 |
| 4 | UP | 2009 | 731,342,744 |
| 5 | THE INCREDIBLES | 2004 | 631,442,092 |
| 6 | RATATOUILLE | 2007 | 623,722,818 |
| 7 | MONSTERS, INC. | 2001 | 562,816,256 |
| 8 | CARS 2 | 2011 | 559,852,396 |
| 9 | BRAVE | 2012 | 538,983,207 |
| 10 | WALL·E | 2008 | 521,311,860 |

## 📍 FINDING NEMO

Pixar's fifth feature film won the 2004 Oscar for Best Animated Feature. Its director and co-writer Andrew Stanton has directed three Disney Pixar productions and the live-action sci-fi movie *John Carter* (2012). His fifth as a director will be Nemo sequel *Finding Dory* (2017).

## BOXTROLLS

Nominated for a 2015 Oscar for Best Animated Feature Film, stop-motion animation The Boxtrolls was based on Alan Snow's novel *Here Be Monsters!* (2005). It was produced by Laika, who created stop-motion adventures *Coraline* (2009) and *ParaNorman* (2012).

## THE NIGHTMARE BEFORE CHRISTMAS

Danny Elfman, the composer of this stop-motion classic, also provides the singing voice for lead character Jack Skellington. The *Nightmare* universe was based on a poem Tim Burton wrote in 1992.

## TOP 10...
# BIGGEST STOP-MOTION ANIMATED MOVIES

The art of creating a moving image by combining thousands of still photos is still a popular form of animation...

| | MOVIE | YEAR OF RELEASE | BOX OFFICE ($ WORLDWIDE) |
|---|---|---|---|
| 1 | CHICKEN RUN | 2000 | 224,834,564 |
| 2 | WALLACE & GROMIT: THE CURSE OF THE WERE-RABBIT | 2005 | 192,610,372 |
| 3 | CORALINE | 2009 | 124,596,398 |
| 4 | THE PIRATES! IN AN ADVENTURE WITH SCIENTISTS! | 2012 | 123,054,041 |
| 5 | THE CORPSE BRIDE | 2005 | 117,195,061 |
| 6 | THE BOXTROLLS | 2014 | 108,255,770 |
| 7 | PARANORMAN | 2012 | 107,139,399 |
| 8 | FRANKENWEENIE | 2012 | 81,491,068 |
| 9 | THE NIGHTMARE BEFORE CHRISTMAS | 1993 | 75,082,668 |
| 10 | FANTASTIC MR. FOX | 2009 | 46,471,023 |

WHO FRAMED ROGER RABBIT? WON

**3 OSCARS**

IN 1989

**TOP 10...**

# BIGGEST CELL/TRADITIONAL ANIMATED MOVIES

Creating an animation with hand-painted, still images is an art form that has lasted for over 100 years...

| | MOVIE | YEAR OF RELEASE | BOX OFFICE ($ WORLDWIDE) |
|---|---|---|---|
| 1 | THE LION KING | 1994 | 987,483,777 |
| 2 | THE SIMPSONS MOVIE | 2007 | 527,071,022 |
| 3 | ALADDIN | 1992 | 504,050,219 |
| 4 | TARZAN | 1999 | 448,191,819 |
| 5 | BEAUTY AND THE BEAST | 1991 | 424,967,620 |
| 6 | POCAHONTAS | 1995 | 346,079,773 |
| 7 | WHO FRAMED ROGER RABBIT? | 1988 | 329,803,958 |
| 8 | THE HUNCHBACK OF NOTRE DAME | 1996 | 325,338,851 |
| 9 | MULAN | 1998 | 304,320,254 |
| 10 | SPIRITED AWAY | 2002 | 274,925,095 |

## LILO & STITCH

Missing the 10th place on this Top 10 by less than $2,000 is Disney's *Lilo & Stitch* (2002). This tale of a friendship between a Hawaiian girl and an alien made $273,144,151 at the box office. There have been two direct-to-video sequels and two TV series totalling 151 episodes.

## ◉ POKÉMON

The Pokémon franchise is a multimedia phenomenon. Since the first Game Boy release in 1996, the video game series has sold 242.5 million copies. Over 900 episodes have been produced of the ongoing Pokémon TV series, plus 17 animated feature films.

## TOP 10...

# BIGGEST**ANIME MOVIES**

The term "anime" refers to Japanese animations that are created with hand-drawn images and/or computer graphics...

| | MOVIE | YEAR OF RELEASE | BOX OFFICE ($ WORLDWIDE) |
|---|---|---|---|
| 1 | SPIRITED AWAY | 2002 | 274,925,095 |
| 2 | HOWL'S MOVING CASTLE | 2005 | 235,184,110 |
| 3 | PONYO | 2009 | 201,750,937 |
| 4 | POKÉMON: THE FIRST MOVIE | 1999 | 163,644,662 |
| 5 | PRINCESS MONONOKE | 1999 | 159,375,308 |
| 6 | THE SECRET WORLD OF ARRIETTY | 2012 | 145,570,827 |
| 7 | POKÉMON: THE MOVIE 2000 | 2000 | 133,949,270 |
| 8 | THE WIND RISES | 2014 | 117,932,401 |
| 9 | STAND BY ME, DORAEMON | 2014 | 105,100,000 |
| 10 | ONE PIECE FILM: Z | 2012 | 72,822,122 |

## DORAEMON

Since 1980, there have been 36 animated films made starring the popular Japanese robot cat Doraemon.

PRINCESS MONONOKE
# 134
**MINS**
LONG

STUDIO GHIBLI'S
CREATIVE TEAM
HAS PRODUCED
**21**
**ANIMATED**
FILMS

## 📍 TOTORO

Written and directed by Studio Ghibli co-founder Hayao Miyazaki, the English-dubbed version features Frank Welker as the voice of the blue forest spirit, Totoro. Welker has over 700 credits, including Scooby-Doo and Futurama's Nibbler.

## STUDIO GHIBLI

Founded in 1985 by Hayao Miyazaki, Isao Takahata, Toshio Suzuki, and Yasuyoshi Tokuma, Japanese animation company Studio Ghibli's vast output includes *Spirited Away*. It won Best Animated Featured at the 2003 Oscars.

TOP 10...

# FIRST EVER STUDIO GHIBLI MOVIES

Although Nausicaä was made a year before the studio was officially formed, it is considered a Ghibli production...

| | MOVIE | YEAR OF RELEASE |
|---|---|---|
| 1 | NAUSICAÄ OF THE VALLEY OF THE WIND | Mar 11, 1984 |
| 2 | LAPUTA: CASTLE IN THE SKY | Aug 2, 1986 |
| 3 | GRAVE OF THE FIREFLIES | Apr 16, 1988 |
| 4 | MY NEIGHBOR TOTORO | Apr 16, 1988 |
| 5 | KIKI'S DELIVERY SERVICE | Jul 29, 1989 |
| 6 | ONLY YESTERDAY | Jul 20, 1991 |
| 7 | PORCO ROSSO | Jul 18, 1994 |
| 8 | WHISPER OF THE HEART | Jul 15, 1995 |
| 9 | PRINCESS MONONOKE | Jul 12, 1997 |
| 10 | MY NEIGHBORS THE YAMADAS | Jul 17, 1999 |

## TOP 10...

# BIGGEST HORROR FILMS

From evil aliens to relentless spectres, these are the 10 scary productions that have lured moviegoers the most...

| | MOVIE | YEAR OF RELEASE | BOX OFFICE ($ WORLDWIDE) |
|---|---|---|---|
| 1 | THE SIXTH SENSE | 1999 | 672,806,292 |
| 2 | WAR OF THE WORLDS | 2005 | 591,745,540 |
| 3 | I AM LEGEND | 2007 | 585,349,010 |
| 4 | JAWS | 1975 | 470,653,000 |
| 5 | THE EXORCIST | 1973 | 441,306,145 |
| 6 | SIGNS | 2002 | 408,247,917 |
| 7 | THE CONJURING | 2013 | 318,000,141 |
| 8 | RESIDENT EVIL: AFTERLIFE | 2010 | 296,221,663 |
| 9 | WHAT LIES BENEATH | 2000 | 291,420,351 |
| 10 | THE VILLAGE | 2004 | 256,697,520 |

## THE BABADOOK

Australian writer-director Jennifer Kent's chiller *The Babadook* (2014) made $4,867,792 at box offices.

JAWS TOOK
## 159
**DAYS**
TO SHOOT

## ⦿ DEMON DOLL

This possessed doll was featured in *The Conjuring*, but it's the focus of this film's prequel, *Annabelle* (2014). It made $255,273,813 at the box office, more than 39 times its $6.5 million budget. Sequel *The Conjuring 2: The Enfield Poltergeist* is due for release in 2016.

## TOLKIEN ADAPTATIONS

New Zealand filmmaker Peter Jackson helmed all six *The Lord Of The Rings* and *The Hobbit* film adaptations of J. R. R. Tolkien's fantasy novels. Released between 2001 and 2014, Jackson's two connected trilogies made $5,849,993,962 at the box office, worldwide.

ALICE IN WONDERLAND IS THE

# 17TH

MOST SUCCESSFUL MOVIE OF ALL TIME

**TOP 10...**

# BIGGEST FANTASY MOVIES

Dominated by adaptations of J. R. R. Tolkien and J. K. Rowling's novels, this list is dedicated to magic, witchcraft, ghouls, and goblins...

| | MOVIE | YEAR OF RELEASE | BOX OFFICE ($ WORLDWIDE) |
|---|---|---|---|
| 1 | HARRY POTTER AND THE DEATHLY HALLOWS PART 2 | 2011 | 1,341,511,219 |
| 2 | THE LORD OF THE RINGS: THE RETURN OF THE KING | 2003 | 1,119,929,521 |
| 3 | ALICE IN WONDERLAND | 2010 | 1,025,467,110 |
| 4 | THE HOBBIT: AN UNEXPECTED JOURNEY | 2012 | 1,017,003,568 |
| 5 | HARRY POTTER AND THE PHILOSOPHER'S STONE | 2001 | 974,755,371 |
| 6 | THE HOBBIT: THE DESOLATION OF SMAUG | 2013 | 960,366,855 |
| 7 | HARRY POTTER AND THE DEATHLY HALLOWS PART 1 | 2010 | 960,283,305 |
| 8 | THE HOBBIT: THE BATTLE OF FIVE ARMIES | 2014 | 951,638,783 |
| 9 | HARRY POTTER AND THE ORDER OF THE PHOENIX | 2007 | 939,885,929 |
| 10 | HARRY POTTER AND THE HALF-BLOOD PRINCE | 2009 | 934,416,487 |

# THE POWER OF POTTER

Lead actor Daniel Radcliffe was 11 years old when he was cast in the first adaptation of J. K. Rowling's *Harry Potter* book series (published 1997-2007). The total box offices takings for the film franchise's seven films is $7,723,431,572. Warner Bros. London-based studio tour The Making of Harry Potter opened 2012, and The Wizarding World of Harry Potter is an interactive attraction at Universal Studios' theme parks in USA and Japan.

## TAKEN TRILOGY

*Taken* star Liam Neeson has more than 100 acting credits. These include playing the titular monster in 2016's *A Monster Calls*, and voicing an animated plastic cop in *The LEGO Movie* (2014).

TAKEN 3 (2015) $325,507,987

TAKEN (2009) $226,830,568

TAKEN 2 (2012) $376,141,306

THE FIRST 4 BOURNE FILMS MADE

## $1.2 BILLION

AT THE BOX OFFICE

# BIGGEST NON-BOND CRIME THRILLERS

007 aside, there are dozens of smash-hit detective tales that have taken the box office by storm...

| | MOVIE | YEAR OF RELEASE | BOX OFFICE ($ WORLDWIDE) |
|---|---|---|---|
| 1 | INCEPTION | 2010 | 825,532,764 |
| 2 | THE BOURNE ULTIMATUM | 2007 | 442,824,138 |
| 3 | TAKEN 2 | 2012 | 376,141,306 |
| 4 | THE FUGITIVE | 1993 | 368,875,760 |
| 5 | GONE GIRL | 2014 | 368,061,911 |
| 6 | MINORITY REPORT | 2002 | 358,372,926 |
| 7 | HANNIBAL | 2001 | 351,692,268 |
| 8 | SEVEN | 1995 | 327,311,859 |
| 9 | RANSOM | 1996 | 309,492,681 |
| 10 | SHUTTER ISLAND | 2010 | 294,804,195 |

## INCEPTION

Written and directed by Christopher Nolan, memory caper *Inception* (2010) won four of its eight 2011 Oscar nominations. It marked the fourth time Nolan had cast Michael Cane in his films, *Interstellar* (2014) being the fifth.

## SEAN CONNERY

The first actor to play novelist Ian Fleming's character was Sean Connery, in *Dr. No* (1962). His 92 acting credits include reprising his Bond role for the 2005 video game *James Bond 007: From Russia with Love*. It sold more than a quarter of million copies in its first three months.

## TOP 10...
# BIGGEST JAMES BOND MOVIES

Ian Fleming debut Bond novel, Casino Royale, appeared in 1952. Ten years later, the first film, Dr. No, was released...

| | MOVIE | YEAR OF RELEASE | BOX OFFICE ($ WORLDWIDE) |
|---|---|---|---|
| 1 | SKYFALL | 2012 | 1,108,561,013 |
| 2 | QUANTUM OF SOLACE | 2008 | 586,090,727 |
| 3 | CASINO ROYALE | 2006 | 599,045,960 |
| 4 | DIE ANOTHER DAY | 2002 | 431,971,116 |
| 5 | THE WORLD IS NOT ENOUGH | 1999 | 361,832,400 |
| 6 | GOLDENEYE | 1995 | 352,194,034 |
| 7 | TOMORROW NEVER DIES | 1997 | 333,011,068 |
| 8 | MOONRAKER | 1979 | 210,308,099 |
| 9 | LICENSE TO KILL | 1989 | 156,167,015 |
| 10 | OCTOPUSSY | 1983 | 67,893,619 |

## ACTORS WHO'VE PLAYED BOND

| | NO. OF TIMES PLAYED 007 |
|---|---|
| SEAN CONNERY | 7 |
| DAVID NIVEN | 1 |
| GEORGE LAZENBY | 1 |
| ROGER MOORE | 7 |
| TIMOTHY DALTON | 2 |
| PIERCE BROSNAN | 4 |
| DANIEL CRAIG | 4 |

## SPECTRE

*Spectre* (2015), Daniel Craig's fourth outing as 007, also features Italian actress Monica Bellucci as Lucia Sciarra. Director Sam Mendes returned for this sequel to *Skyfall* (2012), as did Jesper Christensen, who played the mysterious Mr. White in previous Bond films *Casino Royale* (2006) and *Quantum Of Solace* (2008).

# JACK SPARROW

Johnny Depp's fifth outing as pirate Captain Jack Sparrow, *Pirates of the Caribbean: Dead Men Tell No Tales*, is released in 2017. The actor also provided the voice for the animated LEGO version of the character in *LEGO Pirates Of The Caribbean: The Video Game* (2011).

THE FIRST 4 PIRATES FILMS MADE

## $3.7 BILLION
AT THE BOX OFFICE

TOP 10...

# BIGGEST **PERIOD** **ADVENTURE** MOVIES

If it's set in the past and features perilous adventuring, then it qualifies for a chance to be in this Top 10...

| | MOVIE | YEAR | BOX OFFICE ($ WORLDWIDE) |
|---|---|---|---|
| 1 | PIRATES OF THE CARIBBEAN: DEAD MAN'S CHEST | 2006 | 1,066,179,725 |
| 2 | PIRATES OF THE CARIBBEAN: ON STRANGER TIDES | 2011 | 1,045,713,802 |
| 3 | PIRATES OF THE CARIBBEAN: AT WORLD'S END | 2007 | 963,420,425 |
| 4 | INDIANA JONES AND THE KINGDOM OF THE CRYSTAL SKULL | 2008 | 786,636,0331 |
| 5 | PIRATES OF THE CARIBBEAN: THE CURSE OF THE BLACK PEARL | 2003 | 654,264,015 |
| 6 | KING KONG | 2005 | 550,517,357 |
| 7 | SHERLOCK HOLMES: A GAME OF SHADOWS | 2011 | 545,448,418 |
| 8 | SHERLOCK HOLMES | 2009 | 524,028,679 |
| 9 | INDIANA JONES AND THE LAST CRUSADE | 1989 | 474,171,806 |
| 10 | THE MUMMY RETURNS | 2001 | 433,013,274 |

## THE HUNGER GAMES

American author Suzanne Collins' trilogy of *The Hunger Games* novels (2008-10) have out-sold the *Harry Potter* novels, shifting more than 65 million copies in the USA alone. The film adaptations star Jennifer Lawrence (who won the 2013 Best Actress Oscar for *Silver Linings Playbook*) as protagonist Katniss Everdeen. The fourth and final film of the series, *The Hunger Games: Mockingjay – Part 2*, is due for release November 2015.

**TOP 10...**

# BIGGEST SURVIVAL MOVIES

Dystopian landscapes and a desperate attempt to survive are popular themes in fiction. These are the most successful filmic tales of human endurance...

| | MOVIE | YEAR OF RELEASE | BOX OFFICE ($ WORLDWIDE) |
|---|---|---|---|
| 1 | THE HUNGER GAMES: CATCHING FIRE | 2013 | 864,912,963 |
| 2 | THE HUNGER GAMES: MOCKINGJAY PT.1 | 2014 | 751,414,696 |
| 3 | GRAVITY | 2013 | 716,392,705 |
| 4 | THE HUNGER GAMES | 2012 | 691,247,768 |
| 5 | WORLD WAR Z | 2013 | 540,007,876 |
| 6 | CAST AWAY | 2000 | 429,632,142 |
| 7 | EDGE OF TOMORROW | 2014 | 396,206,256 |
| 8 | NOAH | 2014 | 362,637,473 |
| 9 | APOLLO 13 | 1995 | 355,237,933 |
| 10 | OBLIVION | 2013 | 286,168,572 |

# INDIANA JONES

Created by the mind behind *Star Wars*, George Lucas came up with lecturer-turned-archaeological adventurer Dr. Henry Jones, Jr. as a nod to his love of the action serials of the '30s. In the third film it is revealed that Jones' preferred name of "Indiana" comes from the name of the family dog.

**BOX OFFICE ($ WORLWIDE)**

INDIANA JONES AND THE RAIDERS OF THE LOST ARK (1981)
$389,925,97

INDIANA JONES AND THE TEMPLE OF DOOM (1984)
$333,107,271

INDIANA JONES AND THE LAST CRUSADE (1989)
$474,171,806

INDIANA JONES AND THE KINGDOM OF THE CRYSTAL SKULL (2008)
$786,636,033

## OBLIVION COMIC BOOK

*Oblivion*'s director Joseph Kosinski based his film on a graphic novel that he created, but that hasn't been released. It was originally set to be published in 2012 by Radical Studios, and was key to securing Tom Cruise for the film version as a pitch.

307

## GONE WITH THE WIND

This 238-minute-long drama, adapted from Margaret Mitchell's 1936 novel of the same name won eight Oscars. Rhett Butler (Clark Gable) and Scarlett O'Hara (Vivien Leigh)'s story is regarded as one of the finest on-screen romances of all time.

**TOP 10...**

# BIGGEST DRAMAS

Stories that examine the human condition and our relationships with one another feature strongly in the drama genre...

| | MOVIE | YEAR OF RELEASE | BOX OFFICE ($ WORLDWIDE) |
|---|---|---|---|
| 1 | TITANIC | 1997 | 2,186,772,302 |
| 2 | FORREST GUMP | 1994 | 677,945,399 |
| 3 | THE PASSION OF THE CHRIST | 2004 | 611,899,420 |
| 4 | AMERICAN SNIPER | 2014 | 433,008,447 |
| 5 | CAST AWAY | 2000 | 429,632,142 |
| 6 | THE KING'S SPEECH | 2010 | 414,211,549 |
| 7 | GONE WITH THE WIND | 1939 | 400,176,459 |
| 8 | THE WOLF OF WALL STREET | 2013 | 392,000,694 |
| 9 | SLUMDOG MILLIONAIRE | 2008 | 377,910,544 |
| 10 | AMERICAN BEAUTY | 1999 | 356,296,601 |

## AMERICAN SNIPER

Based on the real life of US Navy SEAL Chris Kyle (played by Bradley Cooper), *American Sniper* won the 2015 Oscar for Sound Editing. As well 67 acting credits, the film's director Clint Eastwood has helmed 34 films since his directorial debut *Play Misty For Me* (1974), which he also starred in.

MAMMA MIA! (2008) FEATURES
**21 ABBA** SONGS

## MOULIN ROUGE

Although set in 1899-1900, Australian filmmaker Baz Luhrmann's third feature film fused modern songs such as Nirvana's "Smells Like Teen Spirit" with theatrical show-music of the era.

## THE MUPPETS

The seventh *Muppets* movie is the most successful of the series. Created by Jim Henson (Sep 24, 1936 – May 16, 1990) in 1955, his comedic puppets' *The Muppet Show* (1976-81) was nominated for 21 Emmys. They still feature in *Sesame Street* (1969-present).

Compare all of The Muppets films' box office takings...

| | BOX OFFICE ($ WORLDWIDE) |
|---|---|
| THE MUPPET MOVIE (1978) | $65,200,000 |
| THE GREAT MUPPET CAPER (1981) | $31,206,251 |
| THE MUPPETS TAKE MANHATTAN (1984) | $25,534,703 |
| THE MUPPETS CHRISTMAS CAROL (1992) | $27,281,507 |
| MUPPET TREASURE ISLAND (1996) | $34,327,391 |
| MUPPETS FROM SPACE (1999) | $22,323,612 |
| THE MUPPETS (2011) | $165,184,237 |
| MUPPETS MOST WANTED (2014) | $80,383,113 |

## TOP 10...
# MOST SUCCESSFUL MUSICALS

Telling stories with singing and dancing began on the stage 150 years ago, with The Jazz Singer (1927) being the first musical film...

| | MOVIE | YEAR OF RELEASE | BOX OFFICE ($ WORLDWIDE) |
|---|---|---|---|
| 1 | MAMMA MIA! | 2008 | 609,841,637 |
| 2 | LES MISÉRABLES | 2012 | 441,809,770 |
| 3 | GREASE | 1978 | 394,955,690 |
| 4 | ENCHANTED | 2007 | 340,487,652 |
| 5 | CHICAGO | 2002 | 306,776,732 |
| 6 | HIGH SCHOOL MUSICAL 3: SENIOR YEAR | 2008 | 252,909,177 |
| 7 | HAIRSPRAY | 2007 | 202,548,575 |
| 8 | MOULIN ROUGE | 2001 | 179,213,434 |
| 9 | INTO THE WOODS | 2014 | 172,635,659 |
| 10 | THE MUPPETS | 2011 | 165,184,237 |

## REAL STEEL ROBOTS

This robot boxing film, set in 2020, was based on Richard Matherson's 1956 short story *Steel*. For the CG robots' boxing moves, motion-capture technology mapped choreography by Olympic gold medallist Sugar Ray Leonard.

MICHAEL MOORE HAS DIRECTED
**7**
FEATURE DOCUMENTARIES SINCE 1989

## ROCKY

The original *Rocky*, released in 1976, just misses out on a Top 10 appearance here with a box office total of $117,235,147. Its lead actor Sylvester Stallone, also wrote the screenplay.

## TOP 10...

# BIGGEST SPORTS MOVIES

By a long way, boxing is the most popular subject when it comes to making a movie about sport...

| | MOVIE | YEAR OF RELEASE | BOX OFFICE ($ WORLDWIDE) |
|---|---|---|---|
| 1 | THE BLIND SIDE | 2009 | 309,208,309 |
| 2 | ROCKY IV | 1985 | 300,473,716 |
| 3 | REAL STEEL | 2011 | 299,268,508 |
| 4 | MILLION DOLLAR BABY | 2004 | 216,763,646 |
| 5 | ROCKY BALBOA | 2006 | 155,721,132 |
| 6 | SEABISCUIT | 2003 | 148,336,445 |
| 7 | REMEMBERING THE TITANS | 2000 | 136,706,683 |
| 8 | THE FIGHTER | 2010 | 129,190,869 |
| 9 | ROCKY III | 1982 | 125,049,125 |
| 10 | ROCKY V | 1990 | 119,946,358 |

## CAVE OF FORGOTTEN DREAMS

Werner Herzog's 2011 documentary *Cave Of Forgotten Dreams* grossed $6,467,348 at box offices worldwide. It captured an investigation inside France's Chauvet Cave, where 3,000-year-old man-made art exists.

**TOP 10...**

# MOST SUCCESSFUL DOCUMENTARIES

Documentary filmmakers are drawn to human stories that ask questions and often reveal answers...

| | DOCUMENTARY | YEAR RELEASED | BOX OFFICE ($ MILLIONS) |
|---|---|---|---|
| 1 | FAHRENHEIT 9/11 | 2004 | 222,446,882 |
| 2 | MARCH OF THE PENGUINS | 2005 | 127,392,693 |
| 3 | EARTH | 2007 | 108,975,160 |
| 4 | JUSTIN BIEBER: NEVER SAY NEVER | 2011 | 99,036,827 |
| 5 | OCEANS | 2010 | 82,651,439 |
| 6 | ONE DIRECTION: THIS IS US | 2013 | 68,532,898 |
| 7 | BOWLING FOR COLUMBINE | 2002 | 58,008,423 |
| 8 | AN INCONVENIENT TRUTH | 2006 | 49,756,507 |
| 9 | SICKO | 2007 | 36,088,109 |
| 10 | CHIMPANZEE | 2012 | 34,823,764 |

MARCH OF THE PENGUINS **80** MINS LONG

## ANY GIVEN SUNDAY

The twelfth most successful sports drama of all time is Al Pacino-starrer *Any Given Sunday* (1999). The football-focused movie made $100,230,832 at the box office and was directed by three-time Oscar-winner Oliver Stone.

## ⦿ THE ROGUE CUT

Although its original version was released May 2014, a new, longer version is released in 2015. *X-Men: Days Of Future Past – The Rogue Cut* has over 17 minutes of new footage, reinstating the plotline featuring Rogue/Marie (played by *True Blood*'s Anna Paquin).

TOP 10...

# BIGGEST **TIME-TRAVEL** MOVIES

With three 2014 films in this list, it was clearly a strong box-office year for time-bending science fiction...

| | MOVIE | YEAR OF RELEASE | BOX OFFICE ($ WORLDWIDE) |
|---|---|---|---|
| 1 | X-MEN: DAYS OF FUTURE PAST | 2014 | 748,121,534 |
| 2 | INTERSTELLAR | 2014 | 672,320,176 |
| 3 | MEN IN BLACK 3 | 2012 | 624,026,776 |
| 4 | TERMINATOR 2: JUDGMENT DAY | 1991 | 519,843,345 |
| 5 | TERMINATOR 3: RISE OF THE MACHINES | 2003 | 433,371,112 |
| 6 | EDGE OF TOMORROW | 2014 | 396,206,256 |
| 7 | STAR TREK | 2009 | 385,680,446 |
| 8 | BACK TO THE FUTURE | 1985 | 381,109,762 |
| 9 | BACK TO THE FUTURE PART II | 1989 | 331,950,002 |
| 10 | AUSTIN POWERS 2 | 1999 | 312,016,858 |

UP TO 2015, HUGH JACKMAN HAS ACTED IN

**31 FEATURE** FILMS

## 12 MONKEYS

Just off this chart is Terry Gilliam's 1995 time-travel thriller *12 Monkeys*, grossing $168,839,459 at the box office. It was inspired by Chris Marker's 1962 French short film *La Jetée* ("The Jetty"). It starred Bruce Willis and Brad Pitt. In 2015, a TV series based on Gilliam's film began on U.S. channel SyFy.

# TOP 10...
# BIGGEST **PREHISTORIC** MOVIES

Dinosaurs have been popular with filmgoers since Harry Hoyt's 1925 silent film The Lost World...

| | MOVIE | YEAR OF RELEASE | BOX OFFICE ($ WORLDWIDE) |
|---|---|---|---|
| 1 | JURASSIC WORLD | 2015 | 1,084,500,00 |
| 2 | JURASSIC PARK | 1993 | 1,029,153,88 |
| 3 | ICE AGE: DAWN OF THE DINOSAURS | 2009 | 886,686,81 |
| 4 | THE LOST WORLD: JURASSIC PARK | 1997 | 618,638,99 |
| 5 | JURASSIC PARK III | 2001 | 368,780,80 |
| 6 | DINOSAUR | 2000 | 349,822,76 |
| 7 | THE LAND BEFORE TIME | 1988 | 84,460,84 |
| 8 | LAND OF THE LOST | 2009 | 68,777,55 |
| 9 | WALKING WITH DINOSAURS | 2013 | 61,021,59 |
| 10 | BABY: SECRET OF THE LOST LEGEND | 1985 | 14,972,29 |

## ⦿ JURASSIC WORLD

Released June 2015, *Jurassic World* is set 22 years after the catastrophic events that took place on Isla Nublar in *Jurassic Park* (1993). Chris Pratt (*Guardians Of The Galaxy, Parks & Recreation*) stars, alongside a wealth of CG and prosthetic dinosaurs, including a 59-ft (18-m)-long Mosasaurus and the genetically modified Indominus Rex.

THE LOST WOR
JURASSIC PARK

## ⦿ WALKING WITH DINOSAURS

Long before the 2013 film, BBC and Impossible Pictures' *Walking With Dinosaurs* franchise began with the 1999 TV series featuring predominantly CG (computer-generated) creatures. Its Arena Spectacular of colossal animatronic dinosaurs has toured the world since 2007.

## TOP 10...
# BIGGEST HISTORICAL MOVIES

Films set in the past often focus on battles or war of some kind, as reflected in this Top 10 of the most popular...

| | MOVIE | YEAR OF RELEASE | BOX OFFICE ($ WORLDWIDE) |
|---|---|---|---|
| 1 | TITANIC | 1997 | 2,186,772,302 |
| 2 | THE PASSION OF THE CHRIST | 2004 | 611,899,420 |
| 3 | TROY | 2004 | 497,409,852 |
| 4 | SAVING PRIVATE RYAN | 1998 | 481,840,909 |
| 5 | GLADIATOR | 2000 | 457,640,427 |
| 6 | THE LAST SAMURAI | 2003 | 456,758,981 |
| 7 | 300 | 2007 | 456,068,181 |
| 8 | PEARL HARBOR | 2001 | 449,220,945 |
| 9 | LES MISÉRABLES | 2012 | 441,809,770 |
| 10 | DJANGO UNCHAINED | 2012 | 425,368,238 |

## ⊙ SAVING PRIVATE RYAN

The five-time Oscar-winning war drama was Steven Spielberg's twentieth film as a director. Here's how successful Steven Spielberg's '90s film were...

| | BOX OFFICE ($ WORLDWIDE) |
|---|---|
| HOOK (1991) | $300,854,823 |
| JURASSIC PARK (1993) | $1,029,153,882 |
| SCHINDLER'S LIST (1993) | $321,306,305 |
| THE LOST WORLD: JURASSIC PARK (1997) | $681,638,999 |
| AMISTAD (1997) | $44,229,441 |
| SAVING PRIVATE RYAN (1998) | $481,840,909 |

## ⊙ LES MISERABLES

The 2012 adaptation of Victor Hugo's 1862 novel featured actors singing live on set. Therefore, months of post-production music editing was required to add a full orchestral score in afterwards. It won Best Music in a Musical Feature Film at the 2013 Motion Picture Sound Editors awards.

## WALL-E

For Pixar Animation Studios' ninth film, *WALL·E*, Oscar-winning Sound Designer Ben Burtt created 2,500 different sound effects. Burtt previously worked on every *Star Wars* and *Indiana Jones* film. *WALL·E* won 47 of its 82 international awards.

THE FIRST 3 HUNGER GAMES FILMS MADE

# $2.3 BILLION

AT THE BOX OFFICE

## EDGE OF TOMORROW

Tom Cruise's 37th film, *Edge Of Tomorrow* (2014) missed this Top 10 with $396,206,256 at the box office. It was based on Hiroshi Sakurazaka's 2004 novel *All You Need Is Kill*.

## TOP 10...

# BIGGEST **FUTURE-SET** MOVIES

Filmmakers' imagination knows no bounds, and the tales of Earth's possible future are still a ripe and popular source of inspiration...

| | MOVIE | YEAR OF RELEASE | BOX OFFICE ($ WORLDWIDE) |
|---|---|---|---|
| 1 | AVATAR | 2009 | 2,787,965,087 |
| 2 | THE HUNGER GAMES: CATCHING FIRE | 2013 | 864,912,963 |
| 3 | THE HUNGER GAMES: MOCKINGJAY PT.1 | 2014 | 751,414,696 |
| 4 | X-MEN: DAYS OF FUTURE PAST | 2014 | 748,121,534 |
| 5 | DAWN OF THE PLANET OF THE APES | 2014 | 708,835,589 |
| 6 | THE HUNGER GAMES | 2012 | 691,247,768 |
| 7 | INTERSTELLAR | 2014 | 672,320,176 |
| 8 | I AM LEGEND | 2007 | 585,349,010 |
| 9 | BIG HERO 6 | 2014 | 546,212,093 |
| 10 | WALL·E | 2008 | 521,311,860 |

## INTERSTELLAR

British filmmaker Christopher Nolan's ninth feature film won Best Achievement in Visual Effects at the 2015 Oscars, and was nominated for awards for its music, sound mixing, sound editing, and production design. Kip Thorne, a friend of fellow theoretical physicists Carl Sagan (Nov 9, 1934 – Dec 20, 1996) and Stephen Hawking, consulted on *Interstellar* for the science behind the story.

## PICTURE CREDITS CONTINUED

89a; Westend61 90br; Wil Meinderts/ /Minden Pictures 15al; Xavier Arnau 166r; Xu Jian 166l; Zuffa LLC 205a & b; **ImagineChina** Niu Shupei 170c; **ISAF** Jeff Crow 68b; **istockphoto.com** Andrew_ Howe 50a; Andrzej Burak 62b; boryak 161a; Devasahayam Chandra Dhas 49a; eROMAZe 8ar; fotoVoyager 161b; gimagphoto 93bl; Glowing Earth Photography 91b; Holger Mette 20b; ivafet 210al; Jim Veilleux 101br; Johannes Gerhardus Swanepoel 6; Karen Massier 101ar; Koonyongyut 93a; Matt Gibson 19b; Mordolff 91ar; Pgiam 149b; sstop 61b; toddtaulman 63a; vasilchenko 163ar; vichie81 190; worakit_63b; **The Kobal Collection** 20th Century Fox/Paramount/Merie Wallace 288bg; 3 Arts Entertainment 315br; Bonne Pioche/Buena Vista/ APC/Jerome Maison 311bcr; Causeway Films/Smoking Gun Productions 302ar; Columbia Pictures 287l; Fox Searchlight/New Regency/Le Grisbi 288bl; Lucasfilm/20th Century Fox 276a, 284bg, 285a; New Line Cinema/Evergreen Media Group 302l; Paramount 276l; Sony Pictures 87ar; Touchstone Pictures 310a; Walt Disney Pictures/Peter Mountain 308ar; **Konami** 107b &l; **Microsoft Xbox** 73a, 75b, 111al, 123al; **Namco** 124a, 141b; **NASA** 256b, 258b, 260ar, 270al & c, 271, 272a, 273b; George Shelton 56b; GRIN 270ar; JPL/USGS 262b; Science/ AAAS 99b; **NOAA** National Climatic Data Center 93l; **Octopus Publishing Group** Philip's 272c; **Photoshot** Collection Christophel 279bl, 313br; / Real Gareth Edwards/Warner Bros/ Legendary Pictures 17l; LFI 303br; Xinhua 197l; **Pokemon/Nintendo** 122, 128a; **Press Association Images** AP 85br, 150r, 280ar; /Alexander Zemlianichenko 259b; /Pavel Rahman 78b, 84b; **Rex Features** Benoit Stichelbaut/bluegreenpictures.com 65l; Eye Ubiquitous 88al; ITV 157b; Jay Hoff 280b; Moviestore Collection Ltd 139ar; Ray Tang 280al; Snap Stills 311ar; **Rockstar Games** 71a; **Science Photo Library** Claus Lunau 146l; Detlev van Ravenswaay 98al, 265b, 269r; Friedrich Saurer 264a; H Singh/ Custom Medical 154a & b; L Calcada/ Nick Risinger/ESO 264b; Solvin Zankl/ Visuals Unlimited Inc 268br; USGS 99ar; **Shutterstock** 13b; charnsitr 117ar; Barone Firenze 105b; Ben Jeays 39a; Byron K Dilkes 38a; Catmando 25a; Christoff 53b; cozyta 168b; D Free 229a; Darren Baker 142; Dave Hunt 19a; Dmitri Malyshev 104a; dwphotos 222; EvrenKalinbacak 54a; fluke samed

292bg; FooT Too 44; Giideon 20c; Gustavo Fadel 55a; Hadrian 282; Ian Grainger 35al; J Stone 249r; Joe Seer 235b; Kirill Umrikhin 76; Mat Hayward 237r; Mathisa 29a; Matt Gibson 24b; Max Earey 52b; Michael Rosskothen 13a, 25b; mooinblack 54b; Netfalls - Remy Musser 39b; Ozphotoguy 69b; Phil Stafford 246l; Reptiles4all 16al; S Bukley 231r; Sergey Kelin 170r; snvv 88b; TDC Photography 224a; Valentyna Chukhlyebova 26a; VanderWolf Images 60b; **Sony Playstation** 71b, 119a & b, 130b, 133a; **SuperStock** 40a; **Thinkstock** istock 183br; James Thew 254; **TopFoto** 64a, 86bl; RIA Novosti 88ar, 148al; **What Architecture** Andy Spain 187c; Wikipedia Commons 100br, 150c; Luciene Lacerda173bl; Martin Roll 56a; (c) New Line Cinema 101bl.

### DATA SOURCES:

**Pages** 13, 25, 26, 27, 34, 42, 43 – data sourced from Luke Hauser & David Martill, Palaeobiologists
**Pages** 16, 70, 72, 74, 87, 138, 139, 140, 163, 218, 219, 220, 221, 252, 253, 261, 284, 285, 287, 288, 289, 290, 291, 292, 293, 294, 296, 297, 298, 299, 300, 301, 302, 303, 304, 305, 306, 307, 308, 309, 310, 311, 312, 313, 314, 315 – data sourced from IMDB.com. Box office information courtesy of The Internet Movie Database (http://www. imdb.com). Used with permission.
**Page** 39 – data sourced from Florida Museum Of Natural History
**Pages** 71, 73, 75, 104–137 – data sourced from VGChartz.com
**Pages** 166, 169, 171, 178, 179, 189 – data sourced from Council on Tall Buildings and Urban Habitat
**Pages** 262, 263, 264, 265, 266, 267 – data sourced from NASA (https:// solarsystem.nasa.gov)
**Pages** 224, 225, 226, 227, 228, 229, 230, 231, 232, 233, 234, 235, 236, 237, 238, 239, 240, 241, 247, 250, 251 – Billboard's Top 10 lists of 2014 Compiled by Nielsen Music. Copyrighted © 2015. Prometheus Global Media. 117320:0515AT

**Please note:** Most figures, like cinema takings, are reported in US dollars, so for accuracy they have been kept in that currency throughout this book.

**Paul Terry would like to thank:** all of the contributing sources for their support and fascinating data, especially paleobiologists Luke Hauser and David Martill for always amazing me with all new, fantastic prehistoric information; my brilliant Editor Polly Poulter for her tireless support and content skills; my Editorial Director (and fellow horror fan) Trevor Davies for continued support with this book series; the fantastic T-10 team of designers, picture researchers, sub editors, proofreaders, and marketeers for doing such a superb job; to everyone at Octopus Books and Firefly; and last, but by no means ever least, to my frequent collaborator Tara Bennett, for keeping me smiling throughout the intense Top 10 process – I'm glad there were (*Sleepy Hollow*) monsters to hunt down together in between collating all of these facts and figures.

Top 10 of Everything 2016

Written & Researched by Paul Terry

Top 10 of Everything was devised and created by Russell Ash

An Hachette UK Company
www.hachette.co.uk

First published in Great Britain in 2015 by Hamlyn, a division of Octopus Publishing Group Ltd
Carmelite House
50 Victoria Embankment
London EC4Y 0DZ

www.octopusbooks.co.uk

**Editorial Director** Trevor Davies
**Editor** Pollyanna Poulter
**Creative Director** Jonathan Christie
**Design** The Oak Studio Limited
**Cover Design** Paul Shubrook
**Production Controller** Sarah-Jayne Johnson